History of Universities

VOLUME XXIX/1

2016

History of Universities is published bi-annually

Editor:
Mordechai Feingold (California Institute of Technology)

Managing Editor:
Jane Finucane (Trinity College, University of Glamorgan)

Editorial Board:
R. D. Anderson (University of Edinburgh)
L. J. Dorsman (Utrecht University)
Thierry Kouamé (Université Paris 1 Panthéon-Sorbonne)
Mauro Moretti (Università per Stranieri di Siena)
H. de Ridder-Symoens (Ghent)
S. Rothblatt (University of California, Berkeley)
N. G. Siraisi (Hunter College, New York)

A leaflet 'Notes to OUP Authors' is available on request from the editor.

To set up a standing order for History of Universities contact Standing Orders, Oxford
University Press, North Kettering Business Park,
Hipwell Road, Kettering, Northamptonshire, NN14 1UA
Email: StandingOrders.uk@oup.com
Tel: 01536 452640

History of Universities

VOLUME XXIX/1
2016

OXFORD
UNIVERSITY PRESS

OXFORD
UNIVERSITY PRESS

Great Clarendon Street, Oxford, OX2 6DP,
United Kingdom

Oxford University Press is a department of the University of Oxford.
It furthers the University's objective of excellence in research, scholarship,
and education by publishing worldwide. Oxford is a registered trade mark of
Oxford University Press in the UK and in certain other countries

Published in the United States of America by Oxford University Press
198 Madison Avenue, New York, NY 10016, United States of America

British Library Cataloguing in Publication Data
Data available

Library of Congress Control Number:

ISBN 978–0–19–877991–9

Printed in Great Britain
by Clays Ltd, St Ives plc

Contents

Articles

Eclecticism as a Vibrant Philosophical Program: Claude Bérigard and Mauro Mancini on the University of Pisa

*Renée Raphael**

Seventeenth-century innovators devoted much energy to disparaging early modern universities as stale institutions whose members upheld traditional ideas at all costs. In his 1613 *Letters on Sunspots*, Galileo Galilei (1564–1642) criticized 'enemies of innovation', who were ready to credit him with every error, no matter how excusable, as a capital offence, for 'it now seems to be the case that it is better to err with the masses than to speak alone, albeit correctly'.[1] In his 1637 *Discourse on the Method*, René Descartes (1596–1650) likened himself to an architect, designing a town from scratch; he chose not to build on the inherited wisdom of the past— that taught systematically in the period's universities—but to demolish it and start anew.[2]

Historians of the last decades have turned with equal vigour to the task of rehabilitating the reputations of these early modern Peripatetics. Many period innovators, they have shown, were educated and worked in universities. Teaching, too, was not as wedded to tradition as once assumed,

* Research for the article was supported by a Fulbright IIE Fellowship and a Villa I Tatti fellowship. In addition, the piece was greatly improved by the comments of the two anonymous reviewers and, in an earlier stage, through conversations with Anthony Grafton.
[1] Galileo Galilei, *Le opere di Galileo Galilei*, ed. Antonio Favaro (20 vols, Florence, 1890), v. 102, 95.
[2] René Descartes, *Oeuvres de Descartes. Correspondence*, ed. Charles Adam & Paul Tannery (11 vols, Paris, 1996), vi. 9–11; John Cottingham, Robert Stoothoff & Dugald Murdoch, ed. and trans., *The Philosophical Writings of Descartes* (3 vols, Cambridge, 1985), i. 115–16. On Descartes's relationship with tradition and innovation, see John Cottingham, 'A New Start? Cartesian Metaphysics and the Emergence of Modern Philosophy', in Tom Sorell (ed.), *The Rise of Modern Philosophy: The Tension between the New and Traditional Philosophies from Machiavelli to Leibniz* (Oxford, 1993), 145–66.

but new speculation and findings entered the curriculum. At first these transformations occurred under the rubric of traditional Aristotelian philosophy, with novel findings being considered with regard to questions standard to the scholastic curriculum. By the end of the seventeenth century, however, many universities had embraced the philosophical teachings of Descartes or Newton.[3] Even traditional natural philosophy, moreover, allowed for empirical investigation and could anticipate and respond to the ideas of those, like Descartes, who portrayed themselves as rejecting all of Aristotelianism.[4]

These broad characterizations belie a more complex and nuanced relationship between contemporary Aristotelianism, the New Science, and the universities. Charles Schmitt has argued that early modern Aristotelianism was a multivalent enterprise, one which drew freely upon multiple intellectual traditions to smooth over inconsistencies and obviate problems.[5] Following Schmitt, we can take the term Aristotelianism to designate a study of the natural world consciously modelled on Aristotle's programme, one whose agenda—the set of questions and subjects studied—were developed from Aristotle's writings and those of his medieval commentators. This precision, however, does not obviate the fact that historical actors were sensitive to and made astute use of the multiplicity of meanings which could be ascribed to the term. Cesare Cremonini (1550-1631), professor of natural philosophy at Ferrara and Padua, for example, defended some his most heterodox positions from criticism by arguing that they were based on literal readings of Aristotle.[6] Galileo was an

[3] Key contributions to this literature include Laurence W.B. Brockliss, *French Higher Education in the Seventeenth and Eighteenth Centuries: A Cultural History* (Oxford, 1987); Mordechai Feingold, *The Mathematicians' Apprenticeship: Science, Universities, and Society in England, 1560–1640* (Cambridge, 1984); Paul F. Grendler, *The Universities of the Italian Renaissance* (Baltimore, 2002). For an overview of the transformation of teaching in response to new ideas, see Laurence Brockliss, 'Curricula', in H. De Ridder-Symoens (ed.), *A History of the University in Europe*, ii: *Universities in Early Modern Europe (1500–1800)* (Cambridge, 1996), 563–620; Roy Porter, 'The Scientific Revolution and Universities', in De Ridder-Symoens (ed.), *Universities in Early Modern Europe*, 531–62; Mordechai Feingold, 'The Mathematical Sciences and New Philosophies', in ed. Nicholas Tyacke (ed.), *The History of the University of Oxford*, iv: *Seventeenth-Century Oxford* (Oxford, 1997), 319–448.

[4] Craig Martin, *Renaissance Meteorology: Pomponazzi to Descartes* (Baltimore, 2011); Dennis Des Chene, *Physiologia: Natural Philosophy in Late Aristotelian and Cartesian Thought* (Ithaca, NY, 2000), esp. 12–13.

[5] Charles B. Schmitt, 'Eclectic Aristotelianism', in *Aristotle and the Renaissance* (Cambridge, 1983), 89–109, 91. Recent calls have been made to expand this notion of Renaissance Aristotelianism even more broadly to recognize the influence of the vernacular tradition: David A. Lines, 'Rethinking Renaissance Aristotelianism: Bernardo Segni's Ethica, the Florentine Academy, and the Vernacular in Sixteenth-Century Italy', *Renaissance Quarterly* 66/3 (2013): 824–65.

[6] Grendler, *Universities of the Italian Renaissance*, 294–6.

outspoken critic of contemporary university Aristotelians, but he often went out of his way to identify himself as a true follower of Aristotle. In his *Dialogue on the Two World Systems*, for example, Galileo criticized contemporaries for remaining dependent on Aristotle's words and for taking Aristotle as their guide when he was not always the person best suited for such a role.[7] Galileo's implication, as he argued in a letter to the Pisan professor Fortunio Liceti (1577–1657), was that he himself was a good Aristotelian and that Aristotle himself, were he to return to the realm of the living, would agree.[8]

As these anecdotes might suggest, it has also been difficult to articulate the relationship between proponents of the New Science and those of university Aristotelianism. In the case of Italy, nowhere is this more apparent than in the often contentious discussion exploring Galileo's relationship to the Aristotelian tradition. To take but two examples, Michele Camerota and Mario Helbing have shown how Galileo was shaped by and at times thrived within the world of the universities; he also placed his own most promising students in, and even supported potential detractors' bids for, university positions.[9] In contrast, Mario Biagioli has argued that Galileo deliberately turned away from a university audience and assumed a sympathetic audience of courtiers and 'free thinkers' in works such as his *Dialogue*.[10]

---

[7] Galilei, *Opere*, vii. 59–60, 78, 81.

[8] Ibid., xviii. 51. Described in Stillman Drake, *Galileo at Work* (Chicago, 1978), 408–10; John L. Heilbron, *Galileo* (Oxford, 2010), 351.

[9] Michele Camerota, *Galileo Galilei e la cultura scientifica nell'età della Controriforma* (Rome, 2004), 75–82; Michele Camerota & Mario Helbing, 'Galileo and Pisan Aristotelianism: Galileo's "De Motu Antiquiora" and "Quaestiones de Motu Elementorum' of the Pisan Professors", *Early Science and Medicine* 5/4 (2000), 319–65; Michele Camerota, 'Flaminio Papazzoni: Un Aristotelico bolognese maestro di Federico Borromeo e corrispondente di Galileo', in Daniel A. Di Liscia, Eckhard Kessler & Charlotte Methuen (eds), *Method and Order in Renaissance Philosophy of Nature: The Aristotle Commentary Tradition* (Aldershot, 1997), 271–300; Galilei, *Opere*, xx. 517–18. For similar arguments stressing Galileo's relationship with university Aristotelianism, see Alastair C. Crombie, *Augustine to Galileo* (Cambridge, MA, 1961); Charles B. Schmitt, 'Experience and Experiment: A Comparison of Zabarella's View With Galileo's in De Motu', *Studies in the Renaissance* 16 (1969), 80–138; Charles B. Schmitt, 'The Faculty of Arts at Pisa at the Time of Galileo', in *Studies in Renaissance Philosophy and Science* (London, 1981), 243–72; Alastair C. Crombie, 'Sources of Galileo's Early Natural Philosophy', in Maria Luisa Righini Bonelli & William R. Shea (eds), *Reason, Experiment and Mysticism in the Scientific Revolution*, (New York, 1975), 157–75; Adriano Carugo & Alastair C. Crombie, 'The Jesuits and Galileo's Ideas of Science and of Nature', *Annali dell'Istituto e Museo di Storia della Scienza di Firenze* 8 (1983): 3–67; W.A. Wallace, *Galileo and His Sources: The Heritage of the Collegio Romano in Galileo's Science* (Princeton, 1984); Mario Helbing, *La filosofia di Francesco Buonamici, professore di Galileo a Pisa* (Pisa, 1989).

[10] Mario Biagioli, *Galileo, Courtier: The Practice of Science in the Culture of Absolutism* (Chicago, 1993), 216–17. For similar arguments stressing Galileo's break with university scholarship, see Stillman Drake, *Galileo Studies: Personality, Tradition, and Revolution* (Ann

These continuing debates have not prevented historians from agreeing that innovative claims entered the university curriculum largely via an indirect route whereby new speculation was discussed under the guise of established lines of inquiry. Such a finding was initially celebrated by historians eager to revise former interpretations of early modern universities as static moribund institutions; the fact that innovative doctrine was taught at all in the university classroom was a cause for celebration.[11] Subsequent scholarship has sought to understand the nature of the reception of the New Science within the university setting by identifying the factors, be they institutional regulations, the comprehensiveness of Aristotle's writings, the inertia of the pedagogical system, or religious vows and beliefs, which constrained professors from embracing novelty without inhibition.[12]

For these historians, eclecticism—the amalgamation of ancient and modern philosophy which is so prevalent in university teaching of the period—has often been viewed as anything but a rigorous intellectual stance, instead portrayed as an option of last resort, a disingenuous compromise, or even the result of intellectual laziness.[13] The true innovator, free from institutional and doctrinal constraints, would have embraced the New Science; the true traditionalist would have opposed it.

Arbor, 1970), esp. 95–9; William R. Shea, *Galileo's Intellectual Revolution: Middle Period, 1610–1632* (New York, 1977), esp. p. viii.

[11] For a summary of this historiography, see Porter, 'The Scientific Revolution and Universities', 531–5.

[12] For some key examples, consider Brockliss, *French Higher Education in the Seventeenth and Eighteenth Centuries*, 341–2; Alfredo Dinis, 'Was Riccioli a Secret Copernican?', in Maria Teresa Borgato (ed.), *Giambattista Riccioli e il Merito Scientifico dei Gesuiti nell'Età Barocca* (Florence, 2002), 49–77; Marcus Hellyer, *Catholic Physics: Jesuit Natural Philosophy in Early Modern Germany* (Notre Dame, 2005), 6–7. Other early modern scholars who embraced eclectic approaches have been celebrated as anomalies who managed to straddle the worlds of traditional and innovative approaches, Ugo Baldini, 'Tra due paradigmi? La "Naturalis philosophia" di Carlo Rinaldini', in Luigi Pepe (ed.), *Galileo e la scuola galileiana nelle università del Seicento* (Bologna, 2011), 189–222.

[13] For two discussions of early modern eclecticism specifically, see Ian Maclean, 'Cardano's Eclectic Psychology and Its Critique by Julius Caesar Scaliger', *Vivarium* 46/3 (2008), 392–417; Willem Otterspeer, 'The University of Leiden: An Eclectic Institution', *Early Science and Medicine* 6/4 (2001), 324–33. While Maclean celebrates the eclectic contributions of Cardano and Scaliger for their later influence, he also appears to dismiss the intellectual content of their contributions, arguing that despite Cardano's claims to novelty and Scaliger's humanist credentials and self-confidence, 'no great change has occurred in the range of questions asked about the soul and in the evidence adduced to determine their answers' (413). Maclean argues that both Cardano and Scaliger were able to distinguish between interpretation and philosophical argument, but 'the conceptual scheme which they found most congenial was that of the Stagyrite, no matter how far they were prepared to modify it' (414). Otterspeer views eclecticism more positively, arguing that Leiden's adoption of an experimental method of education was shaped by its embrace of an eclectic approach to scholarship and pedagogy (esp. 331–3).

Taking as a case study the teaching materials of two professors at the University of Pisa, I argue for a contrary vision of eclecticism. For these professors, the university was a place of vibrant intellectual exchange, not because its members embraced novelty, but because they fostered debate and discussion between old and new ideas. Claude Bérigard's 1643 *Circulus Pisanus* reveals his impression of the University of Pisa as a lively site of knowledge production, one which offered opportunities for dialogue between professors and students and fused humanist, scholastic, and new learning. The teaching notes of Mauro Mancini reveal how he relied on novel speculation to renovate and reformulate traditional philosophical teaching. For these professors, the intellectual landscape was not a battleground between new and old methods, but a site where old doctrine was revived and reformulated in response to the new. The project of updating Aristotle by bringing contemporary speculation to bear on his writings was seen as a worthy and noble endeavor, one which allowed interlocutors to join in a long-running scholarly conversation with roots in antiquity.

The University of Pisa in the Seventeenth Century

The University of Pisa was founded in 1343, while Pisa was an independent city-state.[14] After the city lost its independence to Milan in 1399, and then to Florence in 1406, economic support for the university declined, and it was eventually closed. Following the example of the rulers of Venice and Milan, however, Lorenzo de Medici decided to move the Florentine university outside the city. In 1473, the University of Pisa, now controlled by the Florentine state, was reopened with only a handful of introductory and humanistic positions left in Florence.

Throughout the sixteenth century, the university expanded both its faculty and student body. Between 1474 and 1495, for example, Pisa enrolled about 200 to 320 students annually and employed between 30

---

[14] The most detailed account of the history of the University of Pisa and her professors is found in A. Fabroni, *Historiae Academiae Pisanae* (Pisa: Cajetanus Mugnainius, 1791). Recent work on the university's history is found in Elena Amatori (ed.), *Storia dell' Università di Pisa* (2 vols, Pisa, 1993); Grendler, *Universities of the Italian Renaissance*, chap. 3. For a discussion of the university in the sixteenth century, see Camerota & Helbing, 'Galileo and Pisan Aristotelianism'; Helbing, *La filosofia di Francesco Buonamici*; Charles B. Schmitt, 'The Studio Pisano in the European Cultural Context of the Sixteenth Century', in Charles Webster (ed.), *Reappraisals in Renaissance Thought* (London, 1989), 19–36; Charles B. Schmitt, 'The University of Pisa in the Renaissance', in Webster (ed.), *Reappraisals in Renaissance Thought*, 3–17; Schmitt, 'The Faculty of Arts at Pisa at the Time of Galileo'. Except when indicated, the account that follows is based on Grendler, *Universities of the Italian Renaissance*, chap. 3.

and 32 professors. These numbers rose substantially over the next century, so that by the 1560s, the annual student body averaged 600 and was taught by a faculty that numbered approximately 45. This increase in student enrolment and faculty hiring was accompanied by institutional efforts to heighten the university's prestige. Along with Padua, Pisa shared the honour of creating the first university botanical garden, which opened in late 1544 or 1545. Though Medici policy specified that most faculty positions be filled by Florentines and other Tuscans, concerted efforts were made to hire innovative and well-known professors, particularly in the faculties of arts and medicine. Some of the most notable of these scholars included Realdo Colombo of Cremona (c. 1510-59), who taught anatomy and surgery at Pisa from 1546 to 1548, and Gabriele Falloppia of Modena (1523–62), who taught for three years before leaving for Padua in 1551. These intellectual developments were complemented by a series of administrative reforms. University statutes governing all aspects of academic policy were developed in the mid-sixteenth century, while both the Florentine government and private benefactors constructed residential colleges to provide free board and lodging for select university students.[15]

Historians have differed in their evaluations of the University of Pisa in the seventeenth century. For some, the Pisan university in the period was in decline, with teachers who preferred private over public teaching and students who often chose new, religious schools over the established institution.[16] In a similar vein, others have emphasized the conservative, reactionary nature of the university by stressing the animosity between supporters of Galileo and professors at Pisa and elsewhere.[17] In other venues, scholars have portrayed the University of Pisa in a more positive light, emphasizing the openness of its faculty who embraced Galileo's legacy even in the face of restrictions imposed by the Catholic Church. A significant number of Pisan professors of natural philosophy and mathematics advertised their interest in novel currents in philosophical thought, especially atomism.[18] Pisan professors also interacted with the

---

[15] Danilo Marrara, 'Gli Statuti di Cosimo I: Premessa', in Amatori (ed.), *Storia dell' Università di Pisa* i. 571–6.

[16] Grendler, *Universities of the Italian Renaissance*, 477–83.

[17] On the relationship between Galileo and natural philosophers at Pisa, consider Biagioli, *Galileo, Courtier: The Practice of Science in the Culture of Absolutism*, 159–244; Giorgio Stabile, 'Il Primo Oppositore del Dialogo: Claude Bérigard', in Paolo Galluzzi (ed.), *Novità Celesti e Crisi del Sapere* (Florence, 1984), 277–82.

[18] For examples, see Susana Gomez Lopez, 'Donato Rossetti et le Cercle pisan', in Egidio Festa, Vincent Jullien & Maurizio Torrini (eds), *Géométrie, atomisme et vide dans l'école de Galilée* (Fontenay/Saint-Cloud, 1999), 281–97; Susana Gomez Lopez, *Le passioni degli atomi. Montanari e Rossetti: una polemica tra galileiani* (Florence, 1997); Susana Gomez Lopez, 'Dopo Borelli: la scuola galileiana a Pisa', in Pepe (ed.), *Galileo e la scuola galileiana*, 223–32.

larger Tuscan intellectual community, including the recently-formed Accademia del Cimento, which represented itself as carrying out a programme of experimentation inspired by Galileo.[19]

Claude Bérigard: Pisa as a Place of Vibrant Intellectual Exchange

Claude Bérigard (Claudius Bérigardus) (*c.*1590-1663) studied natural philosophy and medicine in Aix before being summoned to the Tuscan court in 1626 to serve as a secretary to the Grand Duchess Christina.[20] The following year, at the urging of Christina's confessor, Bérigard was appointed an extraordinary professor of natural philosophy at the University of Pisa. Seven years later, he took over the chair previously held by Scipione Chiaramonti to become an ordinary professor of natural philosophy, a post he held until 1639, when he moved to the University of Padua. Bérigard's motivations for leaving Pisa are obscure. In comparison to Pisa, Padua offered greater economic security and prestige. However, the continuing affection held for Galileo in Tuscany also may have been a factor in his decision. In 1632, Bérigard had written *Dubitationes in dialogum Galilaei Galilaei*, the first published critique of Galileo's *Dialogue on the Two World Systems*. Though some scholars have argued that Bérigard was compelled to write at the direct insistence of Ferdinand II, the Grand Duke of Tuscany who was both Galileo's and Bérigard's patron

---

[19] On the Cimento, see W.E.K. Middleton, *The Experimenters: A Study of the Accademia Del Cimento* (Baltimore, 1971); Marco Beretta, Antonio Clericuzio & Lawrence M. Principe (eds), *The Accademia Del Cimento and Its European Context* (Sagamore Beach, 2009).

[20] On Bérigard's life and scholarly work, see Alberto M. Ghisalberti (ed.), 'Beauregard, Claudio Guillermet', in *Dizionario Biografico degli Italiani* (Rome, 1960-), vii. 386–9; Maria Bellucci, 'La Filosofia Naturale di Claudio Berigardo', *Rivista Critica di Storia della Filosofia* 26 (1971), 363–411; Francesco Bottin, 'Claude Guillermet Bérigard (*c.*1590-1663)', in Giovanni Santinello, C.W.T. Blackwell & Philip Weller (eds), *Models of the History of Philosophy*, i: *From Its Origins in the Renaissance to the 'Historia Philosophica'* (Dordrecht, 1993), 147–9; Antonio Favaro, 'Oppositori di Galileo: IV. Claudio Berigardo', *Atti del Reale Istituto Veneto* 79/1 (1919–20), 39–92; Pietro Ragnisco, 'Da Giacomo Zabarella a Claudio Berigardo ossia Prima e Dopo Galileo nell'Università di Padova', *Atti del Reale Istituto Veneto* 52/1 (1893–4), 474–518; Bernard Rochot, 'Bérigard, Claude Guillermet de', in Charles C. Gillispie (ed.), *Dictionary of Scientific Biography*, (16 vols, New York, 1970–80), ii. 12–14; Maria Laura Soppelsa, *Genesi del Metodo Galileiano e Tramonto dell'Aristotelismo nella Scuola di Padova* (Padua, 1974), 92–112; Anabella Checchini Degan, *Nuovi Studi su Claude Beauregard* (Padua, 1971); Jean-Pierre Niceron, *Mémoires pour servir à l'histoire des hommes illustres dans la république des lettres, avec un catalogue raisonné de leurs ouvrages* (42 vols, Paris: Briasson, 1728–42), xxxi. 123–7; Stabile, 'Il Primo Oppositore del Dialogo: Claude Bérigard'; Georgio Stabile, *Claude Bérigard (1592-1663): Contributo alla storia dell' atomismo seicentesco* (Rome, 1975).

at the time, the act inevitably garnered Bérigard unfavourable attention from many of Galileo's supporters.[21]

The *Dubitationes* offers one window into Bérigard's attitudes to the Aristotelian tradition. Written as an open letter to the Academia dei Lincei, the book had a titlepage prominently identifying both Bérigard and Galileo as members of the Pisan university.[22] Bérigard criticized Galileo's stance in the *Dialogue* by arguing that, contrary to the latter's representation, there were insufficient arguments to support the heliocentric hypothesis of the Earth's motion; he took specific issue with Galileo's reliance on the telescope to make astronomical arguments and with his explanation of the tides. The thesis underlying Bérigard's critique focused on Galileo's character of Simplicio, whom Bérigard chastised for being portrayed as overly simple and for ceding too readily to the other interlocutors' pro-Copernican claims, thereby giving the impression that there no longer remained effective arguments to support the Earth's immobility.[23] The publication of the *Dubitationes* prompted contemporaries, including Marin Mersenne, to label Bérigard as one of Galileo's adversaries.[24] Galileo seems to have been less convinced that the *Dubitationes* reflected a real antagonism on Bérigard's part, describing the book in a letter to Elia Diodati as a critique but one written 'against his desire' in order to curry favour.[25]

After moving to Padua, Bérigard published a four-volume course on natural philosophy which he titled *Circulus Pisanus*.[26] The 1643 first edition *Circulus* was printed in four separate volumes, each dedicated to a different patron.[27] Together these four initial volumes treated the *Physics* (addressed in two volumes, one sub-titled *In priores libros Phys. Arist.*, the second *In octauum librum Physicorum Aristotelis*), *De generatione*, and *De*

---

[21] For this argument, see Stabile, 'Il Primo Oppositore del Dialogo: Claude Bérigard'.

[22] C. Berigardus, *Dubitationes in Dialogum Galilaei Galilaei* (Florence: Petrus Nestus, 1632), titlepage.

[23] Soppelsa, *Genesi del Metodo Galileiano*, 94–7; Stabile, 'Il Primo Oppositore del Dialogo: Claude Bérigard', 280–1.

[24] Soppelsa, *Genesi del Metodo*, 96.

[25] Galilei, *Opere*, xvi. 115. On the circumstances which may have prompted Bérigard to write, see again Stabile, 'Il Primo Oppositore del Dialogo: Claude Bérigard'.

[26] This first edition was printed in Udine by Nicolò Schiratti, who saw into print more works by seventeenth-century Paduan professors than did the Paduan printing houses: Favaro, 'Oppositori di Galileo: IV. Claudio Berigardo', 59–60.

[27] The first commentary on the *Physics*, titled *In priores libros Phys. Arist.* is dedicated to Grand Duke of Tuscany Ferdinand II (1610–70). The second commentary on the *Physics*, titled *In octauum librum Physicorum Aristotelis*, as well as that on *De Anima*, were dedicated to Cardinal Carlo de' Medici (1595–1666), the son of Ferdinand I and Queen Christina and uncle to Ferdinand II and Prince Leopold. The commentary on *De ortu* is dedicated to Prince Leopold, brother of Ferdinand II.

anima. Two additional volumes, dedicated to Aristotle's *De caelo* and *In libros meteorologicos*, were published in 1647. A second, expanded and modified version of the work was printed in Padua in 1661.[28] As specified in the university's statutes, each of these texts treated by Bérigard was read as part of Pisa's natural philosophical course; ordinary professors of natural philosophy were required to cover the *Physics*, *De anima*, and *De caelo* during the first year of the course, while *De generatione* was read by extraordinary professors in the second year.[29] Each volume was further subdivided into individual chapters, also labeled as *circuli*, which correspond not to Aristotle's book divisions but to major topics treated by the Greek philosopher.

With his prefatory material and titles, Bérigard suggested that he intended the *Circulus* to be representative and commemorative of his teaching at the University of Pisa. Publishing teachers' 'notes' in this way was a common practice in early modern Europe. Seen into print either by the professors themselves or by their students, these collections of notes most often consisted of commentaries on the established texts that formed the subjects of university courses.[30] The emphasis Bérigard placed on his university teaching in his *Circulus* suggests that he intended the work to be read as belonging to this genre. For example, the common title to each work, *Circulus Pisanus Claudii Bérigardi Molinensis Olim in Pisano, iam in Patavino Lyceo* (*Pisan Circle of Claudius Bérigardus Molinens, Once at the Pisan, now at the Paduan Lyceum*) links Bérigard to the two Italian universities where he taught natural philosophy. Several of his dedicatory letters also stress the twelve years he taught at Pisa as evidence for his competence in producing such a text.[31]

The genre in which Bérigard chose to write, however, makes his work somewhat unusual. Unlike many teaching texts intended to commemorate a professors' lectures, which often follow the Scholastic practice of dividing Aristotle's works into *quæstiones* organized by topic or book,

---

[28] On the contents of the second edition, see Bellucci, 'La Filosofia Naturale di Claudio Berigardo'; Bottin, 'Claude Guillermet Bérigard (c.1590–1663)'; Favaro, 'Oppositori di Galileo: IV. Claudio Berigardo', 63–70; Ragnisco, 'Da Giacomo Zabarella a Claudio Berigardo'; Soppelsa, *Genesi del Metodo Galileiano*, 31–7.

[29] Danilo Marrara, 'Gli Statuti di Cosimo I: Il Progetto e il Testo Definitivo', in Amatori (ed.), *Storia dell' Università di Pisa* i. 615–16.

[30] Ann Blair, 'Student Manuscripts and the Textbook', in Emidio Campi et al. (eds), *Scholarly Knowledge: Textbooks in Early Modern Europe* (Geneva, 2008), 47–57.

[31] 'In hac palæstra duodecim annis exercitatus non minus duxi religioni hoc certamen philosophicum Pisis habitum SERENISSIMO FERDINANDO summo eius parenti non consecrare, quàm veteres athletæ nefas arbitrabantur desudatos Pisæ labores Iovi Olympio non offerre': C. Bérigard, *Circulus Pisanus*, i: *In priores libros Phys. Arist.* (Udine: Nicolae Schiratti, 1643), dedicatory letter.

Bérigard's *Circulus* is a dialogue. Bérigard employed two characters, Charilaus, who represented the views of Aristotle, and Aristaeus, those of Aristotle's ancient opponents all rolled into one.[32] It has been argued that the dialogue was an outdated form by the late seventeenth century, one whose decline was prompted both by methodological criticisms of the ambiguity and unsystematicity of the genre and by ideological arguments associated with the Catholic Church's post-Tridentine censorship policies.[33] In choosing to write a dialogue on natural philosophy, Bérigard was certainly aware of the parallels with Galileo's previous 1632 *Dialogue* and 1638 *Two New Sciences*, where, at least in the former case, Galileo is usually described as having chosen the genre for the safe epistemological space it offered to explore arguments surrounding the Copernican world system.[34] It was also common in pedagogical texts to employ a simple dialogue between master and pupil to convey philosophical topics; Gregor Reisch's 1503 *Philosophical Pearl* is an obvious example of this style of work.[35] Bérigard's *Circulus* does not follow such a simple form; his interlocutors advance arguments but rarely give the type of clear-cut opinions on the various topics in question found in student textbooks. Instead, Bérigard's use of the dialogue may have mimicked Galileo's, in that the dialogue served as a means to explore the intricacies of novel and at times controversial hypotheses. Though Bérigard tended to endorse orthodox viewpoints—e.g. a geocentric world system and the impossibility of a natural void—the dialogue genre allowed him to present to his readers the strength of opposing claims.

The prefatory material Bérigard included in his *Circulus* suggests that the larger humanist intellectual tradition also served as an important impetus for his choice of genre. Since the fifteenth century, Florence had been a centre of humanist scholarship, which involved not only the teaching of Greek by Byzantine scholars and the recovery and study of

[32] 'Ut verò magis elucescat quidquid veritatis est in utraque philosophia, operæ pretium existimavi duos introducere philosophos Charilaum, & Aristæum, quorum ille placita peripatetica, iste veterum opinionem tueatur': ibid., 2. 'Accedit illud quoque venia dignum, quod octavum librum phys. libros duos de ortu, & interitu, & tres de anima primos emittam, ut tentamentum favoris publici, quo si benignè excipiantur, in promptu sunt aliæ partes in priores phys. de principÿs, de cœlo, & de meteoris, in quibus duos Philosophos, quos appellare libet Charilaum, & Aristæum, illum Aristotelis, hunc antiquorum causam agentem introduco': C. Bérigard, *Circulus Pisanus*, ii: *In octauum librum Physicorum Aristotelis* (Udine: Nicolae Schiratti, 1643), 2–3.
[33] Virginia Cox, *The Renaissance Dialogue: Literary Dialogue in Its Social and Political Contexts, Castiglione to Galileo* (Cambridge, 1992), 84.
[34] Ibid., 79, 182n54.
[35] Andrew Cunningham & Sachiko Kusukawa (eds), *Natural Philosophy Epitomised: Books 8–11 of Gregor Reisch's 'Philosophical Pearl' (1503)*, trans. Andrew Cunningham & Sachiko Kusukawa (Farnham, 2010), pp lix–lxvi.

ancient texts, but also humanist criticism of Scholastic style and scholarship. Humanism has been understood in radically different ways, defined at times in terms of ideology, profession, and methodology. Here I take it to refer to a broad intellectual and cultural movement which shaped a range of disciplines in the early modern world through a set of practices aimed to recover and recreate the content and scholarly methods of ancient knowledge.[36] These practices, which included the emulation of ancient literary genres, such as dialogue, had not abated in the seventeenth century, and humanist and scholastic approaches, sometimes seen as antithetical, were actually fused in many contexts by this period.[37]

Bérigard's vision for his *Circulus* was located centrally in such a project to combine humanistic with traditional approaches. In the preface to the volume *In octauum librum Physicorum Aristotelis*, Bérigard emphasized his desire to let philosophical truth shine forth by reviving ancient debate between Aristotle and his predecessors:

> I wanted to confront the philosophy of the ancients with that of the Peripatetics so that, from their conflict, sparks would fly out to reveal the truth which is now covered in shadows. But in order that that which is older [and] now nearly condemned should clash with the other, which is at its full strength and wins favour from the name of its author and his commentators as well, I did not think to produce a separate philosophy of Anaximander, Democritus, Anaxagoras, Empedocles, or any other, as if it were a crippled Philosophy. But I combined whatever each of them had which seemed worthy of being brandished against Aristotle, however they understood it, into one, just like a refurbished soldier, fitted out with his reasons as if with arms, so that, by means of this [soldier] seeking out vehemently the Peripatetic adversary and evading his weapons carefully, we should see which of them ought to carry home the palm of victory.[38]

---

[36] For this definition, I draw from Jill Kraye, 'Preface', in id. (ed.), *The Cambridge Companion to Renaissance Humanism* (Cambridge, 1996), p. xv; Eugene F. Rice & Anthony Grafton, *The Foundations of Early Modern Europe, 1460–1559* (New York, 1994), 78, 83–7. Some key works on the humanist movement in Florence include Hans Baron, *The Crisis of the Early Italian Renaissance: Civic Humanism and Republican Liberty in an Age of Classicism and Tyranny* (Princeton, 1966); Anthony Grafton, *Leon Battista Alberti: Master Builder of the Italian Renaissance* (New York, 2000); James Hankins, *Plato in the Italian Renaissance* (Leiden, 1990), Parts I and IV; Ronald K. Witt, *In the Footsteps of the Ancients: The Origins of Humanism from Lovato to Bruni* (Leiden, 2000).

[37] Eric W. Cochrane, *Tradition and Enlightenment in the Tuscan Academies, 1690–1800* (Chicago, 1961), chap. 4; E.W. Cochrane, 'Science and Humanism in the Italian Renaissance', *The American Historical Review* 81/5 (December 1976), 1039–57; Grendler, *The Universities of the Italian Renaissance*, 267–313.

[38] 'Veterum Philosophiam cum Peripatetica committere volui, ut ex utriusque conflictu assistant veluti quædam scintillæ, unde veritas tenebris involuta quodammodo deprehendatur. Sed ut illa vetustior iam ferè explosa pugnet in alteram non tantùm viribus integris, sed etiam autoris & interpretum suorum nomine favorabilem, non putavi producendam

By claiming that pitting Aristotle against his ancient opponents in dialogue, a genre revived by the humanists, would reveal greater truth than a straightforward exposition of accepted natural philosophical doctrine, Bérigard revealed his application of humanistic techniques to traditional Scholastic subject matter. His decision to unite Aristotle's opponents into one character demonstrates an eclectic approach to questions of natural philosophy, which seems to set Bérigard, an early seventeenth-century scholar, apart from both earlier Platonists and later Epicureans.

No less clearly does Bérigard's language indicate his debt to the humanist tradition. Throughout his prefatory material, Bérigard developed an elaborate metaphor linking his interlocutors to ancient athletic contests. These comparisons were developed in the excerpt above, in which his characters were refurbished 'soldiers' whose intellectual dispute is described by the Latin verb *pugnare* ('to combat or give battle to'). The winner of this struggle would carry home the victory palm, an ancient symbol of glory in battle.

In choosing this analogy, Bérigard most likely expected his readers would be familiar with classical references identifying ancient Pisa, the area around Olympia, as a possible site for the Greek Olympic Games.[39] According to this tradition, the Olympic Games were founded by Pelops after he secured Hippodamia's hand in marriage by beating her father Oenomaus, the king of Pisa, in a chariot race. Bérigard made this analogy explicit by quoting the Roman poet Statius in a later passage:

> And in fact the title of *Circulus Pisanus* did not allow anything else, [the *Circulus Pisanus*] in which the Teachers of the College, like so many pairs of noble gladiators, descend into the philosophical arena, not, as elsewhere to observe the clash of their pupils, but so that, by criticizing one another in turn and by battling most fiercely, they might debate about their own affairs, in a struggle occasionally not less violent than those which once Statius Papinius described, of 'the fatal chariot race Oenomaus set for his daughter's suitors, who quaked to hear his snorting teams behind'.[40]

---

esse separatim Anaximandri, Democriti, Anaxagoræ, Empedoclis, aut alterius veluti delumbem, Philosophiam, sed quod ex singulis visum est non indignum, quod Aristoteli opponeretur, sive ita, sive aliter intellexerint, in unum contuli velut militem interpolem rationibus suis instructum tanquam armis, quibus Peripateticum adversarium petendo vehementer, & eius tela cautè declinando, videatur uter victoriæ palmam referre debet', Bérigard, *Circulus Pisanus*, ii: *In octauum librum Physicorum Aristotelis*, 1–2.

[39] 'Olympic Games', in John Roberts, (ed.), *The Oxford Dictionary of the Classical World* (Oxford, 2005), 515; 'Pisa', in N.G.L. Hammond & H.H. Scullard, (eds), *The Oxford Classical Dictionary* (Oxford, 1970), 835.

[40] 'Nec vero aliud patiebatur inscriptio Circuli Pisani, in quo Doctores Collegæ veluti totidem paria nobilium Gladiatorum descendunt in arenam philosophicam, non ut alibi conflictum discipulorum spectaturi, sed ipsi inter se alternis invehendo, propugnandoque

Bérigard relied on this citation of Statius' *Silvae* to link his colleagues to ancient Pisa and her athletic contests. Not only did he compare their disputations to the chariot races run by Oenomaus, but Bérigard selected a quotation from Statius that emphasized the connection between the Olympic Games and ancient Pisa. As is clear in the excerpt above, Statius referred to Oenomaus's daughter Hippodamia as 'Pisaea'.

The metaphor also allowed Bérigard to comment on the culture of his former university. In the 'Circulus Pisanus', according to Bérigard, the teachers of the college were accustomed to descend into the philosophical arena to sort out their own opinions on correct natural philosophical opinion. Bérigard thus implied that these Pisan professors were not just passive transmitters of a set body of knowledge, but rather, they were active participants in the life of the mind.

The comparison also facilitated Bérigard's expression of his own fascination with the method of disputation, or formal debate, practised at Pisa. In the above excerpt, Bérigard conveys his own admiration for Pisan professors, who, it seems, did the debating themselves, rather than merely serve as spectators for their students. This portrait is strengthened by the work's title of *Circulus Pisanus*. In addition to its associations with ancient spectacles and games, the term *circulus* references the practice of 'circular disputations' (*disputationes circulares*), a type of informal disputation common to many Italian universities. As described in the university statutes, these disputations provided the occasion for students and professors to discuss and debate the material recently presented in lecture. They were called 'circular' disputations because participants were required to sit facing each other in a circle.[41] Bérigard's own references to the

acerrimè disceptant de rebus suis, non minori interdum contentione, quàm quos aiebat olim Statius Papinius, *Pisæa lege trementes Currere, & Oenomae fremitus audire sequentis*': Bérigard, *Circulus Pisanus*, ii: *In octauum librum Physicorum Aristotelis*, 2. Italics mine, to indicate quotation from Statius, *Silvae*, I.2.41–42. Translation of Statius taken from Betty R. Nagle, *The Silvae of Statius* (Bloomington, 2004), 42.

[41] For information on circular disputations in Italian universities in general with specific reference to enforcement and scheduling at Padua, see Grendler, *Universities of the Italian Renaissance*, 156. The University's statutes included a section specifying how and when these circular disputations would be conducted. For the text of the statutes, see Marrara, 'Gli Statuti di Cosimo I: Il Progetto e il Testo Definitivo', 616–17. The possibility that circular disputations had their origins in similar academic exercises practised in the mendicant *studia* and Parisian colleges is discussed in Alfonso Maierù, *University Training in Medieval Europe* (Leiden, 1994), 64. According to Mango Tolomei, circular disputations at Pisa involved professors and students who gathered in a circle and discussed with enthusiasm various questions and problems relevant to the material presented in lecture, Elsa Mango Tomei, *Gli Studenti dell'Università di Pisa sotto il Regime Granducale* (Pisa, 1976), 61. Spagnesi claims they involved one professor defending a list of prepared and circulated theses against arguments and objections posed by students and fellow colleagues, Enrico Spagnesi, 'Il Diritto', in Amatori (ed.), *Storia dell'Università di Pisa* (Pisa, 1993), 222–5.

disputations as practised at Pisa indicate that this choice of title was a deliberate one, designed to allude to and express his admiration for this exercise.[42] His emphasis on the active role of professors in disputations would suggest that Pisa's image of itself was of a place more intimate and collegial than some other universities.

Bérigard's prefatory material thus conveys his admiration for the University of Pisa as a place where professors and students worked together actively to seek philosophical truth. The university, in his eyes, was neither a place of bitter division between faculties or between those who supported novelty and those who clung to tradition, nor a place of stodgy conservatism. Rather, it was a site of intellectual vigour. As good humanists, professors looked to the ancients for inspiration, viewing themselves as inheritors of their tradition of philosophical debate. Moreover, just as Bérigard saw himself and his colleagues as continuing ancient practices, so, too, did he portray contemporary developments as relevant to traditional philosophy.

The content of Bérigard's dialogues reinforces his celebration of Pisa as a place where ancient debates came to life through those of contemporary scholars. Throughout, Bérigard brought recent writings and discoveries to bear on his elaboration of traditional philosophical themes. Bérigard's interlocutors, for example, debated William Harvey's 1628 *De motu cordis*, explicitly citing and explaining Harvey's work in the context of Aristotle's *De anima*. Although Bérigard did not mention or endorse Harvey's theory of circulation, he did adapt some of Harvey's experimental and theoretical findings regarding the relationship between the heart and the arterial pulse to strengthen his argument that the soul does not

According to Verde, professors were fined for failing to participate in the circular disputations and students were prohibited from interrupting debate between their instructors, Armando F. Verde, 'Il secondo periodo de Lo Studio Fiorentino (1504–1528)', in Paolo Renzi (ed.), *L'università e la sua storia. Origini, spazi istituzionali e pratiche didattiche dello Studium cittadino* (Siena, 1998), 105–31, 117.

[42] In his dedicatory letter to Ferdinand II, for example, Bérigard referred to the practice of circular disputations: 'Sic ego nefas existimavi, SERENISSIME FERDINANDE, in hoc certamine philosophico Pisis inito aliud invocare nomen quàm Meduceum, cuius auspiciis palæstra Pisana Pisæ Olympiæ parentis suæ splendorem & gloriam superavit, non pugilatione, luctatione, curriculisque equorum, sed quod præstantius est literaria concertatione. Quippe tales hìc spectantur disceptationes, quas Pisanos circulos iam appellant, ut iurisprudentia demonstrationibus mathematicis vix concedat, medicina non iam facultas videatur, sed scientia, philosophia verò divina, atque humana mirum in modum illustrior evaserit, & copiosior. In hac palæstra duodecim annis exercitatus non minus duxi religioni hoc certamen philosophicum Pisis habitum SERENISSIMO FERDINANDO summo eius parenti non consecrare, quàm veteres athletæ nefas arbitrabantur desudatos Pisæ labores Iovi Olympio non offerre', Bérigard, *Circulus Pisanus*, i: *In priores libros Phys. Arist.*:dedicatory letter.

need a faculty to move the blood.[43] Passages from Day 1 of Galileo's *Two New Sciences* were also discussed by Bérigard's interlocutors in connection with their debates on the nature of the void and of rarefaction. In these instances, specific examples—Galileo's device to measure the strength of the void and his solution to the paradox of Aristotle's wheel—were described without attribution to Galileo as examples which bolstered arguments contrary to Aristotle's.[44] In these passages, Bérigard has his interlocutors discuss in detail the implications of Galileo's examples without fully endorsing them. At the same time, the interlocutors meander from one topic to another, often offering no clear-cut final statement in their discussion. Bérigard appears to have been more concerned with the dialogic process of debate, drawing out the implications of all sides of the argument, rather than with inculcating a definite notion of the right answer, as one finds, for example, in texts intended for student consumption.

A slightly different approach was taken when Bérigard addressed the question of the Earth's immobility with reference to Copernicus's heliocentric hypothesis. As in the instances when he discussed Harvey's *De motu* and Galileo's *Two New Sciences*, Bérigard allowed his interlocutors to explore in detail opinions for and against the Earth's motion. He referenced arguments for the Earth's immobility which had been advanced since antiquity, including observations on the distinctions between the Earth and heavenly bodies and the behavior of projectiles such as arrows and stones on the Earth's surface.[45] He followed this opening litany with more recent arguments advanced by pro-Copernican contemporaries,

---

[43] Roger French, *William Harvey's Natural Philosophy* (Cambridge, 1994), 250–1.

[44] Renee Raphael, 'Teaching through Diagrams: Galileo's 'Dialogo' and 'Discorsi' and His Pisan Readers', *Early Science and Medicine* 18/1–2 (2013), 214–22; Renee Raphael, 'Reading Galileo's *Discorsi* in the Early Modern University', *Renaissance Quarterly* 68.2 (2015): 558–96.

[45] 'Primum absurdum est quod in hypothesi Copernicana sensus videndi perfectus circa obiectum suum, scilicet lumen et motum factum in medio convenient et iusta distantia decipiatur, maximo philosophici criterii damno. Videmus enim Terram nos esse unam ex stellis errantibus, quoniam istae lucidae sunt, illa obscura. Videmus nos esse in medio positos, ut secundum Anaxagoram coelestia omnia contemplemur. Videmus lapides e summa turre demissus cadere secundum muri rectitudinem, non autem oblique, ut accideret si Terra moveretur. Videmus proiecta in altum ad lineam, recidere ad pares angulos in eundem locum. Videmus sagittas aut glandes plumbeas vibratas ad ortum, occasum, meridiem, et septentrionem ad destinatum punctum tendere, perinde ac si Terra esset immobilis. Videmus nubes aves et pisces sese in aere et aqua sustinere velut immobiles. Videmus nihil excuti a Terra, ut sit in iis quae vertigine aguntur. Videmus nihil molestiae nobis asserti a vento perpetuo quem excitari oporteret a velocissimo Terrae motu tam diurno quam annuo': C. Berigard, *Circulus Pisanus Claudii Berigardi... De Veteri et Peripatetica Philosophia in Aristotelis Libros de Coelo* (Udine: Ex typographia Nicolai Schiratti, 1647), 134–5.

including Galileo, explaining in detail, for example, Galileo's claims in the *Dialogue* that the motion of the sunspots and the tides can be explained as a result of the Earth's motion.[46]

Alterations in the second edition of Bérigard's *Circulus* reveal even more strongly Bérigard's desire in the dialogue to use the genre to offer a multi-faceted and detailed account of the intellectual positions at stake. The most notable change in the second edition is the addition of new arguments on behalf of the heliocentric hypothesis. In this 1661 edition, Bérigard elaborated on his earlier account of the response of Copernicans to individuals who claimed that, were the Earth to be in motion, its motion would be violent and thus impossible to sustain. In the first edition, Bérigard had responded merely that the motion of the Earth is natural, for the parts of the Earth move together around the Earth, just as sunspots move around the Sun.[47] In the second edition of the text, Bérigard expanded his explanation, drawing on concepts of relative motion. He argued, on behalf of the Copernicans, that heaviness and lightness and the motions which they engendered were relative, just as a torch lighting the path of a swiftly moving ship looks different depending on whether one observes it from the ship's deck or the shore.[48] Similarly, in another section of his exposition, Bérigard added details to the Copernican claim that the heliocentric planetary arrangement allows for a more natural and harmonious agreement with nature compared to the Ptolemaic system. Among other arguments, Bérigard noted the fact that the

[46] Prima quae pertinent ad sensum, petitur a Solis maculis, quae quoniam circa Solem menstruo fere circum ictu se revolvunt, et circulorum quos describant convexam parten detorquere mox videntur in contrarium, quam priore semestri faciebant, ex eo Terrae mobilitatem vult inferre. Multi valde laborant ut his assentiantur experimentis: propterea quod macularum inconstans aberratio ita certitudinem flexus obturbat, ut prope solus Galilaeus semestrem illam varietatem deprehenderit. . . . Secunda ratio petitur a modo quo sit aestus maris lib. Meteor. confutando': ibid., 137.

[47] 'Tertio dicimus hunc motum fore violentum Terrae: nam si esset naturalis, partes eius omnes similem motum participarent. Respondent omnes partes moveri quidem circa Terram, sed non circa se, sicut maculae Solis non circa se ipsas, sed circa Solem convertuntur': ibid., 136.

[48] 'Quod vero Terra gravis ferri debeat ad medium universi, respondens neque gravem esse neque levem, proinde non minus quare reliqua sidera posse moveri circa Solem: partes autem Terrae dici posse graves aut leves, quatenus ab ipsa seiunctae fortius aut debilius attrahuntur: quod etiam de partibus aliorum siderum dici potest: nam motu recto ferri possunt ad suum totum, et simul cum suo roto ferri in orbem. In quo motu recto est haec sensus hallucinatio, ut qui motus est parabolicus, seu inflexus, iudicetur rectus. Quare si fax accensa noctu demittatur e summo malo navis velociter motae, a nauta quidem et vectoribus iudicabitur motus rectus, ab iis vero qui sunt in littore, parabolicus. Si vero e summa turri demittatur, rectus videbitur ab omnibus in Terra existentibus, parabolicus vero ab iis tantum, qui si Deo placeret, extra Terram collocarentur': C. Berigard, *Circulus Pisanus Claudii Berigardi . . . De Veteri et Peripatetica Philosophia in Aristotelis Libros de Coelo* (Padua: Typis Pauli Frambotti Bibliopolae, 1660), 350.

apparent retrograde motion of the superior planets can be best explained by the Earth's movement into a position between them and the Sun.[49]

Though Bérigard framed his dialogue as a discussion between Aristotle and his ancient opponents, he did not conceal the fact that his characters inhabited a thoroughly contemporary world. What seemed to interest Bérigard was the way his interlocutors—and, by extension, he and his colleagues at Pisa—continually recreated the dialogue of the ancients, and he was eager to draw parallels between contemporary and historical events. In his statement opening the exchange regarding the question of the Earth's motion, for example, Aristaeus proposed that the condemnation of the Copernican doctrine may have been an elaborate ruse to guard its intellectual worth. Bérigard, through Aristaeus, proposed that Copernicus's condemnation by the Catholic Church may be analogous to Plato's condemnation of Homer in his *De summo bono doctrina*. Aristaeus reasoned that just as Plato's criticism of Homer may have been a ploy to reserve Homer for himself and select wise philosophers, so, too, might the condemnation of the heliocentric hypothesis have been intended to preserve Copernicus's thoughts for a privileged group of illuminated individuals.[50] Later Bérigard followed many of his contemporaries, including Copernicus himself, in arguing for the ancient provenance of Copernicus's heliocentric hypothesis, emphasizing that modern adherents of the Copernican system were following in a long line of distinguished predecessors. Bérigard attributed the notion of the Earth's motion to a host of ancient thinkers, including Pythagoras, Aristarchus, Heraclides, and Plato, and then listed the modern authors, including William Gilbert, Simon Stevin, and Johannes Kepler, whom he identified as proclaimed Copernicans.[51] In the 1661 edition of his *Circulus*, Bérigard updated this

---

[49] 'Denique progressus, regressus, institutionesque planetarum per solidos eccentricos et epicyclos consentiunt quidem calculis astronomicis, sed repugnant naturali coelorum dispositioni. Contra vero apud Copernicum explanantur haec omnia facile et mirifice congruunt naturae rerum, ut videre licet in figuris ad hoc constructis, ubi ostenditur nunquam planetas superiores esse retrogrados, nisi cum Terra interposita est ipsis ac Soli: quod optime declaratur Terrae motu, cur enim aliis in locis non sunt retrogradi? Eadem causa est quod Mars et planetae superiores tunc reperiuntur maxime propinqui Terrae, maximique nobis apparent circa mediam retrogradationem? Nam si hoc ab epicyclis proveniret, Martis retrogradatio non esset 12 graduum, Iovis 10 et Saturni 7': Ibid., 351–2.

[50] 'Copernicus hodie damnatus a multis videri possit, ut quondam Homerus a Platone, qui in lib. De summo bono, eum a republica sua unguentis quidem delibutum et coronatum, sed tamen dimitti voluit, fortè ut commodius in loco solo sibi ac sapientibus retineret.' Berigard, *Circulus Pisanus Claudii Berigardi . . . De Veteri et Peripatetica Philosophia in Aristotelis Libros de Coelo* (1647), 133.

[51] 'Non minus illi sensu quam ratione comprobare nituntur opinionem veterum quorundam Pythagoreorum, Heraclidis, Philolai, Nicetae, Cleanthis, Aristarchi Samii, sunt enim alter Aristarchus, qui apud Plutarchum de facie in Luna Cleanthem violate religionis ab Atheniensibus debuisse postulari ait, quod immoto caelo Terram circa se et Solem volui

list of modern Copernicans to include Georg Joachim Rheticus, Christoph Rothmann, Philipp Landsbergen, Wilhelm Schickard, Michael Maestlin, Ismaël Bullialdus, and Martinus Hortensius.[52] This emphasis on the parallels between the world of the ancients and contemporary scholarship reinforces the image presented in the prefatory material of Pisa as a vibrant place of intellectual exchange because of professors' commitment to reviving the debates of the ancients. In Bérigard's depiction, this intellectual community was a lively one precisely because of its eclecticism; it neither clung to nor completely rejected the new but continually revived traditional learning through new speculation.

Mauro Mancini: Teaching a Restored Aristotle

Bérigard's prefatory material and dialogue reveal his conception of the university as a site of vibrant intellectual exchange whereby ancient philosophy was read and reformulated by applying new speculations to it. The surviving teaching notes of Mauro Mancini, who served as an extraordinary professor of philosophy from 1692 to 1694, and then as ordinary professor of natural philosophy at Pisa from 1694 to 1703, reveal the continuing appeal of such an approach, albeit in a different guise, towards the end of the century. Amongst Mancini's surviving papers is a collection of reading notes and a teaching treatise, which he entitled 'Aristotle Restored, a New Philosophy from the Old'.[53]

Examination of the content and organization of Mancini's text reveals that, for him, a natural philosophical course which 'restored Aristotle' took much of its organizational framework, underlying questions, and even

---

probare conatus esset. Theophrastus apud Plutarchum in septima quaest. Platon. testatur Platonem iam senem poenituisse, quod mundi medium tribuisset Terrae, qui locus est praecellentissimus, praesto simoque competere debet. Eam opinionem iam collapsam revocavit Copernicus, quem secuti sunt Origanus, Gilbertus, Stevinus, Keplerus, et alii, quorum rationes, praeter alias a se inventas, refert Galilaeus Dial. De duobus System. iisque magis quam contrariae sententiae argumentis favere videtur': Ibid., 137.

[52] 'Eam opinionem iam collapsam revocavit Copernicus, quem secuti sunt Ioachimus Rheticus, Rhotmannus, Landsbergius, Schickardus, Maestlinus, Bullialdus, Hortensius, Gilbertus, . . . ': Berigard, *Circulus Pisanus Claudii Berigardi . . . De Veteri et Peripatetica Philosophia in Aristotelis Libros de Coelo* (1660), 350.

[53] 'Aristoteles restitutus Philosophia de Veteris Nova': Mancini, 'De Physica' n.d., 51a, Biblioteca Medicea Laurenziana Ms. Ashb. 1623. A separate set of notes (perhaps for his teaching as extraordinary professor of philosophy) at the front of the manuscript has the date 1692, but no date is given for the part of the manuscript entitled *De physica*: Mancini, 'De Physica'.

conceptual content from Aristotle. This Aristotelian core was supple-
mented and modified by appeals to new philosophical principles and
ideas, derived primarily from the mechanical philosophies of René Descartes and Pierre Gassendi. The way Mancini chose to integrate old and
new in his teaching was not unusual in the period; professors throughout
Europe followed a similar eclectic strategy for incorporating new material
into the traditional curriculum.[54] My argument is for a new interpretation
of this pattern of incorporation, namely that Mancini, like Bérigard,
actively chose to adopt an eclectic approach, not out of intellectual laziness
or subterfuge, but because he saw it as a valid and proper way of doing
good philosophy.

Mancini retained, on the whole, the same *quaestiones* as did previous
commentators and teachers of Aristotelian natural philosophy. He began
by discussing what physics and the object of philosophy were. He then
explained basic categories of Aristotelian natural philosophy, including the
principles of natural bodies, the difference between form and matter, and
the definition and principles of the terrestrial elements. Mancini went on
to treat a variety of subjects drawn from Aristotle's *Meteorology, On
generation and corruption,* and *On the heavens.* Rather than divide his
treatise according to the titles and books of Aristotle's writings, Mancini
moved from one subject to the next as the topics related to each other,
noting at the end of various chapters, for example, how the subject treated
in the current chapter would be expanded upon in subsequent sections.[55]

Revealing his own conception of a 'restored' Aristotle, one shaped by
contemporary speculation and investigation, Mancini did modify the
relative weight assigned to different subjects in his course. He allotted
little or no time to topics which had been standard in courses on Aristotelian natural philosophy at Pisa earlier in the century; for example,
Mancini devoted no explicit section of his treatise to discussing Aristotle's
typology of causes and the distinction between nature and art. Instead he
paid more attention to the topic of motion, devoting five sections of his
text to motion, movers, and their causes.[56]

Mancini's use of the mechanical philosophy to supplement his exposition of Aristotle is evident in the section of his text entitled 'On nature'.
Aristotle defined nature well, said Mancini, when he said that it was 'the

---

[54] See note 3.

[55] Mancini closed his discussion of the section entitled 'De natura': with the following
remark: 'ut suo loco de natura loci nos explicabimus, cum modo potius de continuo ad
methodum substinendam sit habenda discussio', Mancini, 'De Physica', 67r.

[56] The sections that deal with motion are titled, for example, 'De Motu, et de Mobili'
(69r), 'De Causa continuati Motus' (70v), 'De Motu Gravium, et de ipsorum reflexione'
(74r), and 'De Reflexione Corporum' (76r).

beginning and cause of motion and of rest of its subject in which it is primary, both through itself and not according to circumstance'.[57] After discussing Aristotle's definition in more detail, Mancini explained what a 'natural body' was. Here he departed from the Aristotelian notion relating a 'natural body' to a principle of motion and embraced a definition promoted by more recent mechanical philosophers. According to Mancini, a natural body can be easily recognized, for 'it is an extended substance, one that is impenetrable, quantitative, and physically indivisible'. A perceptible natural body is simply a 'substance extended in three appointed dimensions, namely by length, width, and depth', a definition which calls to mind Descartes's notion that matter is identical with geometrical space and has extension as its only property.[58]

This combination of Aristotelian and mechanical philosophy permeates Mancini's teaching text. For example, in his discussion of the subject of motion and moveables, Mancini similarly started with Aristotle, noting the importance of considering the different types of causes (material, formal, efficient, and final) which Aristotle had defined.[59] Only once this Aristotelian basis was established did Mancini move on to address motion in mechanical terms. He argued that the first subjects to be discussed were 'the causes of motion in the universe and the laws of nature in the collision of bodies'. He would then treat of other subjects, including that which 'relates to the motion of heavy bodies'.[60]

With respect to the cause of motion, Mancini rejected the opinions of recent writers who assigned the first cause of motion to the shape of bodies. Instead, echoing Descartes and Gassendi, Mancini claimed that the absolutely primary cause of motion was God. Secondary causes certainly play their parts, for motion depends instrumentally on the shape, medium, and a thousand other things which move the body

---

[57] 'Natura optime definitur ab Aristotele, quod sit principium, et causa motus, et quietis eius subiecti in quo est prima et per se et non secundum accidens', Mancini, 'De Physica', 66r. For Aristotle's definition, see *De physica* II.I, 192b.

[58] 'corpus autem diverso modo consideratur prout per se est substantia extensa in triplici dimensione constituta scilicet longitudine, latitudine et profunditate, haec simpliciter tria constituunt perceptibile corpus naturale', Ibid., 66v. On Descartes's notion of matter (in comparison to Gassendi's), see Margaret J. Osler, *Divine Will and the Mechanical Philosophy: Gassendi and Descartes on Contingency and Necessity in the Created World* (Cambridge, 2004), 9.

[59] 'Unde definivit Aristoteles causam quod sit illud ex cuius activitate sequatur aliud per verum influxum. Distinguitur causa quadrupliciter, alia enim dicitur causa materialis alia dicitur causa formalis alia efficiens et alia finalis': Mancini, 'De Physica', 69r.

[60] 'His adductis et praehabitis de motu sermonem facimus. Primum itaque causas motus in universum, ac naturae leges in corporum collisione exponemus, tum quae ad motum rerum gravium pertinent': ibid., 66v.

to motion, but these secondary causes ultimately depend on God.[61] To strengthen his argument, Mancini drew on the example of a watch, whose wheels are moved by weight or by a driving mechanism coiled within the drum. The cause of the watch's measurement of time is all the wheels, but the true primary cause is heaviness (*gravitas*) which moves first the greater wheels and then the smaller ones. Though we might be inclined to end the argument here, Mancini stated that the primary cause was God, 'the first workman of matters in things which ought to be moved'.[62]

Having established God as the primary cause of motion, Mancini turned to causes which can be assigned physically apart from him. The first of these is the 'fluidity of bodies', by which a 'body hit by another is moved and flows in a continuous motion'.[63] The first and principal cause of motion is thus, according to Mancini, the 'ether and a very subtle substance, which is either fiery or of the sun', here, perhaps, an allusion to Stoic physics.[64] By the restless, driving nature of this fleeting, spiritual substance, bodies are moved to generation and corruption, to impact and motion, to advance and decay.[65]

At this point, Mancini relied on these mechanical notions to inform his reading of Aristotle. He noted, first, that this explanation of ether 'is the universal cause of motion, which is given by Aristotle, for bodies moving

[61] 'Unde causa motus primaria debere assignari, quae causa quid sit inquirentes, relictis recentiorum sententiis, adducentibus in corporum figuris motus necessitatem dicimus, primam rerum causam in quacumque generatione; hoc est in quocumque motu a primo rerum Opifice pendere, secundario vero, et instrumentaliter pendere a figura, a medio et a caeteris mille, quae corpus ad motum promovent... Observandum tamen quod Deus in ratione motus consideratur ut causa absolute primaria non excludens secundarias causas, quae ab ipso tanquam propriae dependent': ibid., 69v. On the role of God in Gassendi's physics, see Osler, *Divine Will and the Mechanical Philosophy*, 48–56. For one instance in which Descartes stated that God is the primary cause of motion, see C. Adam and P. Tannery, eds., *Oeuvres de Descartes* (Paris: L. Cerf, 1964), VIII, 61–62.

[62] 'sit exemplum de Horologio, cuius rotae moventur a pondere vel ab impellente alite intra timpanum horologii convoluto, ad mensuram enim temporis omnes rotae sunt causae; Primaria vero Causarum Causa est gravitas illa praeponderans, quae primo maiores, secundo minores movet rotas, quasi nos pro prima omnium agente causa pondus praeponderans adducamus, quod stet loco Dei primi rerum Opificis in rebus quae moveri debent': Mancini, 'De Physica', 69v–70r.

[63] 'Circa Causas, quae extra Deum physice possint assignari potissima erit corporum fluiditas, cuius lubricitate corpus corpore repercussum in continuo motu agitatur et fluit': ibid., 70r.

[64] Samuel Sambursky, *Physics of the Stoics* (New York, 1959), 1–7.

[65] 'si vero primam principalemque causam ipsius motus exquiramus non nisi aetheream subtilissimamque substantiam, quae vel ignea sit vel solaris, proponimus, uno verbo est quoddam volatile spirituosum cuius inquieta natura agitante cuncta moventur corpora ad generationem, et corruptionem ad impulsum et motum, ad incessum et prolapsum': Mancini, 'De Physica', 70r.

themselves naturally'.[66] With this statement, Mancini reinterpreted Aristotle using mechanical principles. The notion of an ether becomes, in his teaching text, Aristotle's underlying principle of motion. Applying this analysis to the example of the watch, Mancini stated that the watch's wheels are naturally immobile but are moved by the balance spring (lamina), which is rolled up within the watch's drum. Mancini claimed that the balance spring contains spirits and aetherial parts which are violently contracted as it is rolled up; the balance spring and thus the wheels are moved as these spirits strive to return the balance spring to its correct shape.[67]

In the next section 'On the cause of uninterrupted motion', Mancini was more explicit about the textual sources on which he drew in explaining his philosophy. According to Mancini, followers of Democritus explained continuous motion by 'spirits moveable by themselves which, driven by the motor, are joined in the moveable in motion'. Cartesians attribute continuous motion to 'some law of nature impressed and delimited by the Motor through which the thing perseveres until it is removed by an external cause or contrary barrier'. Others, in contrast, explain continuous motion by 'an impressed impetus or impressed quality which brings about motion according to the impression'. Mancini endorsed an opinion, which he attributed to Aristotle, namely that it is an impetus impressed by the thing doing the projecting which is the cause of continuous motion. For example, it is the hand which communicates velocity to a stone, and the thing it communicates is called 'impressed impetus'.[68]

Mancini continued by providing various examples of this impressed impetus. He noted, for example, that on a moving ship which strikes sand,

[66] 'Haec est universa motus causa, quae datur ab Aristotele corporibus naturaliter se moventibus, ad differentiam, segnium corporum quae motu nativo donata non sunt, sed moventur a praefatis corporibus in quibus inest motus', Ibid., 70r–v.

[67] 'Sit exemplum iam usitatum de Horologio, cuius rotae per se immobiles moventur a lamella involuta intra timpanum, quae lamella sic involuta spiritus coarctat ad reluctationem, et impulsum faciendum. loquor de spiritibus et partibus aethereis, quae in [*unreadable*] lamella sunt utpote dici posset de arcus tensione, cuius aethereae partes violenter contractae extra propriam figuram conantur propriam redire': Ibid., 70v.

[68] 'Democritici ad spiritus per se mobiles confugiunt qui a motore impulsi mobile consociantur in motu. Cartesiani referunt rationem continuati motus ad quamdam naturae legem impressam ac determinatam a Motore per quam res perseverat in eo statu donec ab extranea causa, sive obice contrario removeatur. Alii impetum impressum volunt, seu qualitatem impressam, quae motum efficiat secundum impressionem. Aristoteles vero ab Aere exterius consequente [*unreadable*] continuitatem motus [*unreadable*]: unde nos eius adherentes sententiae statuimus pro Conclusione, quod impetus a proiciente impressus mediante aere sit causa motus continuati, ubi enim manus deseruit ipsimet lapidi imprimit eandem velocitatem a manu proicientis communicatam eamque vocamus impetum impressum': Ibid., 70v–71r.

the individuals and objects on the ship will continue to move because of the impression of the ship's motion. Similarly an arrow shot upwards on a moving ship will fall to the same place, because the ship's motion is impressed on it. The same is true of a rock which is thrown down from the mast of a moving ship and falls to the bottom of the mast.[69]

In Day 2 of his *Dialogue*, Galileo assigned the contrary argument—that motion is not impressed by the ship on the arrow—to followers of Aristotle. According to him, Aristotle and his followers claimed that on moving ships arrows and other projectiles would fall far from their place of projection; as such, because projectiles thrown vertically on the Earth's surface return to the place from which they were thrown, the Earth must be at rest. Galileo's own view—that projectiles are impressed with the motion of the object carrying them, be it a ship or the Earth—had been addressed by Copernicus and proposed already by fourteenth-century Scholastics, including Nicole Oresme (*c*. 1320-5—1382).[70] The experiments also were associated with more contemporary writers; Gassendi had described his own experiments dropping heavy objects from the top of a moving ship's mast in a letter to Louis-Emmanuel de Valois in June 1641 which was published with his posthumous *Opera omnia* in 1658.[71] Mancini's attribution of these examples to Aristotle can thus be read, alternately, as a 'restoring' of opinions to Aristotle previously articulated by his commentators but overlooked by more recent writers, or, in a similar vein as the attribution of recent writers' arguments to elucidate Aristotle's original writings.

Mancini relied similarly on Aristotelian and mechanical explanations in his discussion of the void. He began, once again, by citing Aristotle's definition of the void as 'a place not filled by a body'. According to Mancini, Aristotle had distinguished between two types of voids. The

---

[69] 'sit exemplum de Navi celerrime currente quae si forte in Arenam impingat, et sistatur etiam si navis vere quiescat ob motum precedenter impressum movet illos, qui sunt in navi, quia adhuc quiescente navi perseverat motus impressio, simili ratione cum a stante in Navi emittatur sursum sagitta quantumque [*unreadable*] currat navis, in eundem locum navis recidit, et hoc a motu impresso motoris, si non velimus dicere quod Aer precedentur mutilatus ac motione conflictus violentiam maiorem prestet sagittae, qua forsan ipsa sagitta impressionem habeat a motore. Confirmamus hanc veritatem ex eo quo si quis fuerit in vertice Abetis, ac saxum proiciat in navim ad directionem longitudinis eiusdem Abetis etiamsi violenter currat Navis nec spatium quidem per minimum a directione ipsius abetis perfugitur a saxo': Ibid., 71r.

[70] On these arguments and their origins, see Edward Grant, *Planets, Stars, and Orbs: The Medieval Cosmos, 1200–1687* (Cambridge, 1994), 639–67.

[71] P. Gassendi, *Opera Omnia in Sex Tomos Divisa* (Lugduni: sumptibus Lavrentii Anisson & Ioan. Bapt. Devenet, 1658), vi. 108–9. French translations of the letters can be found in Pierre Gassendi, *Pierre Gassendi, 1592–1655: Lettres Latines*, trans. Sylvie Taussig (Turnhout, 2004).

first was one designated by the term *coacervatum* ('heaped up'), a void which was formed by a great space filled with no body. The second was a void *disseminatum* ('disseminated'), or a number of small empty spaces between bodies.[72] These distinctions originated not with Aristotle himself but with his later commentators, and they continued to be employed in the seventeenth century.[73]

As he moved on to consider the question of whether such a void could be produced, Mancini turned to recent experimental evidence. He described experiments with mercury tubes reported by the Accademia del Cimento, Boyle's accounts of his air-pump, and other experiments which had demonstrated a limit to the ascent of air.[74] While their creators had claimed that such experiments demonstrated the possibility of creating a void in nature, Mancini dismissed these arguments by stating that aetherial substances can be found within these so-called void spaces.

While such an explanation calls to mind the similar arguments made by other seventeenth-century professors of natural philosophy, including Bérigard, Mancini justified his account through the writings of Descartes.[75] Descartes also had argued that the apparently empty space above the mercury was not empty at all, but rather filled with the subtle and fast-moving tiny particles he identified as his 'first element' which, he claimed, entered through the pores of the glass.[76] Indeed Mancini went on

---

[72] 'Vacuum eg definitur ab Aristotele quod sit locus non repletus corpore. Dupliciter consideratur aliud coacervatum, et aliud disseminatum. Coacervatum dicitur, quando multum loci spatium nullo corpore expers est. Disseminatum vero, quando inter corpora dantur spatiola nullo corpore plena', Mancini, 'De Physica', 78v.

[73] On medieval precedent and its relevance to seventeenth-century discussion, see Edward Grant, *Much Ado about Nothing: Theories of Space and Vacuum from the Middle Ages to the Scientific Revolution* (Cambridge, 1981), 67–100, 182–255. On Gassendi's discussion, see Osler, *Divine Will and the Mechanical Philosophy*, 183.

[74] 'Pro explicatione Conclusionis antequam ad obiectiones deveniamus scire est, quod Aeris corpus eo ingredi potest, quo nos ingredi solidum non credimus; immo quod Aeris pars subtilior, quae vocatur aether eo loci subingreditur; quo aer ingredi non potest: Unde quoquo modo vergant hanc Conclusionem Philosophi absolute vacuum dari posse non assignant, cum potius immaginari, quam demonstrari vacuum possit. Varia sunt de vacuo experimenta, quorum ope vacuum dari demonstrasse credunt operatores, attamen vacuum absolute absque etiam aetherea substantia intus latitantiae nullatenus possunt probare... Variae tamen experientiae ducuntur in obiectionem naturae Conclusi; Unde dicant flammam vidisse praecipitare in vacuo ut Asserit experimentum Accademiae florentiae; sicuti de Machina pneumatica Doctissi Boile; immo Philosophorum aliqui demonstrarunt experientia Aerem nonnisi ad determinatum ascensum mensurae posse pervenire: Unde eo excesso vacuum necessario dari asserant, sicuti quod corpora, quae adinvicem a nobis dicuntur contigua eo motu agitari, quo per spatiola vacui disseminata corpus potest magis acutum introduci, et per consequens ibi dari vacuum, ubi disunita contiguitate corpus ultro compenetrat': Mancini, 'De Physica', 79r–v.

[75] For similar responses to these experiments, see, for example, Hellyer, *Catholic Physics*, chap. 7.

[76] Daniel Garber, *Descartes' Metaphysical Physics* (Chicago, 1992), 138.

to cite Descartes specifically, though his statement does not reveal that he read the French philosopher very carefully; Mancini confusingly attributed to him the opinion that small void spaces (*spatiola vacui disseminata*) are necessary to bring about motion in a more flexible body.[77] Mancini rejected this view and instead supported an opinion he attributed to Aristotle—and one with which Descartes also would have agreed—that such small spaces are actually plena. Turning to Aristotle once again, Mancini cited him in support of the opinion that such phenomena only prove 'a struggling void of a small moment', one in which air itself does not enter. Instead, Mancini argued that such spaces are filled with the more subtle and purer part of air, namely aether, which fills the space, making it only a relative void.[78]

In this discussion of the void, Mancini began with Aristotle and his definitions of the void and argued, following Aristotle, for the impossibility of creating an absolute void in nature. The arguments and reasoning Mancini provided to support his conclusions, however, derived from new speculation and experiment, namely citations of contemporary authors and evidence from recent experiments with mercury tubes and the air pump and responses to them.

Because of the way Mancini combined old and new in his teaching, it may be tempting to read Mancini's eclectic 'restoration' of Aristotle as a subterfuge, an attempt to pay lip service to Aristotle while endorsing aspects of Descartes's and Gassendi's mechanical philosophies. Such a conclusion has been advanced on behalf of other seventeenth-century scholars to explain their outward conformity with Aristotelian doctrine in the face of their apparent adherence to novel speculation.[79] Adopting

---

[77] 'Spatiola vacui disseminata, quae a Cartesio, et aliis sunt adducta ad rerum motum efficiendum flexibiliori corpore plena esse voluit Arist: sua tenendo sententia, quod Deus et natura nihil faciant frustra': Mancini, 'De Physica', 79a. According to modern scholars, Descartes very firmly denied the possibility of any void from 1630 on and had no qualms about explaining motion in a plenum: Garber, *Descartes' Metaphysical Physics*, 116–55.

[78] 'Respondetur quod haec est similia pariter experimenta vacuum probare nitentia parui momenti existimantur ab Aristotele: cum eo loco, quo Aer tendere non possit pars aeris subtilior ac purior perveniat, quae Aether nuncupatur, quod inter corpora contigua nonnisi relative vacuum dici potest, quia fluidum ac flexile corpus intermediat', Mancini, 'De Physica', 79b.

[79] Consider, for example, de Ceglia's evaluation that Biancani's claim to be providing a commentary on Aristotle using the writings of Galileo was a mere 'ploy': Francesco Paolo de Ceglia, '"Additio Illa Non Videtur Edenda": Giuseppe Biancani, Reader of Galileo in an Unedited Censored Text', in Mordechai Feingold (ed.), *The New Science and Jesuit Science: Seventeenth Century Perspectives* (Dordrecht/Boston, 2003), 162. In a recent contribution, Dinis outlines and moves beyond a tradition of scholarship that portrayed Riccioli as a secret Copernican, Dinis, 'Was Riccioli a Secret Copernican?', esp. 49–50. Laurence Brockliss insinuates the same for professors of philosophy in French universities at the turn of the eighteenth century, noting that while they had adopted Cartesian philosophy,

such logic, it could be argued that Mancini wanted to endorse some version of a mechanical philosophy, but that he was constrained by religious and secular authorities at Pisa to remain outwardly wedded to Aristotle and his texts. Alternatively, some might see in Mancini an awkward attempt to fuse Aristotle with the writings of Gassendi and Descartes. Such a project has been attributed to other university professors in the period with respect to various novel strands of philosophizing.[80]

This latter reading approaches Mancini's conception of his natural philosophical project, but it stops short of expressing it in full. By calling Mancini's natural philosophy a 'fusion' of mechanical speculation with Aristotelianism, it minimizes the intellectual validity of the eclectic approach. It also ignores Mancini's own professed conception of his project as a restoration of Aristotle, one that involved the application of recent philosophical speculation and experimental findings to questions and problems initially proposed by Aristotle. The notion that new philosophy could speak to the old was a common one in Pisa. Mancini shared this opinion not only with Bérigard but also with Carlo Rinaldini (1615–98), who served as a professor of natural philosophy from 1649 to 1667. While at Pisa, Rinaldini began work on a treatise of philosophy which was intended to cover all the canonical parts of natural philosophy, in addition to a volume on questions of physical mathematics. The first part of this work was published in 1681 as *Philosophia rationalis*; it treated questions of logic. Three of the four volumes of the second part were published at the end of Rinaldini's life, under the title of *Naturalis philosophia*. Ugo Baldini has claimed that Rinaldini's *Naturalis philosophia* allows a glimpse into how 'a contemporary of elevated philosophical and scientific culture perceived the Scientific Revolution'. Rinaldini viewed the relationship between old and new in remarkably similar terms as did Bérigard and Mancini, seeing the two projects of Aristotelian and the New Science as capable of being integrated.[81]

That Mancini could have understood Descartes's, Gassendi's and others' writings as relevant to his exposition of Aristotle is not surprising,

---

'all professors at the turn of the eighteenth century went out of their way to pretend that they had not really deserted Aristotle at all': Brockliss, *French Higher Education in the Seventeenth and Eighteenth Centuries*, 352.

[80] See, for example, Hellyer, *Catholic Physics*, 2; Carla Rita Palmerino, 'La fortuna della scienza galileiana nelle Province Unite', in Pepe (ed.), *Galileo e la scuola galileiana*, 61–79, 78.

[81] 'ma osservare che esso espresse il modo in cui un contemporaneo di elevata cultura filosofica e scientifica percepì la rivoluzione scientifica: supponendo possibile una (parziale) continuità delle forme del discorso sulla natura, egli assunse che i due paradigmi fossero integrabili': Baldini, 'Tra due paradigmi? La "Naturalis philosophia" di Carlo Rinaldini,' 221–2.

given that these innovators were familiar with the questions and topics traditionally associated with Scholastic teaching. Mancini would have been led to combine Aristotle, Descartes, and Gassendi in a curriculum structured by Aristotle through the common framework—consisting of definitions, methodological tenets, and topics—shared by Aristotle, Gassendi, and Descartes.[82] Nor is it unthinkable that Aristotle be reinterpreted according to the findings of more recent thinkers, for the notion that recent writing and findings could be used to clarify one's interpretation of Aristotle lies at the heart of the Scholastic enterprise. It was the project underlying the work of Aristotle's medieval commentators, and it was the same project in which Manini participated. His was not necessarily a 'conservative' intellectual enterprise nor was it an attempt by a secretive 'innovator' to hide his mechanist sympathies. Instead Mancini engaged in what was likely a common seventeenth-century project, namely the improvement of one's understanding of the natural world using all tools possible, both old and new.

Period innovators were vocal in their disparagement of traditional university teaching. Their rhetoric painted a picture of the early modern landscape as one divided between innovators and traditionalists. Modern historians have rehabilitated the reputation of the university and its members by revising period innovators' assessments of their peers. They have often done so, however, by implicitly embracing the same criteria as those individuals whose judgments they claim to overturn. In particular, they have followed period innovators in taking the acceptance of novel doctrine and methodologies and the rejection of traditional ones as markers of intellectual vigor. Early modern universities, according to this analysis, are thus not stale, moribund institutions—as period innovators claimed—because their members relied on empirical evidence, embraced (or at least taught) novel doctrine, and began to incorporate quantitative, mathematics in their courses on philosophy.[83] What separated period innovators from the university professors who taught their ideas was a series of restrictions—doctrinal, institutional, and religious—which constrained professors in what they could teach in the classroom. One necessary corollary of this argument has been the denigration of the intellectual output of these university professors. The implicit argument has been that if only these professors were not impeded by these outside

---

[82] Margaret J. Osler, 'New Wine in Old Bottles: Gassendi and the Aristotelian Origin of Physics', *Midwest Studies In Philosophy* 26/1 (2002), 167–84, esp. 167; Osler, *Divine Will and the Mechanical Philosophy*, 48, 103–5, 124.

[83] For one example of this tendency, see Porter, 'The Scientific Revolution and Universities', esp. 557–60.

factors, then they would have been fully contributing members of the rising movement to overturn established learning.

The writings of Bérigard and Mancini suggest, however, an alternative conception of their eclectic approach. For these two professors, intellectual engagement did not necessarily involve the embrace of the new at the expense of the old, where an eclectic middle ground was an unsatisfying compromise. Rather, it comprised an active search for truth, one which involved the amalgamation of a variety of truth claims and practices. According to their writings, Mancini and Bérigard regarded the University of Pisa as an intellectually stimulating environment precisely because its members were involved in this eclectic project of updating Aristotle. Bérigard and Mancini portrayed the university as a site where ideas were thrown together in battle so that truth could emerge. The ultimate victor was not a specific side, but truth. Although they acknowledged their debt to the ancients, it seems wise to refrain from labelling Mancini or even Bérigard as an 'Aristotelian', a 'Cartesian', or a 'Gassendian'. Instead, they were individuals trying to use available tools to describe their method and the content of their philosophizing to students.

Department of History
University of California, Irvine

Central European Polemics over Descartes: Johannes Placentinus and His Academic Opponents at Frankfurt on Oder (1653–1656)

Pietro D. Omodeo

Between 1653 and 1656 a heated polemic over Cartesianism and the reconcilability between Descartes's views and traditional university curricula burst out at the University of Frankfurt on Oder, at the so-called *Academia Viadrina* in Brandenburg.[1] The protagonist was the Bohemian-Polish mathematician Jan Kołaczek, latinized as Placentinus, a committed supporter of Cartesian philosophy, who had to face the attacks and the vexations of his colleagues from the Faculties of Philosophy and Theology. His opponents accused him of overturning a well-established scholarly tradition—mainly resting on Aristotelianism—and subverting the university statutes. They denounced him to the academic and political authorities for the dissemination of unprecedented ideas, and went so far as to reprimand his philosophical and cosmological teaching from the pulpit. Placentinus reacted with provocative writings and public demonstrations, such as the distribution of pro-Cartesian publications in the market place in front of the Church. He eventually overcame his adversaries by making a clever recourse to academic mechanisms and practices, such as the use of disputations to defend and propagate his theses, and by taking advantage of political ties, in particular the patronage of Friedrich Wilhelm of Brandenburg. I will reconstruct the details of these events, so far neglected

[1] I would like to thank Rodolfo Garau for critically reading an early version of this essay, Prof. Klaus Geus for his advice on Latin translations, and Louis Berger and Lindsay Parkhowell for their revision of the text. I am very thankful to Urs Schoepflin and the library staff of the Max Planck Institute for the History of Science for their support, especially for the digitalization of the archival documents discussed in this paper.

in the studies on the early reception of Descartes, on the basis of Placentinus's early publications as well as on a series of documents (including letters and reports issued by the competing parties) preserved in the archives of Potsdam (*Brandenburgisches Landeshauptarchiv*, hereafter referred to as BLHA) and Berlin (*Geheimes Staatsarchiv Preußischer Kulturbesitz*, hereafter GStA PK).[2]

I see this essay as a contribution to the investigation of the early reception of René Descartes in Central European academic institutions. At the beginning of the last century, Josef Bohatec, the first scholar who stressed the importance of reconstructing this line of reception, pointed out the intermingling of Cartesian and Aristotelian themes in this environment and coined the expression *cartesianische Scholastik*, or 'Cartesian Scholastic', in order to refer to it. According to him, the reason for this Cartesio-Aristotelian fusion was the necessity, perceived by the most 'moderate' among the followers of Descartes, to connect the new philosophy with theological dogmatics. In fact, in the century or so after Philip Melanchthon reformed the Lutheran university curricula, Lutheran theology had been systematized through Aristotelian categories.[3] However significant his study was as the first monograph exclusively dedicated to this issue, Bohatec neglected the social dynamics and the institutional constraints, as well as the scientific controversies and the negotiations that led to such an intellectual bias and to the reworking of Cartesian thought to make it suitable for university teaching. More recent studies have brought into focus the antagonisms of the age, especially related to the Cartesian controversies in the Netherlands and in France.[4] As to Germany, particular attention has been dedicated to the scholarly tradition of the University of Duisburg, where Cartesian philosophy was introduced into the studies of philosophy and medicine.[5] Yet a complete overview of the early reception

---

[2] I will mainly base my reconstruction on documents preserved in Potsdam BLHA as 'Acta betreffend Placentini', signature Rep. 86 Universität Frankfurt an der Oder, Nr. 45, and in Berlin GStA PK as 'Acta des Königl. Geheimen Staats-Archivs betreffend der Philosophorum [zu Frankfurt a. O.] Irrungen unter sich (1655-1659)', signature I HA Rep.51, Universität Frankfurt Oder, Nr. 94.

[3] Josef Bohatec, *Die cartesianische Scholastik in der Philosophie und reformierten Dogmatik des 17. Jahrhunderts* (2 vols, Leipzig, 1912), 4. The early reception of Descartes in German universities and gymnasia is discussed at 51–62.

[4] I will limit myself to mentioning, among the most important studies, Theo Verbeek, *Descartes and the Dutch: Early Reactions to Cartesian Philosophy 1637–1650* (Carbondale/Edwardsville, 1992) and Roger Ariew, *Descartes among the Scholastics* (Leiden, 2011), especially Chap. 9, 146–50: 'Cartesians, Gassendists, and Censorship'.

[5] Francesco Trevisani, *Descartes in Germania: La ricezione del cartesianesimo nella Facoltà filosofica e medica di Duisburg* (Milan, 1992) and Massimiliano Savini, *Johannes Clauberg: Methodus cartesiana et ontologie* (Paris, 2011). Cf. also Wolfgang Hübener, 'Descartes-Zitate bei Clauberg: Zum Quellenwert frühcartesianischer Kontroversliteratur für die Descartes-forschung', *Studia Leibnitiana*, 5/2 (1973), 233–9.

of Descartes, which brings together studies on individual scholars and local scholarly constellations, along with an analysis of additional primary sources and archival research, is still a desideratum.

Placentinus's name is almost absent from the studies on Cartesianism. Bohatec, for one, did not dedicate to this scholar more than a couple of lines: 'The Professor of mathematics in Frankfurt/Oder, Johannes Placentinus [. . .], was a follower of the Cartesian Scholastic'.[6] As a matter of fact, Placentinus authored in 1656 a work entitled *Syncretismus philosophicus inter Renatus Des-Cartes et Aristotelem institutus* (*Philosophical Syncretism Established between René Descartes and Aristotle*). Still, the consensus between Descartes and Aristotle as suggested by this title is only superficial. As I will show, this publication marked the conclusion of a furious Cartesian controversy in which Placentinus had been attacked for the irreconcilability of his views with the Aristotelian tradition and he, in response, had scorned Aristotle and his followers. Therefore we must ask whether his syncretistic publication was merely opportunistic, a concession made by Placentinus to his adversaries, or rather a provocation; only a reconstruction of the details of the controversy can offer us an insight into the features and the meaning of Placentinus's 'Scholastic Cartesianism' and, by extension, tell us something more about early academic responses to the philosophy of Descartes. I will investigate the reasons for the opposition to this philosophy in a Lutheran University with a Reformed *Landesherr*, and point to the tensions between local traditions and European-wide networks of scholars and ideas.[7] Placentinus, in fact, had received his education at leading university centres, especially in the Netherlands. Thus, in the midst of the polemics, he proudly claimed to be part of an international community of Cartesians ranging from the Netherlands to Sweden, France, and other German provinces. In the following pages I will introduce him and his early work, and focus on the institutional mechanisms that enabled him to circulate new conceptions at the crossroads of a confessionalized academy, the princely court, and the wider Republic of Letters.

Placentinus's Curriculum Studiorum

Jan Kołaczek of Leszno (or Lissa) was appointed as *professor ordinarius* of mathematics at Frankfurt in 1653. His Latinized name, as indicated in the

---

[6] Bohatec, *Die cartesianische Scholastik*, 61: 'In Frankfurt a. d. O. war der Mathematiker Joh. Placentinus Lesnensis (1653–1665[sic!]) Anhänger der cartesianischen Scholastik'.

[7] Cf. Kenneth G. Appold, 'Academic Life and Teacing in Post-Reformation Lutheranism', in Robert Kolb (ed.), *Lutheran Ecclesiastical Culture, 1550–1675* (Brill, 2008), 65–116.

official letter of appointment by Friedrich Wilhelm of Brandenburg, was
'Johannes Placentinus Lesnensis Polonus'.[8] At the time of his appointment, he was in his early twenties. His birth year, inferred from indirect
evidence, was either 1629 or 1630.[9] Placentinus's family was of Bohemian
origin, as indicated in some documents in which he is mentioned as
'Bohemo-Polonus' or 'Lasna-Bohemus'.[10] His parents, belonging to the
religious minority of the Bohemian Brothers, absconded to Leszno in
1637 in order to escape religious persecution in their country of origin. In
Leszno, a few years after their arrival, their fellow countryman, Jan Amos
Komeński (better known as *Johannes Comenius*) established a school
organized around his pedagogical principles (1640).[11] Arguably, Placentinus received his first education in this Gymnasium.[12] The lack of documentary evidence does not permit us to assess his confessional situation
nor whether he maintained contacts with the network of Bohemian
emigrates.

Placentinus studied at several Baltic, German, and Dutch gymnasia
and universities, among them Gdańsk (1648), Königsberg (1649), Groningen (1651), Leiden (1652), and Heidelberg (1653).[13] From the introduction of one of his most provocative Cartesian contributions, *Renatus
Des-Cartes Triumphans* (*René Descartes Triumphant*, Frankfurt/Oder,
1655), we know that he studied Cartesian philosophy at Groningen
under the supervision of the Greek and history professor Tobias Andreae
and the theologian Samuel des Marets (Lat. *Maresius*). At Leiden, he

---

[8] GStA PK I HA Rep. 51, Universität Frankfurt Oder, Nr. 92, 1560–1730, without
folio numeration. The original Slavic name can be inferred from a manuscript document
of 1667, signed 'Placentinianum, alias Kolaczkianum' (GStA PK, I HA Rep. 51, Nr. 95,
'Scrutinium longitudinis locorum').

[9] I derive these possible birth dates from his enrolment at the University of Groningen
on 2 July 1651. In the album it is indicated that, at the moment of the enrolment,
Placentinus was 21 years old. Historisch Genootschap te Groningen, *Album Studiosorum
Academiae Groninganae* (Groningen, 1915), 64: 'Johannes Placentinus Lesnensis, a[nni]
21, Theol[ogia] et Mathem[atica], Gratis, quia exul'.

[10] Such expressions appear in Placentinus's registration as a rector at Frankfurt on Oder
in 1659 and 1665. See *Aeltere Universitäts-Matrikeln, Universität Frankfurt a. O.*, ed. Ernst
Friedländer (3 vols, Leipzig, 1887–91), ii. 72, 106.

[11] Comenius's *Leges Illustri Gymnasii Lesnensis* can be found in *Veškerých Spisů Jana
Amosa Komenského*, ed. Josef Reber (Brno, 1911), 1–10.

[12] Cf. Ludwik Chmaj, 'Jan Placentinus-Kołaczek: Nieznany Kartezjanin XVII wieku',
Archiwum historii filozofii i myśli społecznej, 1 (1957), 71–81.

[13] *Catalogus Discipulorum Gymnasii Gedanensis (1508–1814)*, ed. Zbigniew Nowak &
Przemysław Szafran (Warsaw/Poznań, 1972), 161; *Die Matrikel der Albertus-Universität
zu Königsberg i. Pr.*, ed. Georg Erler (3 vols, Leipzig, 1908–17), ii. 506; Historisch
Genootschap te Groningen, *Album Studiosorum Academiae Groninganae*, 64; *Album Studiosorum Academiae Lugduno Batavae 1575–1875*, ed. Martin Nijhoff (Leiden, 1875), 422;
and *Die Matrikel der Universität Heidelberg*, ed. Gustav Toepke (7 vols, Heidelberg,
1884–1913), ii. 316, n. 68.

studied under the theologian Abraham van der Heyden (*Heidanus*) and the philosopher Johannes de Raey.[14] He also maintained contacts with Poland, as is witnessed by his correspondence with the Gdańsk astronomer Johannes Hevelius.[15]

As soon as he arrived in Germany, he set about disseminating the mathematical and philosophical views he had learned in the Netherlands. But this proved an arduous task from the very beginning. Two days after he matriculated at Heidelberg, on 27 June 1653, Placentinus was prevented from giving private lectures unless he agreed to be evaluated by the Faculty of Philosophy. He declared willing to undergo the examination. However, in the following semester he moved to Frankfurt on Oder. Perhaps he did not pass the examination, or he found it more convenient to move to the territories of Friedrich Wilhelm, who was a Calvinist ruler favorable to influences coming from the Dutch Republic.

The Electoral Prince's cousin, Elizabeth of Palatinate, was the affectionate correspondent to whom René Descartes dedicated his *Principia philosophiae* (1644) and for whom, as the French philosopher declared, he composed *Les Passions de l'âme* (1649).[16] Notably, Placentinus later dedicated to her a book on geography, *Geotomia* (Frankfurt/Oder, 1657), signing the dedicatory epistle as 'a very humble and devoted client of Your Very Serene Highness' (*Serenissimae Celsitudini Vestrae humillimus et devotissimus Cliens*). Thus, Placentinus's name should be added to the list of scholars and philosophers who corresponded with her, along with the physician Franciscus Mercurius van Helmont, and the philosophers Nicolas Malebranche and Gottfried Wilhelm Leibniz.[17]

Friedrich Wilhelm of Brandenburg frequented Elizabeth's family during his formative years in the Netherlands (1634-8). He later maintained close ties with her and obtained her election as abbess of Herford, which was under his jurisdiction (30 April 1667). Therefore, it should not surprise us that this Prince received with benevolence a Cartesian educated

---

[14] Johannes Placentinus, *Renatus Des-Cartes Triumphans, id est, Principia Philosophiae Cartesianae in Alma Viadrina ventilata atque defensa a Johanne Placentino Lesnensi, Mathematum Professore Ordinario* (Frankfurt/Oder, 1655), unnumbered folio, but f. 3r ab incipit.

[15] One letter is printed in Placentinus, *Physicalischer und Astrologischer Bericht von denen erschrecklichen... Winden* (Frankfurt/Oder, 1661), ff. E3r-E4r. Hevelius's letter (Gdańsk, 2 March 1661, following the Gregorian calendar) dealt with celestial singularities observed that year: a comet, a nova, and a parhelion ('seven suns') that were visible in Gdańsk on 20 February at about 11 am. Seven manuscript letters are preserved in the *Observatoire de Paris* among Hevelius's letters. I thank Patricia Radelet de Grave for this valuable information.

[16] On Elizabeth and Descartes, cf. Stephen Gaukroger, *Descartes: An Intellectual Biography* (Oxford, 1995), chap. 10.

[17] Gerd van den Heuvel, 'Elisabeth und die Philosophen', in Helge Bei der Wieden (ed.), *Elisabeth von der Pfalz, Äbtissin von Herford, 1618–1680* (Hannover, 2008), 59–76.

in the Netherlands. As we shall see, his support was fundamental for Placentinus's early career.

The Conditions for the Appointment at Frankfurt on Oder

Placentinus enrolled at the *Academia Viadrina* in the Winter Semester of 1653/4.[18] On 3 December 1653 he submitted a mathematical disputation under the auspices of the Professor of Greek, Georg Mollemanus (or Mellman). The title of this short publication is quite generic: *Disputatio mathematica exhibens themata ex universa mathesi* (*Mathematical Disputation Presenting Issues from All Mathematics*). It entails a series of theses pertaining to different fields of mathematics.[19] Although Placentinus exposed these new theses in a very cautious manner, his opponents accused him of spreading novel theories nonetheless. When they said that he had disguised these theories at the moment of his appointment, he replied that on the occasion of his first disputation he had not openly expressed his views on purpose in order to avoid polemics:

> Mr. Placentinus has recently revealed to an eminent and reliable person the only real and true reason why he started treating such novel doctrines in disputations. As that person told him (Placentinus) that he should respect the Statutes and his oath, he (Placentinus) answered that he had behaved in that manner, because in the examination he had been too strictly required to present disciplinary definitions, in an attempt to downplay [*deprimieren*] his intelligence, as if he knew absolutely nothing. Hence, [on that occasion] he aimed to prove that he had some knowledge.[20]

Even under these circumstances, Placentinus's first disputation is not completely devoid of interest. Some theses refer to theoretical and

---

[18] *Aeltere Universitäts-Matrikeln*, ed. Friedländer, 38.

[19] The theses concern the following fields, then seen as belonging to mathematics: arithmetic, geometry, geodesy, astronomy in general, spherical astronomy, planetary theory, astrology, geography, music, optics, and statics, as well as civil and military architecture.

[20] GStA PK, I HA Rep.51, Universität Frankfurt Oder, Nr. 94, *Acta des Königl. Geheimen Staats-Archivs betreffend der Philosophorum [zu Frankfurt a. O.] Irrungen unter sich (1655–1659)*, f. 62r-v: 'Alleine waß die rechte unt echte Ursache sey, Warumb H[err] Placentinus solcher newerung *disputando* sich unterfangen, daß hat Er noch newelich, gegen eine vornehme und glaubwürdige Person an den tag gegeben: Von welcher, als Ihme (Placentino) für gehalten worden, daß Er den *Statutis*, und seinem *Pacto*, wol hette mögen nachkommen, Er (Placentinus) geantwortet, Er hette es darumb gethan, Weil mann in *Examine*, die *Definitiones Artium* zu scharff von Ihm erfordert, und sein *ingenium* deprimiren wollen, als wüste Er gar nichts: so hette Er es wollen sehen laßen, daß er etwas könte'.

technical innovations of the time; others even hint at cosmological and natural novelties at odds with the views that were traditionally imparted to students. For instance, Placentinus stressed the computational advantages of John Napier's logarithms in astronomy, geodesy, and geography.[21] One of his theses on statics is an objection to the Aristotelian theory that no body is heavy *per se*.[22] Rather, he supported the relativity of heaviness in line with the neo-Archimedean advances of mechanics that culminated with Galileo Galilei.

Placentinus showed a marked interest in optics and in the explanation of the properties of lenses. This reveals his attentiveness to the advances of telescopic astronomy.[23] In the corollaries, on the Moon and the tides, Placentinus emphasized the analogy between the lunar asperities and terrestrial mountains and valleys, which is a step toward the affirmation of the principle of cosmological homogeneity.[24] Copernican themes emerge from the astronomical theses that the distance of the fixed stars cannot be determined (th. 16), that the Earth is not necessarily at the centre of the solar orbit (th. 17), and that the *motus spiralis* of the Sun (that is, its variation of declination during the year) is not an effect of some motion accomplished by the Sun itself (th. 19).[25] The first of these astronomical theses refers to the Copernican enlargement of the dimensions of the cosmos to account for the absence of observable stellar parallax in spite of the circumsolar path of the Earth.

Placentinus asserted the existence of celestial orbs, although he remarked that they are not solid (th. 21). As we shall see, this ought to be understood as a reference to the Cartesian vortex theory which he supported.[26] He also advanced the epistemological claim that planetary theory can be treated not only a posteriori but also a priori. A position such as this echoes Kepler's project of an a priori foundation of the heliocentric system, as well as Descartes's rationalistic philosophy.

In the title page of his first disputation, Placentinus mentioned his promoter, Professor Mollemanus, with reverence as: 'my patron and supporter whom I shall always revere' (*patronus et fautor suus perpetim venerandus*). Yet, despite this apparent agreement between the two, Mollemanus would soon turn out to be one of his harshest adversaries. Another scholar who would later oppose him, Magister Elias Grebnitz, dedicated a eulogy to him. The poem, printed at the end of the four-folio

---

[21] Placentinus, *Disputatio mathematica exhibens themata ex universa mathesi* (Frankfurt/Oder, 1653), f. A2r, th. 8 and f. A2r, th. 12.
[22] Ibid., f. A4r, th. 48.   [23] Ibid., f. A4r, th. 43–4.
[24] Ibid., f. A4v, Cor. 3.   [25] Ibid., f. A2v.
[26] On Descartes's vortex theory and its reception, see E.J. Aiton, *The Vortex Theory of Planetary Motions* (London/New York, 1972).

long disputation, began with the following verses emphasizing Placentinus's education in the Netherlands: 'Oh Placentinus, brought to us by the waves of the Dutch sea,/whose wealth you, oh lucky one, bring to our shore'.[27]

This mathematical disputation ensured Placentinus his position in the Philosophical Faculty. On 12 December, the rector, the theologian Conradus Bergius, and his colleagues (*Rector, Magistri undt Doctores*) officially announced their intention to appoint him as a professor of mathematics ('Johannes Placentinus wirdt zum Professore Mathematum vorgesehen und bestatiget').[28] The Prince ratified this decision on 18 December, under the condition that Placentinus obtain the title of *Magister* from Frankfurt as soon as possible.

Placentinus received his Master's degree in May of the following year. On 27 April 1654, the dean and the professors of the Philosophical Faculty asked the Electoral Prince for permission to confer the degree onto him ('Verleihung des akademischen Grades eines Magisters der Philosophie'). In the letter, they extolled the merits of their illustrious colleague, referring to him as 'our colleague, whom we particularly love for the strength of his intelligence, and for his dexterity in the study of the mathematical science and its teaching'.[29]

In spite of these effusive references, there were already signals of the incipient conflict. Some philosophers were concerned about Placentinus's philosophical views, as emerged from a later denunciation (a *Kürzer relation und supplicatum*) penned by Mollemanus and some colleagues of the Philosophical Faculty (*Decanus, Senior und Professores d[er] Philo [sophischen] Fac[ultät]*) and sent to the Brandenburg chancellor Thomas von Knesebeck on 26 January 1655.[30] As one reads in the report, on 5 December 1653—that is, two days after the submission of his mathematical disputation—the Philosophical Faculty received Placentinus and communicated to him that the assignation of the vacant chair of

---

[27] Placentinus, *Disputatio mathematica*, f. A4v: 'Placentine, maris Batavi prolatus ab unda,/Eius opes nostram felix deducis in oram'.

[28] GStA PK I HA Rep.51, Universität Frankfurt Oder Nr. 92, Phil. Fak., 1560–1730, without numbering.

[29] GStA PK I HA Rep.51, Universität Frankfurt Oder Nr. 96, Bd. 1 1605–1700, f. 111v: 'Dn. noster Collega qui ob praestans ingenium, praeclaram in matheseos studio scientiam docendique dexteritatem, nobis omnibus unice est in amoribus'.

[30] Two copies of this denunciation are still extant. One is preserved in BLHA, Rep. 86 Universität Frankfurt an der Oder, Nr. 45. The second copy, from which I will quote, is preserved in GStA PK, I HA Rep.51, Universität Frankfurt Oder, Nr. 94, *Acta des Königl. Geheimen Staats-Archivs betreffend der Philosophorum [zu Frankfurt a. O.] Irrungen unter sich (1655–1659)*, ff. 56r–63v. In the following I will refer to this document as *Kürzer relation (26 Jan. 1655)*.

mathematics depended on the following three conditions: first, he had to improve his 'erudition'; second, he had to obtain the Master's degree; third, he should refrain from teaching philosophical novelties to the students. The latter limitation sheds light on Placentinus's reasons for prudence in his first disputation, and goes as follows:

> He should abandon all strange and abnormal opinions differing from the genre of philosophy that is accepted in our [university]. In the case that he adheres to some new doctrines [*opiniones*], he should keep them for himself and should certainly renounce disseminating them among the students.[31]

Despite this admonishment, when Placentinus presented his first teaching programme on 27 December 1653, he still tried to introduce some *novitates* in the form of astonishing theses on sunspots and comets, which his adversaries would later denounce.

> Irrespective of that [of his colleagues' admonishments], he soon began to spread his novel theories through the press in his first inaugural programme on 27 December 1653. Among other things, he brought forward [the following thesis] [. . .]: 'In the solar body, spots are sometimes generated, sometimes corrupted, sometimes converted into flames [*faculas*]. Fixed stars are often generated all of a sudden and gradually disappear so that they degenerate into comets'.[32]

He probably published these views in *Observatio Eclipseos Solaris peracta in Alma Viadrina... 1654* (*Observation of a Solar Eclipse Accomplished at the Academia Viadrina*, Frankfurt/Oder 1654), which is catalogued in the *Staatsbibliothek zu Berlin* as 'Kriegsverlust' (i.e., as lost during World War II).

Controversies on Terrestrial Motion, Tides, and Cartesian Philosophy

More than one hundred years after the publication of Nicholas Copernicus's *De revolutionibus orbium coelestium*, the astronomical theses that the Earth *might not* occupy the centre of the solar orbit and that the daily rotation does

---

[31] *Kürzer relation (26 Jan. 1655)*, f. 56*v*: 'Daß er alle frembde, ungewöhnliche, und vom *Philosophandi genere apud nos recepto* abweichende *opiniones* fahren laßen solte. Hette er etliche newe *opiniones*, so solte Er dieselben für sich behalten, mit nichten aber unter die studiosos proseminiren'.

[32] Ibid., ff. 57*r*-*v*: 'Deßen aber ungeachtet, hat Er bald in seinem ersten *programmate inaugurali* den 27 Decemb[ris] 1653 seine *novitates per typum* zu spargiren angefangen, und unter andern lin. 3 et seqq. fürgebracht: "In corpore solari maculae mox generantur, mox corrumpuntur, mox in faculas convertuntur. Stellae fixae saepius ex improviso apparent, ac paulatim disparent, sicque in cometas degenerant"'.

not depend on the motion of the starry heaven were far from surprising to a northern European Reformed audience. At Frankfurt Placentinus's predecessor, David Origanus, had already defended the thesis of a magnetic axial rotation of the Earth at the beginning of the century. At Rostock and at Helmstedt, the Copernican system had been taught alongside the Ptolemaic and the Tychonic since the end of the sixteenth century. Kepler had defended and developed the heliocentric theory at the imperial court of Prague, whereas his competitor, Christian Longomontanus, professor of mathematics at Copenhagen, had revised the geoheliocentric theory of his master Brahe including the axial rotation of the Earth. In the second decade of the seventeenth century, terrestrial motion was discussed in disputations at the Gymnasium of Stettin, and Peter Crüger freely presented different sets of astronomical hypotheses at the Gdańsk Gymnasium. By the time of Placentinus's appointment at Frankfurt, Crüger's most renowned pupil, Johannes Hevelius, had already published his epoch-making lunar maps in the *Selenographia* (Gdańsk, 1647). Here, he discussed at length the most important telescopic novelties of the time and defended the heliocentric system.[33] In spite of this wide discussion of Copernicus's hypotheses in northern Europe, Placentinus's teaching of terrestrial motion encountered the violent reaction of his colleagues.

On 21 January 1654, Placentinus printed a disputation *de Terra*, 'which was comprised of many novel doctrines', as his adversaries claimed.[34] This disputation was probably the collection of *Mathematico-Physical Theses on Earth* (*Theses mathematico-physicae de Terra*, catalogued as 'Kriegsverlust' in the *Staatsbibliothek* of Berlin).[35] Nonetheless, it is not difficult to reconstruct Placentinus's views on this matter from the denunciations of his opponents as well as from his later publications: *Discussio mathematica erotematis, An Terra moveatur? (Mathematical Discussion of the Question: Does the Earth Move?)* (Frankfurt/Oder, 1655) and *Dissertatio, delationem Terrae annuam, et circumgyrationem diurnam circa proprium centrum, probans (Dissertation, in Which the Annual Shift of the Earth and the Daily Circumvolution around Its Own Centre Are Demonstrated).*[36]

---

[33] Cf. Pietro Daniel Omodeo, *Copernicus in the Cultural Debates of the Renaissance: Reception, Legacy, Transformation* (Leiden, 2014).

[34] *Kürzer relation (26 Jan. 1655)*, f. 57*v*: 'in welcher viel newes dinges enthalten'.

[35] One copy of this dissertation is preserved in the British Library, St. Pancras (London, UK) according to its catalogue.

[36] The *Dissertatio* is printed as an appendix to Placentinus, *Vier Nachdenkliche Fragen und* Instantien *aus denen* Physicali*schen und* Astronomi*schen Wissenschaften genommen* (Frankfurt/Oder, 1659).

According to his adversaries' report (the *Kürzer relation* of 26 January 1655), after the publication of these theses the dean of the Philosophical Faculty called Placentinus to order. He reminded him of his oath of obedience (*juramentum de obedientia*) and of the statutes' prescriptions.[37] According to Placentinus's later report on the facts, three colleagues were particularly severe with him, 'M. Mellman, M. Lesle, und M. Becman', professors of Greek, logic, and physics (i.e., natural philosophy) respectively.[38] They tried to prevent him, he writes, from disseminating his Cartesio-Copernican doctrines. Nonetheless, Placentinus defended them on 28 January 1654.

His enemies denounced the most scandalous ones ('welche... nur verwirrunge einführen' [which bring only confusion]). Some of them are Copernican: thesis two, that the Earth is a planet ('daß die Erde ein Planet sey'), and thesis four, that it is one of the wandering stars ('daß sie ihres *situm inter stellas erraticas* habe'). Other theses are derived from Descartes's *Principia philosophiae*, such as theses six and eight which concerned the vortex theory explaining the origin of the Earth and its revolution about the Sun. The philosophers also mentioned the theory of the three Cartesian material elements as one of the absurdities that should not be taught to 'innocent' youth. It is evident that the Copernican theory was still seen as an undesirable paradox in this German university more than one hundred years after its first publication, and its philosophical foundation on new, Cartesian doctrines made it even more unacceptable.

In spite of these polemics, Placentinus received his Master's degree in the spring of that year. In the following summer, he left for Prussia to marry his future wife.[39] After he had returned, he embarked on a new controversial disputation, concerning tidal theory, which he defended on 19 July 1654.[40] His explanation was based on the Cartesian elements and the doctrine of the vortices. The judgement of the Frankfurt philosophers was even sarcastic: 'To sum up, vortices are here and vortices are there. They fill the ears but not the intellect'.[41]

---

[37] *Kürzer relation (26 Jan. 1655)*, f. 57*v*–58*r*.

[38] GStA PK Rep.51, Nr. 94, f. 49*r*.

[39] As far as I have been able to ascertain, the name of Placentinus's wife is not reported in the documents.

[40] A copy of that disputation is preserved as an appendix to the aforementioned *Vier Nachdenkliche Fragen* under the title *Dissertatio, Fluxum et Refluxum Oceani, demonstrans* (*Dissertation, in Which the Flux and Reflux of the Ocean is demonstrated*). The correspondence between this appendix and the disputation of 1654 can be established through a comparison with the quotations in the denunciation against Placentinus of January 1655.

[41] *Kürzer relation (26 Jan. 1655)*, f. 58*v*. '*Summa Vortices* sind hinter und *Vortices* sind vorn. *Aures implentes, non intellectum*'.

For his enemies, one of the most alarming aspects in his philosophy was the *méthode*. In their first extensive denunciation they repeated several times that he had 'unduly' addressed cosmological and natural issues *more geometrico*. Moreover, to their increasing chagrin, on 29 October 1654 he announced a new programme, specifically directed against the professor of natural philosophy (*professor physices*), Philipp Beckmann (*Philippus Becmannus*),[42] who was the brother of the rector. Placentinus called his own principles 'more solid' (*solidiora*) than those of his adversaries who stuck to a traditional Aristotelian frame. Also, he was able to treat physics in mathematical terms and with mathematical evidence.[43] As is reported, he disregarded the philosophy of his adversaries, calling their quarrels vulgar and insubstantial (*vulgares et leviusculas ratiunculas*).[44] After he realized that the professor of natural philosophy was printing a disputation *De Mundo* defending traditional views, he rapidly prepared a counter-disputation entitled *De delatione Terrae*. His colleagues blocked its publication and attempted to censure it.[45] This began a quarrel that involved the Faculty dean, Johannes Walter Lesle, and the rector, the theologian Friedrich Beckmann, devout men concerned with moral rectitude and orthodoxy.[46]

---

[42] Philipp Beckmann's confirmation as professor of physics (8 April 1653) is to be found in GStA PK, I HA Rep.51, Nr. 92, 1560–1730. He is mentioned as 'Dessaviensis, Medicus Anhaltinus'. He was confirmed in his position along with M. Johannes Waltherus Lesle *Dantiscanus Borussus* (logic) and M. Erasmus Scultetus, *Pastor Botaniensis in Silesia* (rhetoric).

[43] *Kürzer relation (26 Jan. 1655)*, f. 59r: 'In *Programmate contra Professorem Physices*, am 29. Octob[ris] Sontages nach mittage angeschlagen, nennet Er seine *principia solidiora et reapse vera*, und verspricht auß bloßer zunötigung, *Physicam ad evidentiam mathematicam* zu reduciren'.

[44] Ibid., 61v: 'Es ist auch sehr schimpflich, das *Autor eodem* in *Prologo* [in der disputation *De delatione Terrae*], die, seiner sententz von hocherfahrenen *Philosophis* entgegen gesetzte gründe verachtet, und *vulgares et leviusculas ratiunculas* nennet'.

[45] Ibid., f. 59r: 'Als Er vernommen, daß *Professor Physices* eine *disputationem de Mundo* in die druckerrey gegeben, hat Er sie daselbst durch gelesen, und eylendes den andern tag drauf seine *disputation de Delatione Terrae* zum verdruß, in der druckerey gebracht: darin nicht allein vorbesagte *novitates*, sondern auch stachelworte gefunden worden, so gar, daß auch der herr Magnificus [Rector], nach dem es Ihm zu ohren gebracht, solche *disputation* der Censur Unsers *Decani* zu vbergeben rathsam erachtet'.

[46] The 'spirit' of these two theological minds is revealed by their extant publications. Friedrich Beckmann promoted a *Dissertatio theologica de exorcismi* (Beckmann, Frankfurt/ Oder, 1689) dealing with exorcism and baptism, also hinting at the expulsion of the devil in connection with diseases (6: 'Exorcismi et artis, quae Daemones fugantur et morbi curantur, inventionem ad Salomonem refert'). Johannes Waltherus Lesle Scoto-Borus. Dantiscanus defended and presided over theses on justification, predestination, and Providence. I consulted e.g. Johann Waltherus Lesle, *Disputatio theologica de Dicto Rom. V. vers. 18. 19. Sicut per unam offensam reatus venit in omnes homines* (Frankfurt/Oder, 1651); Lesle, *De Providentia Dei* (Frankfurt/Oder, 1666); and Lesle, *De Justificatione hominis peccatoris coram Deo* (Frankfurt/Oder, 1667).

The 1654 Censure of the Disputation
on the 'delatio' of the Earth

After his adversaries interrupted the printing of his disputation *De dela-tione Terrae* (13 November 1654), Placentinus wrote a letter of protest to the Prince (23 November) asking for his intervention. He accused the rector of attacking him for personal reasons. He wrote that rector Beck-mann first took away the manuscript from the typesetter and passed it to Lesle for censure. Not satisfied with this, he hung the title of the dispu-tation at the entrance door of the Church and tore it apart during the Mass. According to Placentinus, this aroused the indignation of several people, in particular of his students.[47] Rector Beckmann even menaced the printer with corporal punishment if he were to complete the publica-tion of the censured disputation.[48]

Friedrich Wilhelm of Brandenburg quickly intervened in defence of the persecuted *mathematicus*, writing the following injunction to the philo-sophers (Cöln an der Spree, now Berlin, 2 January 1655):

> We cannot see any reason why he, as an appointed professor, should be deprived of his right [*Facultät*] to hold and print disputations, especially since he has submitted these same [disputations] to public examination by doctoral holders. Thus, We graciously order that you should not hinder or disturb Placentinus in any manner, neither in his defence and dissemination of mathematical truth nor in his academic studies.[49]

As a response, the philosophers sent a detailed account to chancellor Knesebeck, offering their version of the facts. This is the *Kürzer relation* of 26 January 1655. They declared that the theses Placentinus intended to propound were incompatible with both the statutes of the Philosophical Faculty and with the oath the mathematician made upon appointment. Therefore, rector Beckmann had decided that the disputation could not be defended unless all philosophical novelties were expunged. In particu-lar, Placentinus had to renounce his 'geometrical mode of disputation', as well as his definitions, postulates, and axioms. Among the most suspect ones, the censors mentioned the definition of body (*corpus*) as *res extensa*

---

[47] GStA Rep.51, Nr. 94, f. 64r.   [48] Ibid., f. 64r.

[49] Ibid., f. 55r-v. 'Nun können wir nicht absehen, warumb ihm, alß einem bestalten *Professori*, in seiner *Facultät, disputationes* zu halten und drucken zu lassen, gewehret werden will; Bevorab da er dieselbe *pubblico Doctorum examini subijciret*. Ergehet derowegen Unser gnädigster befehlich hiemit an euch, ihr wollet es dahin nichts, daß ihme *Placentino*, weder in *defendenda et propaganda veritate mathematica*, noch in seinen andern *studijs Academicis* einige hinderung oder molestien zugefüget werden mögen'.

(def. 1); Placentinus's claim he had abandoned 'prejudices' and based his arguments solely on reason (postulate 1);[50] and his assumption that God set matter in motion at the beginning of the world (post. 3). Moreover, they attacked Placentinus's distinction between 'local motion' (*motus localis*) and *delatio* (that is, 'shift'), which they decreed was sophistic. This conceptual subtlety permitted him to argue that the Earth does not move of local motion while fluid celestial matter shifts it around the Sun and twists it about its axis. He conceived of the Earth by analogy with a small object such as a straw (*festuca*) transported by the stream of a river. These theses directly descended from Descartes's cosmology. In particular, they remind us the Cartesian *fable cosmogonique*, according to which the 'mobile immobility' of the Earth has a clear aim: that of removing the heliocentric system from the censure of theologians resting on biblical literalism.

Placentinus's Cartesio-Copernicanism

The Prince's intervention in favour of Placentinus settled the controversy for a while and gave Placentinus a new impetus. On 24 February 1655 a student of his, Samuel Kaldenbach, submitted the disputation *An Terra moveatur?* on terrestrial motion. On that occasion, Placentinus figured as president in the disputation, and used it as an occasion to expound his own views.

Kaldenbach remarked in his beginning that there is no reason to stick to certain philosophical assumptions if others are more compelling and are therefore more likely. No natural thesis should be wiped out a priori because of its novelty. Arguments should decide which theory rests on more solid foundations. In fact, as Galileo teaches, truth can be gained by means of argumentation.

> In the first dialogue *On the System of the World* [. . .] Galileo Galilei wisely says: 'Philosophy itself will greatly benefit from our disputations. In fact, if we propose true [theses], it [philosophy] will grow through the addition of new [knowledge]. By contrast, if we propose something false, the old

---

[50] Cf. Descartes's dedicatory letter of the *Meditationes* 'Sapientissimis clarissimis viris Sacrae Facultatis Theologiae Parisiensis Decano et Doctoribus', in René Descartes, *Meditationes de prima philosophia*, in *Oeuvres*, ed. Charles Adam & Paul Tannery (11 vols, Paris, 1983), vii. 4 (emphasis added): 'Ita, quamvis eas quibus hic utor, certitudine et evidentia vereor tamen ne a multis satis percipi non possint, tum quia etiam longiusculae sunt, et aliae ab aliis pendent, tum praecipue quia *requirunt mentem a praejudiciis plane liberam*, et quae se ipsam sensuum confortio facile subducat'.

doctrines [*sententiae*] will be reinforced through the refutation of these false propositions'.[51]

The first thesis of the disputation affirms terrestrial motion (or, rather, the motion of the terrestrial element) and follows all astronomers and natural philosophers who 'Copernicize' (*Coperniturientes*).[52] The subsequent theses go into detailed analysis which serve as punctual responses to the objections of Scholastic adversaries. The difference of local motion and *delatio* is reaffirmed (th. 3). Placentinus claimed that this distinction should be familiar even to traditional philosophers for Peripatetic philosophy assumes that heavenly bodies do not move by themselves but are transported by celestial spheres (th. 5).

Another anti-Copernican objection Placentinus considered rests on the assumption that the element 'earth' strives toward the gravitation and cosmological centre and that this is its unique 'natural' motion. Following Galileo (whom he explicitly mentioned), Placentinus objected that the displacement of a body can indeed result from the composition of more than one motion, although the Aristotelians thought that this is at odds with the natural order (th. 9). Furthermore, there is no reason to believe that the Earth, as a centre, cannot move. Does not the Ptolemaic theory admit the spinning of the centres of the epicycles? Why should a centre be at rest and not turn? (th. 10) Additionally, there is no compelling reason to consider the Earth to be the universal centre of all heavy bodies. If it were so, all the stars, seen as heavy bodies, should converge toward it (th. 11). Placentinus also replied to those who argued that terrestrial motion cannot last, because it is violent. He objected that terrestrial motion is not disruptive, because it is allotted to a *corpus agitabilis* (movable body). Rather, motion fulfills the potentialities of such a body and leads it to perfection (th. 13).[53]

A reference to the mechanical works by Archimedes, Heron, and Pappus (and a reference to Bernardino Baldi mentioning them) served Placentinus in his wish to dispel the anti-Cartesian objection that the Earth could not be transported by an elemental, heavenly matter which is lighter than our planet. In fact, mechanics and pneumatics show many

---

[51] Placentinus, *Discussio mathematica erotematis, an Terra moveatur?... Pres. Dn. Johannes Placentino... Respondebit exercitii gratia Samuel Kaldenbach... Polono... D. 24. Febr.* (Frankfurt/Oder, 1655), f. A2r: 'Scite *Galilaeus Galilaei dial. I de mund. Syst.* p. 29 *Ipsa Philosophia*, inquit, *nostris e disputationibus nonnisi beneficium recipit. Nam si vera proponimus, nova ad eam accessio fiet: sin falsa, refutatione eorum sententiae priores tanto magis stabilientur*'.

[52] Ibid., f. A2r.

[53] Ibid., f. A3v: 'Vis enim ista sit in loco proprio secundum naturam corporis agitabilis, estque perfectiva non destructiva: quod ipsum apparet etiam in aere, etc'.

cases where the mover *is* lighter than the moved object (th. 14).[54] According to Gilbert (and Kepler), the Solar force (*Solis virtus*) also acts as a mover that is much lighter than the planets it sets in motion.[55]

Placentinus concluded that terrestrial motion is a well-founded thesis (th. 17).[56] He emphasized that reason rather than authority should decide on this issue.[57] This appeal to competence would become a leitmotiv in his work. On the *retro* of the frontispiece of many of his publications, he printed the following quotation from Philip Melanchthon: 'The arts shall not be judged relying on the opinions of those who know nothing about them' (*Nec vero judicium de artibus faciendum est ex eorum opinionibus, qui eas ignorant*). In the *Vier nachdenkliche Frage* (1659) with the reprint of his 1654 disputations on terrestrial motion and on the tides, this motto was translated into German and was accompanied by Plato's prohibition, inscribed at the entrance of his Academy: 'Let none ignorant of geometry enter'.

The Cartesian Offensive of 1655

In the fall of 1655, Placentinus orchestrated a proper Cartesian offensive. He pushed ten of his students to defend a series of disputations, one per week for ten weeks, treating one by one all aspects of Descartes's *Principia philosophiae*. These theses were privately discussed in the circle of his pupils. Nonetheless, as we shall see, they raised vehement reactions on the part of the philosophers.

The disputations were grouped in four sections that followed the progression of the Cartesian work.[58] They dealt with epistemology (*de principiis cognitioni humanae*) (first disputation), with the principles of material bodies (*de principiis rerum materialium*) (second disputation), with cosmology in general (*de mundo aspectabili*) (disputations three to five), and with the Earth in particular (*de terra*) (last five disputations). This uneven partition—only one disputation on knowledge theory and

---

[54] Placentinus, *Discussio mathematica erotematis, an Terra moveatur?*, f. A3*v*: 'Non tandem quod violenter movetur semper ab alio se ponderosiore corpore movetur: sed saepe movens mobili levis est'.

[55] Ibid., f. A3*v*: 'Et an Solis virtus tam grave corpus? Sol tamen praecipuus in natura actor, ut erronum promovet cursus, sic hanc telluris conversionem incitat, virtutibus orbium effulsis et lumine: verba sunt *Guilelm. Gilbert. libr. 6 de Magnet. e. 4 p. 216*'.

[56] Ibid., f. A3*v*: 'Rationibus etiam nostram sententiam stabilivissemus, nisi antea id factum esset, et alii illud abunde praestitissent'.

[57] Ibid., f. A4*v*, corollary 2: 'Astronomia cum sit satis superque Artificibus approbata, non eget approbatione ulteriori'.

[58] Cf. Stephen Gaukroger, *Descartes' System of Natural Philosophy* (Cambridge, 2002).

one on general principles against three on the worldly system and five on the terrestrial environment—shows the importance Placentinus gave to cosmology (three disputations out of ten) and to issues connected with the study of the Earth as a planet and as the place where observable elemental phenomena take place (five disputations).

The series of Cartesian disputations was inaugurated on 5 September 1655, when the Polish student Stanislaus Demianovitius defended the *Dissertatio prima, exhibens theses de principiis cognitioni humanae* (*First Dissertation Dealing with Theses on the Principles of Human Cognition*). It began with a brief eulogy of Descartes, 'great mathematician and philosopher' (*summus mathematicus atque philosophus*). The subject of this disputation is the method (*methodum*) employed by Descartes, namely cognition and knowledge theory. It begins with an exposition of the methodical doubt (th. 1-6), which leads to the idea that the first undisputable truth is the existence of the mind revealed by the *cogito* (th. 7). The distinction between *res cogitans* and *res extensa* is thus introduced (th. 8), along with the assertion that the existence of the mind is more evident to us than that of our bodies (th. 11).

One week later, on 12 September, the Brandenburg student Peter Hafnerus dealt with the principles of material bodies in the disputation *Principiorum philosophiae Cartesianae pars secunda exhibens theses de principiis rerum materialium* (*Second Part of the Cartesian Principles of Philosophy Dealing with Theses on the Principles of Material Beings*). It begins by securing the reality of the external world, whose existence has been cast into doubt by the first disputation as part of the methodical doubt. The main argument for the existence of a reality external to the mind is that sensations do not originate from within us. Therefore, we have to admit an extra-mental reality affecting the mind (th. 1). The disputation then deals with the properties of matter. One learns that the first and most evident properties are not sensible qualities such as hardness or colour; rather, the fundamental property of material beings is their tridimensional extension (th. 4). Body and extension coincide (th. 10). 'Internal space' (*spatium sive locus internus*) and 'corporeal substance' (*substantia corporea*) are one and the same thing (th. 11). Hafnerus's overview of the Cartesian theses on material principles includes the rejection of the physical void (th. 16), the negation of the existence of indivisible atoms (th. 20), the *in-de-finite* extension of the visible world (th. 21) and the principle of cosmological homogeneity, according to which 'the matter of the heavens and of the Earth is one and the same; and there cannot be a plurality of worlds' (th. 22).[59]

---

[59] Placentinus, *Renatus Des-Cartes Triumphans*, f. C2v: 'Una et eadem est materia coeli et terrae; ac plures mundi esse non possunt'.

Theses on motion are also discussed, alongside a presentation of the three Cartesian laws of nature. Motion and natural order, one learns, are interdependent since local displacements produce all transformations visible in nature (th. 24): 'All matter's variations, that is, all its variety of forms, depend on motion'.[60] The presentation of the first two laws looks bizarre to a modern reader. In fact, Placentinus (or his student) misunderstood the correct meaning of Descartes's definition of inertia. The examples illustrating the principle of conservation (first law) refer to the persistency of a material conformation and of circular motion. The importance of the equation of motion and rest as qualitatively equivalent states is thus neglected. Moreover, the straightforwardness of *inertial* motion (second law) looks like a void statement, because the example of centrifugal tendencies of the projectile of a rotating sling is misunderstood. It is interpreted as a radial tendency out of the centre of rotation whereas Descartes referred to it to infer the rectilinear tendency of matter particles along the tangent of the circular motion.[61]

The next three disputations defended by Placentinus's students dealt with celestial phenomena, cosmic order, planets, and comets. They were grouped under the label *De mundo aspectabili* (*Visible World*). Three students defended them: the Prussian Johannes Hackerus, the Silesian Fridericus Ebersbachius, and the Prussian Abraham Hesius, on 19 September, 26 September, and (presumably) on 3 October 1655, respectively.[62] Their theses dealt with planetary hypotheses (Hackerus) and vortex theory (Ebersbachius and Hesius), issues that had already emerged from Placentinus's earlier polemics.

The fourth and most extensive part of the Cartesian series of disputations concerned the Earth. The next five *respondentes*, originally from various German and Polish provinces, were Johannes de Monscavia of Jülich, Christianus Fridericus Salmuth of Anhalt-Dessau, Johannes Laurentius of Silesia, Ulricus Adolphus of Malovitz in Boemia, and Placentinus's fellow citizen, Joannes Vigilantius of Leszno. The first student, Johannes de Monscavia, disputed his theses on 10 October 1655, and the second, Christianus Fridericus Salmuth, presumably on the 17th (the exact day is omitted). After them it is probable that the public disputes were interrupted since no date is indicated for the last disputations.

---

[60] Ibid., f. C2*v*: 'Omnis materiae variatio, sive omnis ejus formarum diversitas pendet a motu'.

[61] Ibid., f. C3*r*, th. 37–9.

[62] Hesius's disputation indicates only the month, October, but not the exact day. Since the disputations had a weekly cadence, it is likely that it was defended on the 3rd.

The five concluding disputations *de Terra* do not only treat the Earth from an astronomical viewpoint. They also cover issues traditionally belonging to meteorology such as the behaviour of the four elements in the sublunary realm. The first of these disputations deals with the terrestrial globe with particular attention to 'air'; the second deals with 'water' and the tides; and the third one with 'fire.' The fourth of these disputations *de Terra* is dedicated to magnetism. The last and final one tackles the *sensibilia*, that is, the qualities of material bodies perceived by human senses. The meaning of this latter disputation is stated as follows (th. 188):

> Since René Descartes did not complete the fifth part of the *Principia* on animals and plants, and the sixth on man (contrary to his intention), we will add only a few theses on the perception of objects. Since we have so far described this Earth and the entire perceivable world as machines, we have considered nothing but figures and motions. But our senses exhibit to us many more phenomena such as colours, odours and sounds. If we simply pass these [qualities] under silence, we would neglect a fundamental aspect of the explanation of material beings.[63]

Can a Cartesian become Dean of the Philosophical Faculty?

Shortly after the series of Cartesian disputations begun, Georg Mollemanus, who was at that time rector, and Magister Lesle undertook a series of countermeasures. On 17 September 1655, Mollemanus wrote a letter denouncing Placentinus to the *Kurfürst* for his dissemination of views that were at odds with the statutes and contrary to the oath taken upon his appointment. Placentinus and his consociates immediately wrote to Friedrich Wilhelm, offering their versions of the facts (Frankfurt/Oder, 27 October). He reported that two weeks earlier (i.e., around 14 October) Mollemanus and Lesle insulted him in public, in the deanery, calling him a perjurer, reckless, and malevolent (*'perjurum* leichtfertigen menschen

---

[63] Placentinus, *Renatus Des-Cartes Triumphans*, Part IV, 4 (*De Terra*), f. A1r. 'Cum Renatus des Cartes, quintam partem principiorum de viventibus et plantis, ac sextam de homine (prout ipsi ante hac in animo fuit), non absolverit; pauca quaedam *de sensuum objectis* hic subjungemus. Quippe hactenus hanc terram totumque hunc mundum aspectabilem, instar machinae descripsimus, nihil praeter *figuras et motus* in eo considerantes; sensus autem nostri multa alia nobis exhibent, colores scilicet, odores, sonos et similia de quibus si plane taceremus, praecipuam explicationis rerum materialium partem videremur omisisse'.

und *male feriatum*).[64] On 26 October, rector Mollemanus penned a furious letter in Latin to chancellor Thomas von Knesebeck urging some censure against the professor of mathematics, who was exceeding the limits of decorum.[65] This action probably interrupted the series of Cartesian disputations. Mollemanus wrote that he had suspected Placentinus's bias toward illicit doctrines from the beginning. In a public ceremony, transferring the position of rector to the jurisprudent Johannes Brunnemannus, Mollemanus reminded all the professors and scholars that, according to the statutes, university faculties had the right and the duty of censuring the works and ideas of the professors. He claimed that this practice was particularly useful in hindering ambitious innovators like Placentinus who attempted to spread obsessive fantasies (*ne obsistat nobis amplius cum phantasmatis suis*). In the letter to the chancellor, Mollemanus observed that censure is a healthy measure and therefore the patient to whom it is administered should not protest (*tamque salutari ne recalcitret sanctioni!*).[66]

The situation was complicated by the fact that Placentinus would soon become dean of the Faculty. According to the statutes, that position was assigned on the basis of a constant turnover of representatives of different 'nations'. Since Placentinus was the only professor inscribed in the *natio Marchica* (of the March of Brandenburg) and it was the turn of this nation to be represented, he should obtain the honorific position without election. Yet, Mollemanus and Lesle urgently transferred a new professor, Grebnitz, from the nation of Silesia to the nation of Brandenburg and proclaimed him dean, even though some colleagues were opposed to their conspiracy. Their reply to Placentinus's protests was that the only condition under which he could be elected was by renouncing his Cartesian ideas, as Placentinus himself reported:

> This affair happened for this reason: because I privately taught Cartesian philosophy, thus fulfilling the order [*mandatum*] of His Princely Serenity that was most graciously communicated to me through His Excellency Hr. von Wolzogen. Actually, they [the philosophers] gave me a condition under which I could become dean, that I should abandon the Cartesian philosophy.

[64] Placentinus to Friedrich Wilhelm of Brandenburg (Frankfurt/Oder, 27 Oct. 1655), in GStA PK Rep.51, Nr. 94, ff. 49–50, f. 49r.

[65] GStA PK, Rep.51, Nr. 94, f. 53r. 'Previdi ego mox ab initio intrantis Academiam Placentini nostri ambitiosum inclarescendi appetitum et pruritum per singularum singularem. Itaque et suasor fui Facultati nostrae censurae ut subderemus invicem scripta nostra'. On Mollemanus's rectorate in the Summer Semester 1655, cf. Friedländer, *Aeltere Universitäts-Matrikeln*, 50.

[66] Mollemanus to Knesebeck (Frankfurt/Oder, 26 Oct. 1655), in GStA PK, Rep.51, Nr. 94, ff. 53–54, f. 53r-v.

I replied that I should obey His Princely Serenity and not them. Did they want to count more than the Serene Prince?[67]

Placentinus's long letter of 27 October 1655 included a series of documents in his support: Mollemanus's aforementioned accusation of 17 September 1655 (as attachment A, f. 47); a transcription of the Prince's letter of 2 January 1655 allowing Placentinus to defend his views (attachment B, f. 46); and the witnesses of the professor of rhetoric *Licentiatus* Erasmus Scultetus (att. C, f. 45), and of the professor of history and poetry Valentinus Crüger (att. D, ff. 37–38), and of an illustrious student, Johannes Joachimus Rollius, son of the mayor (*Bürgermeister*) of Königsberg (att. E, f. 48). On the same day (27 October) the new rector, the Jurisprudent Brunnemannus, summarized the polemic to the Prince. Brunnemannus mentioned the Cartesian problem explicitly, also reporting that Placentinus claimed that the Prince had allowed him to dispute Cartesian ideas.

> Concerning the dean's election, Mr. Magister Mollemanus advanced that Mr. Placentinus first of all infringed the Statutes of the Philosophical Faculty, since he privately defended the Cartesian philosophy in [a series of] disputations after he rejected the Aristotelian philosophy in some disputations. By contrast, Mr. Magister Placentinus objected that his predecessors already defended the thesis of the motion of the Earth. Moreover, [he declared that] His Princely Serenity had graciously conceded him the Permission to present and defend the Cartesian philosophy, partly in written form, through a letter [*rescript*] a copy of which he [Placentinus] showed us, and partly in oral form, through Mr. Ludwig von Wolzogen Freiherr, acting, he claimed, upon orders which Your Princely Serenity had graciously communicated in person.[68]

---

[67] GStA PK, Rep.51, Nr. 94, ff. 50*r-v*: 'Diese aber praetention ist darumb geschehen, weil ich *Philosophiam Cartesianam privatim* dociret, und mandato E. Churfl. D. welches durch Ihr Gnaden hern von Wolzogen freiherr clementissime mir ist angedeutet worden, obtemperiret habe. Sie schlugen mir zwar vor ein condition danlich wenn ich also bald *Philosophiam Cartesianam* fahren ließe, so solte ich *Decanus* werden: aber ich antwortete darauf E. Churfl. D. müßte und wolt ich pariren und nicht ihnen, sie würden ja nicht wollen mehr seyn, alß E. Churfl. D'.

[68] Rector Brunnemannus to Friedrich Wilhelm of Brandenburg (Frankfurt/Oder, 27 Oct. 1655), in GStA PK, Rep.51, Nr. 94, ff. 40–43, f. 41*v*: 'Hingegen hatt H. M. Mollemannus *pro electione Decani* angezogen, das erstlich H. M. Placentinus *contra statuta Philosophicae Facultatis* gehandelt in dem er *relicta Philosophia Aristotelica* in etlichen *disputationibus* die *Philosophiam Carthesianam* [sic!] privatim *in disputationibus* defendirete. Dagegen H. Placentinus eingewand, das die *hypothesin de Terrae motu* auch seine *antecessores* defendiret hätten und von E. Churfl. Durchl. auch die *Philosophiam Carthesianam* [sic!] zum proponiren und zum defendiren gnädigste Concession habe, theils schriftdich wie Er uns dan eine *Copiam Rescripti* gezeiget, theils mündlich durch herren Ludwig von Wolzowen [sic!] Freiherren dem E. Churfl. Durchl. solches gnädigst mündlich befohlen hätte'.

Friedrich Wilhelm tried to calm the polemics with one letter to the Philosophical Faculty (Cöln an der Spree, 28 October 1655) and one to Placentinus (Cöln an der Spree, 31 October 1655). In the latter, the tone was severe. The Cartesian was invited to moderate his tones, in accordance with the Statutes, and to accept that others could have opinions differing from his own. Friedrich invited him to disseminate *only* theses he was capable of defending.[69] The *mathematicus* interpreted this as a concession and did not miss the occasion to demonstrate that he was capable of defending his views, printing his ten Cartesian disputations together under the superlative title of *Renatus Des-Cartes Triumphans*.

An International Network of Cartesians

The *Des-Cartes Triumphans* was dedicated to none other than Friedrich Wilhelm. The dedicatory epistle (Frankfurt/Oder, 7 November 1655) had a polemical and programmatic character. Placentinus began by asserting that he followed a requirement of the Prince in presiding over the Cartesian disputations. He added that he had not taught Cartesian philosophy for ambition or boastfulness. In fact, he knew in advance that he would encounter severe obstacles. His only motivations, as he assured the dedicatee with rhetorical emphasis, were his conscience and the love for truth.[70] Placentinus moreover directed against his adversaries a polemical passage he quoted from his teacher, the Groningen professor Tobias Andreae, who dismissed dogmatic adversaries with the following words:

> They can gather 'as much as they want in the Senate, deliver prescriptions, orchestrate conspiracies, deliver decrees, solicit Academic judgments and theological advices, devise adjudications, and deliver anathemas. We will not give much importance to all that, if they do not first demonstrate that we uttered false and empty [doctrines], and that we were mistaken, being wrong in our judgment'. These are the words annotated by the very famous Tobias Andreae, ordinary professor of History and Greek at Groningen [. . .], at the end of his *Assertion of Cartesian Method* [. . .].[71]

[69] Friedrich Wilhelm to Placentinus (Cöln an der Spree, 31 October 1665), in Brandenburgisches Landeshauptarchiv (BLHA) Potsdam 'Acta betreffend Placentini' (Rep. 86 Universität Frankfurt an der Oder, Nr. 45).

[70] Placentinus, *Renatus Des-Cartes Triumphans*, Dedicatory letter (without page number).

[71] Ibid.: 'At enim eant illi *quantum velint in consilium, conferant capita, ineant comspirationes, cudant Decreta, sollicitent Iudicia Academica, consilia Theologica, fabricent res judicatas, vibrent anathemata, nos omnia illa tanti non faciemus, nisi prius falsa ac vana nos jactasse, ni errasse judicioque lapsos demonstrarint,* Sunt verba Celeberrimi viri Tobiae Andreae, Acad. Groning. Hist. et Gr. Ling. Prof. Ordinarii, Fautoris et Preceptoris mei

In the preface to *Des-Cartes Triumphans*, Placentinus emphasized the international dimension of his network of Cartesian adepts. Andreae was mentioned as 'my supporter and teacher in this philosophy' (*fautor et praeceptor meus in eadem Philosophia*). This professor would later teach Cartesian medicine in Duisburg (1662–9) and be appointed as a professor of medicine at Frankfurt on Oder in 1674. Among his publications, one can find various philosophical and medical disputations.[72]

In the second place, Placentinus mentioned the French diplomat Hector-Pierre Chanut, that 'magnificent and generous man [...] who had an epitaph engraved for Descartes in Stockholm' (*magnificus et generosus vir, [...] qui Cartesio Epitaphium Stockholmiae poni curavit*). Chanut, French ambassador in Sweden, was the person who had introduced Descartes to Queen Christina.[73]

Two theologians came next in Placentinus's list of Cartesians, the Groningen professor Samuel des Marets, remembered as 'my preceptor, whom I shall perpetually acknowledge' (*praeceptor meus aeternum suspiciendus*), and the Leiden professor Abraham van der Heyden. This mention is significant in this context, since these Dutch scholars counted as two major anti-Scholastic opponents of Gijsbert Voet in the famous theological and philosophical polemics that had occupied Descartes in the Netherlands a few years earlier.[74] It shall be remembered that this Dutch controversy led by Voet had also implicated the Copernican system. In particular, it was concerned with the philosophical foundations and the extent to which the Cartesian system could be reconciled with Scripture.[75]

In his Cartesian network, Placentinus also mentioned the Dutch philosopher and physician Johannes de Raey as the one who specifically taught him Cartesian philosophy at Leiden ('praeceptor meus in philosophia

---

in eadem Philosophia olim devenerandi annotata in conclusione *Assertionis Methodi Cartesianae* pag. 770'.

[72] Cf. Tobias Andreae, *Dissertatio philosophico-medica de homine microcosmo* (Duisburg, 1665) and the trilogy of *exercitationes De conjugio mentis et corporis, De cura mentis per corpus* and *de cura corporis per mentem* (Andreae, Frankfurt/Oder, 1679). On Andreae's activity as a Cartesian professor of medicine in Duisburg, cf. Trevisani, *Descartes in Germania*, chap. 3.

[73] Cf. Gaukroger, *Descartes: An Intellectual Biography*, 412–16.

[74] Verbeek, *Descartes and the Dutch*. However, des Marets later took sides against the 'excesses' of the Dutch followers of Descartes. A document of this theology-loaded debate over Cartesianism is Samuel des Marets, *De abusu philosophae Cartesianae, surrepente er vitando in rebus theologicis et fidei, dissertatio theologica* (Groningen, 1670). Cf. Giulia Belgioioso's preface and Igor Agostini and Massimiliano Savini's introduction to the anastatic reprint (Hildesheim, 2009).

[75] Rienk Vermij, *The Calvinist Copernicans: The Reception of the New Astronomy in the Dutch Republic, 1575–1750* (Amsterdam, 2002), 245–6. Cf. J.A. van Ruler, *The Crisis of Causality: Voetius and Descartes on God, Nature and Change*, (Leiden, 1995).

Cartesiana fidelissimus, honoratissimus'). De Raey was a Utrecht pupil of Henry le Roy (Lat. *Regius*), whose *Fundamenta physices* (Amsterdam, 1646) played a major role in the early dissemination of Cartesian natural views.[76] As for de Raey, he published a syncretistic work, *Clavis philosophiae naturalis, seu introductio ad naturae contemplationem Aristotelico-Cartesiana (Key to the Natural Philosophy, or Introduction to the Aristotelian-Cartesian Contemplation of Nature)* (Leiden, 1654), in which he argued for an agreement between the new philosophy and the ancient *auctoritas*. His strategy was to isolate passages from the Aristotelian corpus and to read them through Cartesian lenses.[77]

Placentinus counted among his contacts two physicians: Cornelius van Hogelande, and Gualterus Mirkinius, 'very expert physicians, and very honorable friends' (*medici expertissimi, amici plurimo honorandi*);[78] and two prominent Duisburg professors, Johannes Clauberg and Christopher Wittich. Clauberg, a pupil and friend of de Raey, was a decided defender of Cartesianism who published extensively on metaphysics and developed a logic founded on the principle of clarity and distinction.[79] In the 1650s, while Placentinus was engaged in his *Frankfurter Streit*, Clauberg and Wittich were promoting the philosophy of Descartes at Duisburg, that is, at a university centre which was under the jurisdiction of Friedrich Wilhelm of Brandenburg, just like the *Academia Viadrina*. In those years, Clauberg printed in rapid succession his *Logica vetus et nova (New and Old Logic)* (Amsterdam, 1656), a syncretistic Aristotelian-Cartesian work, *De cognitione Dei et nostri, quatenus naturali rationis lumine, secundum veram philosophiam, potest comparari, exercitationes centum (One Hundred Exercises on our Knowledge of God and of Ourselves, insofar as It Can Be Understood Through the Light of Natural Reason and According to the True Philosophy)* (Duisburg, 1656), and two apologetic writings, *Defensio Cartesiana (Cartesian Defence)* (Amsterdam, 1652) and *Initiatio philosophi sive dubitatio Cartesiana (The Philosopher's Initiation, or*

---

[76] Cf. Verbeek, 'Regius's *Fundamenta Physices*', *Journal of the History of Ideas*, 55/4 (1994), 533–51. Regius was also fundamental for the circulation of Cartesian astronomy. Cf. Aiton, *The Vortex Theory of Planetary Motions*, esp. 65–6.

[77] Cf. Ariew, *Descartes among the Scholastics*, 146–50. Cf. Roger Ariew & Marjorie Grene, 'The Cartesian Destiny of Form and Matter', *Early Science and Medicine*, 2/3 (1997), 300–25, 321–2.

[78] In *Cogitationes, quibus Dei existentia, item animae spiritalitas et possibilis cum corpore unio, demonstrantur* (Leiden, 1676), Cornelius van Hogelande dealt with issues pertaining to life in a very comprehensive manner ranging from God's existence to the connection between spiritual souls and bodies and the mechanical explanation of organic function. Mirkinius defended some *Disputationes physicae* in Groningen in 1651, under de Raey, and some medical disputations one year later.

[79] Trevisani, *Descartes in Germania*, 85–114, and Savini, *Johannes Clauberg*

Cartesian Doubt) (Leiden, 1655). As for Wittich, in 1652, he defended a disputation entitled *[Dissertatio] altera [quae] dispositionem et ordinem totius universi et principalium ejus corporum tradit, sententiamque nobilissimi Cartesii, de vera quiete et vero motu terrae defendit (Second [Dissertation] on the Disposition of the Entire Universe and Its Main Bodies, Also Defending the Opinion of the Very Noble Descartes on the Real Rest and the Real Motion of the Earth)*, printed in Amsterdam in 1653 alongside a theological disputation. Just like Placentinus in 1654, Wittich presented Descartes's natural philosophy as the foundation of the Copernican system.[80] He also authored a scriptural defense of Cartesian philosophy, *Consensus Veritatis in Scriptura Divina et infallibili revelatae cum veritate philosophica a Renato Des Cartes detecta, cuius occasione Liber. II. & III. Principiorum Philosophiae dicti des-Cartes maximam partem illustrantur (Agreement between the Truth in Divine Scripture, Infallibly Revealed, and the Philosophical Truth Discovered by René Descartes, Giving Occasion to Illustrate the Most Part of Books II and III of the Principles of Philosophy by the Aforementioned Descartes)* (Nijmegen, 1659). Hence, Placentinus's publications were not isolated. Rather, they should be read against the background of a Cartesian campaign that was conducted on a European scale by scholars with close Dutch connections.[81]

The last scholar mentioned in Placentinus's list was his friend (*amicus honorandus*) Daniel Lipstorp of Lübeck, who undertook to promote Cartesian philosophy in connection with the Copernican system. In 1653, he had his *Specimina philosophiae Cartesianae (Aspects of Cartesian Philosophy)* printed in Leiden with the addition of a small tract entitled *Copernicus redivivus (Copernicus Restored to Life)*. This pro-Copernican apology reworked a series of theses that Lipstorp had disputed one year earlier at Rostock. His decisive argument for the reconciliation of terrestrial motion and Biblical exegesis was the Cartesian idea of the mobile immobility of the Earth, that is, the distinction between *motio* and *delatio* adopted by Placentinus in 1654. Lipstorp's work contributed to the identification of Descartes's philosophy with Copernicus's astronomy in the natural and theological debates of those years.[82]

---

[80] See Vermij, *The Calvinist Copernicans*, 146–8.

[81] Also Spinoza's *Renati des Cartes principiorum philosophiae pars I et II, more geometrico demonstrata* (1663) can arguably be regarded as a byproduct of the efforts of systematizing Cartesian natural philosophy by reducing it to collections of theses.

[82] Vermij, *The Calvinist Copernicans*, 142–6. Lipstorp was a sort of wandering scholar. In 1653, he was court mathematician and preceptor of the ducal princes in Weimar and some years later, after obtaining a Dutch degree in law, he became professor in Law at Uppsala (between 1662 and 1672). Cf. Siegmund Günther, 'Lipstorp, Daniel', *Allgemeine Deutsche Biographie* 18 (1883), 746.

On 12 November 1655, Placentinus's adversaries of the Philosophical Faculty of Frankfurt wrote a denunciation to Friedrich Wilhelm as a reaction to the publication of the *Des-Cartes Triumphans*. Referring to the Prince's recent injunction to stop all controversies, they regarded this publication, carried out without any previous approbation or censure, as a provocation. They were especially indignant at the 'stacheliches *Prologum*' (insulting preface), which they called a 'Pasquil,' or satire. The preface was included in the letter. The philosophers annotated at the margins of the subtitle—'Principles of Cartesian Philosophy Exposed and Defended at the Oder University' (*Principia philosophiae Cartesianae, in Alma Viadrine, ventilata atque defense*)—the questions: 'When? Where? With Whom?' (*Quando? Ubi? Coram quibus?*). Indeed, the disputations had not been disputed in public. Hence, Placentinus's opponents questioned the legitimacy of his reference to the academic institution in the title page of his Cartesian work.

His position was aggravated by a further provocation. On 11 November, a Sunday, he let an 'arrogant' student disseminate his book in front of the church at the market place.[83] This time the Prince enforced moderation upon Placentinus (28 November).[84] Despite the apparent severity of this gesture, their relationship was not strained; on the contrary, events which succeeded this reproach show that Friedrich Wilhelm was supportive of Placentinus's career and of his cultural programme.

An Extreme Attempt to Ban Cartesianism from Frankfurt

The polemic concerning the acceptability of a Cartesian in the Faculty position of dean was not over. It re-erupted in the next semester. On 24 March 1656, the anti-Cartesian philosophers wrote a long letter explaining why a Cartesian should not obtain such a prestigious academic position and why Placentinus was particularly unfit to obtain it.[85] In addition to earlier allegations (the contravention of the statutes and of his oath), they mentioned his lack of respect towards the new dean, Grebnitz, whom he stubbornly called '*Decanus de facto*' and not '*de jure*'. The denouncers observed that Placentinus's lack of recognition for the legitimacy of a dean acknowledged by the university and confirmed by the Prince would be sufficient to undertake disciplinary measures against him.

---

[83] GStA PK, Rep.51, Nr. 94, f. 27r. [84] Ibid., f. 26. [85] Ibid., ff. 9–14.

Moreover, they accused Placentinus of infringing disciplinary bound-aries. Instead of restricting his lectures to mathematics, he undertook to teach logic on the basis of a Cartesian author, Clauberg. The accusers also recalled that Clauberg bore the cost of his ideas by being expelled from the Gymnasium of Herborn.[86] In addition to logic Placentinus ventured to teach physics, infringing all the rules of disciplinary boundaries.

> On account of the precious oath that we swore on the statutes and our conscience, we cannot accept the election of a man as Dean who so wantonly insists on innovation in everything; who [moves] from mathematics, [a discipline] that requires a man's complete and exclusive dedication, to logic and physics, thereby invading the fields of other professors; who disrespects the Prince's order [*rescript*] from Berlin so much as to incur censure; who confuses the students with unusual and obscure dogmas that fill the ears and not the intellect (so that the Academy falls into poor repute); and who should not become dean and 'teach the old masters their art' ['correct Greek and Latin verses and orations']. [We cannot accept] that he swears the dean's oath, [swearing] that he will uphold the statutes and will guarantee their respect by everybody (something that he cannot do himself according to his principles, fundaments, and hypotheses).[87]

The main disagreement was doctrinal. In the letter of March 1656, the Aristotelian legacy was addressed explicitly. Placentinus's scorn for Aris-totle was incompatible with the university's mission: '[...] We always directed ourselves according to the Statutes that we swore, and we never desired anything but what they express, that is: *None shall deviate from the philosophy that has been transmitted to us*; and: *We will defend unanimity on the Peripatetic doctrine*'.[88] For the first time, the philosophers made an open profession of adherence to the Peripatetic doctrine a criterion of inclusion in the Faculty. In the words of an earlier professor of philosophy at Frankfurt, Christopher Neander, 'Academies will survive for as long as

---

[86] Ibid., f. 10*r*.

[87] Ibid., ff. 13*r-v*.: 'Unser Thewrer in die *statuta* geschworner Eyd und gewißen, wollen es dergestalt ja nicht leiden, daß wir einen Menschen, der so Muttwillig alles zu innoviren sich erkühnet; *post habita Mathesi, quae totum hominem requirit*, in die *Logicam* und *Physicam* anderen *Professoren* eingerumpelt: so viel Churfürstlichen *rescriptis* von Berlin, der *Censur* sich zu untergeben, refrangiret; die Jugend mit ungewöhnlichen finsterseltzamen *dogmatibus, aures, non intellectum implentibus* (darüber die *Academia* in bösen ruff bey den exteris gerahten) beirret; zum *Decanat, corrigendis Graecis et Latinis carminibus et orationibus* nicht geschickt ist p. zum *Decano* erwehlen, oder Ihme das *Juramentum Decani*, daß er die *Statuta* halten, auch verschaffen sol, daß sie von allen gehalten werden (welches er, *secundum principia, instituta, et hypotheses suas* auch nicht halten kan) auferlegen'.

[88] Ibid., f. 10*r-v*: 'Wir haben unß iederzeit nach Unseren beschwornen *Statutis* gerich-tet, und nichts anders, alß was die im munde führen, begehret, nemblich: *Nemo a recepto apud nos philosophandi genere recedat. Item: Tueamur consensus doctrinae Peripateticae*'.

Aristotle continues to be taught in the classes' (*Tamdiu durabunt Academiae, quamdiu Aristoteles audetur in Cathedris*).[89]

In the eyes of Placentinus's opponents, his philosophical heresy repeated and aggravated that previously committed by the Calvinist philosopher Pierre de la Ramée and his followers. They deliberately reminded the Prince that Ramist logic and philosophy were both banned from most German academic centres, including Frankfurt on Oder, during the sixteenth century:

> When, in the time of our predecessors who now rest in God, in 1586, there was an attempt to introduce the doctrines of Pierre de la Ramée in this Academy, they consented unanimously and decreed, under the deanery of Magister David Origanus and the rectorate of Martin Benckendorf, I.U.D. [Doctor in civil and canon law], with a decree published on 7 August, that no-one should be permitted to teach the doctrines of Pierre de la Ramée or of his followers here, nor would the gates be left open for any of the same to attain philosophical honours.
>
> And in spite of this de la Ramée was not the kind of man to throw all of the old *termini* [technical terms] into confusion, unlike Placentinus who comes out with so many bigger, smaller, and mean vortices, first and second elements, threaded particles [*particulae striatae*], and similar fantasies, causing the true meanings of things to be forgotten, so that young people and even their elders cannot understand anything.[90]

The denunciators suggested that the Prince treat the Cartesians in the same manner as the Ramists. This comparison was disingenuous because it was designed to suppress Placentinus's programme by referring to previous controversies and the ban on de la Ramée's philosophy enacted by several German universities.[91]

---

[89] Ibid., f. 13*r*.

[90] Ibid., f. 12*v*: 'Alß zu Unserer in Gott ruhenden *antecessoren* zeit, Anno 1586, in dieser *Academia* des Petri Rami dogmata eingeführet werden wollen: haben sie *unanimi consensu, sub Decanatu M. Davidis Origani, Rectore Martino Benckendorffio* I.U.D. *Calendis Aug.* decretiret, und das *Decretum ad diem 7. Cal. Augusti* publiciret, daß keinem *Docenti* des Petri Rami, und seiner *adseclarum dogmata* alhie zu profitiren gestatet, noch die Pforten zu dem Philosophischen honoribus iemanden derselbigen offen stehen solten. Und war dennoch Ramus nicht ein solcher Mann, der die alten *terminos* über einen hauffen hette Verworffen sollen, wie dieser Placentinus lauter *vortices, majores, minores, medios, crepiret, elementum primum, secundum et particulas striatas*, und dergleichen Phantaseyen, darauß die Jugendt, *obliteratis veris sententiis*, auch elttere Leütte, nichts faßen können'.

[91] On Ramist controversies in Germany, see Howard Hotson, *Commonplace learning: Ramism and its German ramifications 1543–1630* (Oxford, 2007) and Riccardo Pozzo, *Adversus Ramistas: Kontroversen über die Natur der Logik am Ende der Renaissance* (Basel, 2012).

We therefore commit this long report to His Princely Serenity [for] His very intelligent and gracious decision, so as to be informed whether He should prefer, in the future, that if Placentinus or other upstart innovators like him should deviate from the Aristotelian tradition, statutes and princely rescripts acknowledged by us here, then we as a College should take no heed, the circumstances being so, but should and may elect him or his like as dean without doing violence to our oath or consciences, and without suppression of the dean's oath.[92]

It is evident from this document that Placentinus's opponents felt galvanized by the Prince's earlier letter, in which he warned the mathematician to moderate the tone of his polemic after he had distributed copies of the *Des-Cartes Triumphans* in front of the Church. They thought that the time had come to ban him and his philosophical school. Actually, they had misinterpreted the Prince's intentions. Friedrich Wilhelm's response was a brief communication (4 April 1656) taking the side of the professor of mathematics. 'Again Magister Placentinus is allowed to profess the Cartesian philosophy and shall not be excluded from the deanery this year'. This is the indication on the draft copy preserved in the *Preußisches Geheimstaatsarchiv.*[93]

In April, Placentinus was in Königsberg along with Friedrich Wilhelm. On the 19th of April he asked the Prince for funding to cover the expenses he had faced for astronomical observations and geographical measurements. He had invested 60 talers for instruments and for printing, that is to say, an amount of money about one fourth of his annual salary of 264 talers as a professor of mathematics.[94] Friedrich Wilhelm generously conferred upon the *mathematicus* an annual increase of salary of 200 talers on 1 May 1656.[95] This beneficence signalled Placentinus's appointment as a court mathematician and marked his legitimization among his colleagues. On the title page of his next publication, he emphasized his new status: 'Johannes Placentinus, Mathematicus Electoralis Brand. et Prof.

---

[92] GStA PK Rep.51, Nr. 94, f. 13*v*: 'Stellen demnach dieses gantze werk, zu E. Churf. D. hochvernünftigen gnädigsten decision, und erkäntnis, Ob ins künftige, des M. Placentini halber, oder wann andere *novatores* mehr, von der *recepta apud nos Philosophia Aristotelica, Statutis,* und *rescriptis,* abzuweichen Ihnen fürnehmen möchten, Wir uns *Collegialiter* nichts zu bekümmern haben, sondern *rebus sic stantibus,* unserm Jurament und gewißen ohne Schaden, Ihn, oder einen seines gleichen, zum Decano, ohne abnehmung des Decanatjuraments, erwehlen mögen und sollen'.

[93] Ibid., f. 7*r*. 'Dem M. Placentino wird nochmals zugelaßn die Philosophiam Carthesianam zu profitiren u. soll umb das cur[rente] A[nno] des Decanat gar nicht excludiret seyn'.

[94] The relevant document is preserved in GStA PK, Rep.51, Nr. 94, f. 6*r*. Regrettably, the publication on solar eclipses and the determination of longitudes mentioned in the manuscript is now lost.

[95] Ibid., f. 4.

Ordin., p[ro] t[empore] Amplis. Facult. Decanus' (Johannes Placentinus, Mathematician of the Elector of Brandenburg and Ordinary Professor, Presently Illustrious Faculty Dean). This book was a disputation proposing a syncretistic interpretation of Aristotle and Descartes, *Syncretismus philosophicus inter Renatus Des-Cartes et Aristotelem institutus (Philosophical Syncretism Established between René Descartes and Aristotle)*. Rather than a concession, this was a mortal blow to those calling for the preservation of the Aristotelian tradition. This time, none could hinder Placentinus from officially parading his Cartesian views in public, as evidenced by this announcement: '[The disputant] proposes [his theses] for Public Discussion on 19 July [1656], at the usual places and hours' (*Publice ventilandam proponit ad diem 19. Juli, loco horisque solitis*).

Epilogue: Rise and Fall of a Cartesian Mathematician

After the polemics and Placentinus's apogee as a faculty dean and a court mathematician, ten years of intense intellectual and cultural activity followed. He published several mathematical and philosophical works. In 1657, he issued the geographical work *Geotomia sive Terrae sectio exhibens praecipua et difficiliora problemata I. Explorandi Latitudines... II. Inquirendi Longitudines... III. Determinandi distantias... per trigonometriam logarithmicam, soluta* (*Geotomy, or Section of the Earth, Explaining the Main and Most Difficult Problems Concerning 1. the Establishment of Latitudes... 2. the Establishment of Longitudes... 3. the Determination of Distances... Solved with the Support of Trigonometry and Logarithms*, 1657). Given the relevance of cartography in the age of oceanic navigation and of rising colonialism, this work on geodesy bears witness to Placentinus's effort to reach beyond his academic post and appeal to political authorities and the *respublica litterarum* at large. Samuel Hartlib, for one, reacted quite positively as he annotated in his *Ephemerides*

> Placentinus Bohemus Prof*essor* Math*ematics* upon the Oder at Frankford hath published a Booke De Longit*udine* wh*i*ch is thought the best that ever hath been written and should not have beene thus plainly discovered the States of Holl*and* and others having set so great a price and reward for it, wh*i*ch belike this Prof*essor* was ignorant of.[96]

---

[96] *The Hartlib Papers, Ephemerides 1655* Part 2 (*1655 [February-21 April]*). Ref: *29/5/ 15A-28B* http://www.hrionline.ac.uk/hartlib/view?file=main/29_05_15&term0=transtext_ placentin*#highlight (28 January 2015). Hartlib probably refers to an earlier publication of the second section of the *Geotomia*. On his work, networks and legacy, cf. Mark Greengrass,

Placentinus also wrote on biology, life, and ethics from a Cartesian viewpoint in a series of disputations beginning with a *Dissertatio philosophica, probans, calorem et motum membrorum naturalem, in humano corpore; adeoque vitam non procedere ab Anima, quae unica est scilicet rationalis, sed a materia coelesti subtilissima, analoga elemento Solis et stellarum fixarum (Philosophical Dissertation Proving that the Natural Warmth and the Motion of the Limbs in the Human Body and Even Life Do Not Descend from the Soul, Which is Only One and Rational, but from Very Subtle Celestial Matter, Which Is Analogous to the Element of the Sun and the Fixed Stars,* 1659).[97] These publications provoked new polemics, but this time outside Brandenburg. His opponents, based in Wittenberg, publicly presented a series of theses against him.[98] In return, Placentinus organized a series of defensive disputations that still merit scholarly attention.[99]

In the same period of time, Placentinus attained the highest academic position possible. He was rector on two occasions, in 1658 and in 1665. He moreover published a series of successful works in German on uncommon meteorological and celestial phenomena such as windstorms, solar eclipses, and other celestial appearances, merging Cartesian mechanics, meteorology, and astrology.[100] He also continued to train students in Cartesian philosophy, as witnessed by an extant syllabus for the year 1659, announcing the continuation of his 'private college' (*privatim Collegium Fortificatorium continuaturus*).[101]

These were the golden years of Placentinus's life. Regrettably, his career ended in a tragic manner. In 1666, he was declared crazy (*Des Magister Placentini verrückung im haupt, 1666*) and, as a consequence, enchained and committed to house arrest. This meant not only the end of his

Michael Leslie & Timothy Raylor *Samuel Hartlib and Universal Reformation: Studies in Intellectual Communication* (Cambridge, 1994).

[97] Placentinus's approach seems to be a Cartesian reworking of Renaissance doctrines concerning the connection of terrestrial life and heavenly heat. Cf. Hiro Hirai, *Medical Humanism and Natural Philosophy: Renaissance Debates on Matter, Life and the Soul* (Leiden, 2011).

[98] A series of six disputations *de vita hominis* against Placentinus were promoted in Wittenberg by his fellow countryman Samuel Hentschel Lesnensis in 1659 and 1660.

[99] Placentinus, *Dissertatio physica, refutans propositam in Academia Wittenbergensi* (1660) *de origine caloris et motus membrorum naturalis; in humano corpore, adeoque vitae brutae, quae nobis communis est cum bestiis et nonnullis philosophiae Cartesianae speciminibus* (Frankfurt/Oder, 1660).

[100] In 1661 alone, Placentinus had three astrological-meteorological works printed: 1. *Physicalischer und astrologischer Bericht von denen erschrecklichen... Winden*; 2. *Feuer- und Blutrohte Sonne*; and 3. *Newlicher Sonnenfinsternisz Astronomische und Astrologische Observation.*

[101] *Catalogus lectionum publicarum in Universitate Viadrina, Exhibens quid singuli Dn. Professores hac aestate Lecturi sint* (Anno 1659, die 7 Maii), in GStA PK I HA Rep.51, Universität Frankfurt Oder Nr. 4, f. 474.

academic career, but also of his existence as a free man. His wife and daughters were also taken away from him. The most important documents, which are preserved in Berlin, have already been summarized in a recent publication.[102] Still, the connection between these later facts and the earlier polemics has not yet been studied. There is evidence that Placentinus was still capable of working, even after the diagnosis of mental illness and his imprisonment. In fact, after thirty weeks he penned a sober mathematical-astronomical paper for Elizabeth of Palatinate (addressed as 'Benedicta' with reference to her status as abbess of Herford). The manuscript is preserved in the *Preußisches Geheimstaatsarchiv* among the documents concerning his infirmity.[103] Furthermore, it has yet to be considered whether a series of disputations on the relation between mental and bodily health promoted at Frankfurt by Placentinus's teacher and friend Andreae in 1679 relates to his case.[104]

Placentinus died in 1683, after seventeen years of reclusion. In spite of his marginalization and disgrace, some of his friends (*communis mensae convictores*) published a celebratory poem in his honour that included these verses:

Nothing is eternal besides the eternity of the end,
Besides that single thing that is eternal nothingness.
Only you, vicissitude of all things, do not change your changing
You persist immobile, as you will not displace your centre
While you, who are for us more mobile than our destiny, twist us by our centres.
You conduct, transport, and take us away,
Play and deceive us,
Move, remove, and get rid of us.
And you removed [that man] from his cardinal point,
[...]
[who] was irremovable to himself and the others:
Johannes Placentinus,
Philosopher, Astronomer, Mathematician,

---

[102] The documents are preserved in GStA PK, I HA Rep. 51, Universität Frankfurt Oder, Nr. 95. The only secondary source on Placentinus's fate is Andrea Lehmann, '"Nun ist wohl keiner bey dieser Stadt, so den traurigen Zustandt gedachten Placentini nicht von Herzen solte Beklagen". Tragische Ende der Karriere des Mathematikprofessors Johannes Placentini', *Jahresbericht/Forschungsstelle für Vergleichende Universitätsgeschichte (Frankfurt/ Oder)*, 6 (2011), 40–56.

[103] The manuscript (in GStA PK, I HA Rep. 51, Nr. 95) is entitled 'Scrutinium longitudinis locorum Anglis, Gallis, Hispanis, Belgis desideratissimum' and is signed: 'Placentinianum, alias Kolaczkianum, vinculis AntiChristicis ultra triginta septimanas innocenter durantibus, in domo det, quae mutate est in speluncam latronum, breviter consignatum, et humilissime consecratum'.

[104] Andreae, *De conjugio mentis et corporis*, *De cura mentis per corpus* and *de cura corporis per mentem*.

In Philosophy, akin to Aristotle,
In Astronomy, akin to Copernicus,
In Mathematics, akin to Archimedes,
All in One.[105]

Concluding Remarks and Future Research Prospects

Placentinus's transfer of Cartesian philosophy from the Netherlands to a German university offers an insight into the institutional difficulties facing novel ideas in the circulation of knowledge in seventeenth-century middle Europe. In order to realize the philosophical renewal he had in mind, he made recourse to all possible institutional, technical, and social means: teaching, disputations (even multiple disputations covering the natural philosophy of Descartes in its entirety), publications, and patronage. His attempt to establish a Cartesian school in Frankfurt provoked the reaction of his colleagues of the Philosophical Faculty, who accused him of infringing the University Statutes, of neglecting his curricular duties by introducing novel doctrines that the students were not supposed to learn, of printing books without adequate permission, of entering pointless polemics, and of abusing his academic position. They appealed to the authority of the Electoral Prince, patron of the Academia, asking him to solve the controversy and bring Placentinus back to order. This affair shows that university institutions were resistant but not impenetrable to novelties. Loyalty to tradition, in particular to Aristotelianism and to statutes establishing the centrality of Aristotelian philosophy for the education of youth, was a hindrance but not an insurmountable obstacle for *novatores* such as Placentinus. Yet, since Frankfurt on Oder received its legitimation from a political authority embodied in the person of the Electoral Prince, the latter could determine the cultural direction of *his* Academic institution. In the Frankfurt controversy over Descartes, in fact, his role proved decisive. Without princely support, Placentinus's polemical and argumentative capacities would not have been sufficient.

---

[105] Funeral poem in honour of Placentinus, *Radii honoris* (Frankfurt/Oder, 1683): 'Nihil est aeternum extra aeternitatis terminum,/ Nisi hoc unicum, quod aeternum Nihil est./ Tu unica rerum vicissitudo, non mutas vices./ Persistis Tibi immobilis; quia tuo non moveris centro./ Nobis coronide mobilior, nostro nos usque moves centro./ Ducis, traducis, subducis,/ Ludis, illudis,/ Moves, dimoves, amoves/ Et movistis suis cardinibus/ O aulus!/ Virum Tetragonum et sibi et aliis/ Johannem Placentinum/ Philosophum, Astronomum, Mathematicum/ In Philosopho Aristotelem,/ In Astronomo Copernicum,/ In Mathematico Archimedem,/ In Uno Omnes'.

Placentinus's quarrel is revealing of the tension between tradition and innovation at a northern German teaching institution, as well as of the opportunities and limitations of the academic activities of that age. In his struggle for the affirmation of Cartesian but also Copernican ideas, in the years 1653 to 1656, Placentinus had to learn to navigate academic norms, politics, and institutional constraints. In order to be accepted, Placentinus first disguised his adherence to theories that were at odds with Aristotelian cosmology and natural philosophy. Hence, his first disputation was simply aimed at showing his skills, in particular his familiarity with mathematical terminology and problems (as he later acknowledged). The second phase of his attempt to introduce Cartesian conceptions into the University consisted of cautiously defending disputations on cosmological and natural issues, beginning with the explanation of the Copernican solar system and of tides on the basis of Cartesian mechanistic philosophy. The perceived novelty of his geometrical and mechanical approach astounded several philosophers and theologians. Their attempts to censure him and block his publications, alongside Placentinus's sensational reactions, made the polemic rapidly escalate through reciprocal accusations and denunciations. At its peak the polemic also invaded institutional spaces outside the university: Placentinus's private household, where he trained his school of young Cartesians; as well as the press, the Church, the Chancery of Brandenburg, and the Court. Evidently the boundaries of an early modern academic institution were permeable and reached far outside the walls of the university buildings. In the course of events, not only did Placentinus succeed in obtaining the support of some colleagues and of various students, but he also, most importantly, gained external political legitimation from the Prince. His appointment as Court mathematician and the explicit permission of the Prince to access the highest academic honours inaugurated a new phase of his career at Frankfurt. This also led to the insertion of Frankfurt into an international network of scholars, as Placentinus claimed in his *Des-Cartes triumphans*. Whereas he was part of a large northern European community committed to Cartesian reforms of university curricula, his Frankfurt opponents were entrenched in their local context and stuck in their tradition. Apparently, they were not able to accept that Placentinus's Cartesian campaign at Frankfurt was parallelled by similar efforts at Duisburg and that Prince Friedrich Wilhelm of Brandenburg supported these cultural tendencies. Or perhaps they were aware of the Dutch controversies over Descartes and were determined to maintain control over the curriculum in the face of cultural and confessional developments. More research is needed in order in order to reconstruct the facts of the later phases of Placentinus's career, and to explore the reasons and consequences of his mental illness

As to Placentinus's scholastic Cartesianism, it concerned the form of philosophical communication rather than the content. His case also shows that the insertion of Descartes's philosophy into traditional institutions required adaptation to institutionalized forms of knowledge transfer, teaching, and learning. His Cartesian and Copernico-Cartesian writings took the shape of collections of theses to be defended as academic disputations. Arguably, this was employed as a means to make Cartesianism fit to university curricula. Along with the *disputatio*, all other traditional university genres were used in the so-called Scholastic Cartesianism of that age, such as the commentary, the *quaestio*, and the *exercitatio* for teaching purposes. For instance, Wittich's *Annotationes ad Renati Descartes Meditationes (Annotations to René Descartes's Meditations)* (Dordrecht, 1688) can be seen as a transition from the medieval and Renaissance commentary to the modern edition of Descartes's *Meditationes* which also includes a commentary; Andreas Petermann's apology for Descartes, *Philosophiae Cartesianae adversus censuram Petri Danielis Huetii vindicatio, in qua pleraque intricatiora Cartesii loca clare explanantur (Vindication of Cartesian Philosophy against the Censure of Pierre-Daniel Huet, in Which Many Difficult Passages of Descartes are Explained)* (Leipzig, 1690), has the form of the academic *quaestio*, in which questions concerning the problems of Cartesian philosophy are followed by punctual answers and explanations.[106] Original works also emerged from this scholastic environment, as was the case with Clauberg's logic, Lipstorp's views on the foundations of astronomy and mechanics,[107] Wittich's reconciliation of philosophy and theology,[108] or

[106] It should be added that German opponents to Descartes also reformulated his views in the form of Scholastic theses, in order to discuss and reject them. As an example of academic *exercitatio* produced in the context of the Cartesian polemics, one can mention Eckhard Leichner, *Anti-Cartesius, sive de Natura rediviva per vindicationem ab Internecinis Cartesii, ejusque hyperaspistarum Antonii le Grand, Jacobi Rohaulti etc. commentis Exercitationes Sex: Quibus examusim palam fit: Commenta ea omnino esse anti-Philosophica, praesertim autem anti-Physica. Tractatus omnium Facultatum, praecipue vero Medicinae Studiosis hodieque lectu necessarius pariter atque perutilis* (Erfurt, 1686).

[107] Daniel Lipstorp's *Specimina philosophiae Cartesianae* (Leiden, 1653) is a wide-ranging text, organized around important themes of epistemology, natural philosophy and mechanics. This includes a long discussion of the Cartesian method (*de certitudine philosophiae Cartesianae*), of the laws of motion, of air mechanics, and of the weight of the element 'air'. The *Copernicus redivivus* attached to the *Specimina* is a detailed treatment of Copernican astronomy and of the arguments against and in favour of heliocentrism, accompanied by explanatory images. Also, the dedications and the prefaces of these works indicate a network of scholarly contacts including many scholars in Germany (e.g.in Lübeck, Hamburg, and Rostock), with Denmark and with the Baltic provinces of Poland (Gdańsk).

[108] Cf. Christopher Wittich, *Theologia pacifica, in qua varia problemata theologica inter Reformatos theologos agitari solita ventilantur, Simul Usus Philiosophiae Cartesianae in diversis Theologiae partibus demonstratur, et ad dissertationem celeberrimi viri, Samuelis Maresii De abusu Philosophiae Cartesianae in rebus theologicis et fidei modeste respondetur* (Leiden, 1671).

Andreae's medicine.[109] Against this background, Placentinus's efforts to substitute a novel philosophy for the Aristotelian tradition were not isolated. His polemics and their connection with controversies and cultural trends in other countries suggest that there are grounds to reconsider Central Europe as a site for the early reception of Descartes and the role of the so-called Scholastic Cartesianism in the developments of German philosophy.

Max Planck Institute for the History of Science
Berlin

[109] Among other publications, this prominent Cartesian professor of medicine, appointed at Frankfurt on Oder in 1674, authored a book on embalming techniques in epistolary form (Andreae, *Bilanx exacta Bilsianae et Clauderianae Balsamationis* (Amsterdam, 1682)), which reveals his contact with Flemish physicians (in Louvain and in Brussels), with whom he exchanged the reports of experiments.

Nominal Definition in the Seventeenth-Century University Disputations of the German Cultural Space

Meelis Friedenthal

In early modern schools public and private disputations were used as a method of teaching and examination.[1,2] From the second half of the sixteenth century onwards, statutes of Protestant universities[3] generally state that all public disputations had to be printed and made publicly available a few days before the disputation took place.[4] As such we have extensive collections of early modern disputations from all over Europe. For example in the German cultural area it is estimated that there are

---

[1] I would like to thank Steven Tester, Andrea Speltz and three anonymous referees for their kind assistance in putting together this piece.
[2] Ku-ming Chang, 'From oral disputation to written text: The transformation of the dissertation in early modern Europe', *History of Universities* 19/2 (2004), 129–87, 134; Rainer A. Müller, 'Student Education, Student Life', in Hilde De Ridder-Symoens (ed.), *A History of the University in Europe*, ii: *Universities in Early Modern Europe (1500–1800)*, general editor Walter Rüegg (Cambridge, 2003), 326–54, 344–5.
[3] E.g. Peter Baumgart & Ernst Pitz (eds), *Die Statuten der Universität Helmstedt* (Göttingen, 1963), 87; Daniel Heinrich Arnoldt, *Ausführliche und mit Urkunden versehene Historie der Königsbergischen Universität, Erster Theil* (Königsberg, 1746), Beylage nr. 49 (c. XI de disputationibus), 181; Juhan Vasar (ed.), *Tartu Ülikooli ajaloo allikaid. Quellen zur Geschichte der Universität Tartu (Dorpat)*, i: *Academia Gustaviana: a) Urkunden und Dokumente* (Tartu, 1932), 60.
[4] Catholic universities often gave only a list of theses. Andreas Pietsch, '"Pour satisfaire à la curiosité des Princesses & des Dames de la Cour". Grenzarbeiten am wissenschaftlichen Feld im Frankreich des 17. Jahrhunderts', in Martin Mulsow & Frank Rexroth (eds), *Was als wissenschaftlich gelten darf: Praktiken der Grenzziehung in Gelehrten Milieus der Vormoderne* (Frankfurt am Main, 2014), 161–86, 169–70.

around 80,000 printed disputations from the seventeenth century alone.[5] As all disputations had to be approved beforehand, usually by deans of the faculty,[6] these texts reflect quite well the general intellectual atmosphere and the learned consensus in a specific region. They also inform us of the content of the teaching that educated elites received at the universities and thus give a more accurate idea about contemporary mentalities than would a few outstanding or exceptional treatises.[7] These short texts (often two or three sheets in quarto format, i.e. 16 or 24 pages)[8] were designated variously as *exercitium, disputatio* or *dissertatio*, but in this paper the word mainly used is 'disputation'. Early modern disputations differed significantly from today's university dissertations: most of these texts were not written for promotion or to obtain an academic degree (*pro gradu*) and a greater part of these disputations were in fact written by professors or masters who acted as presider (*praeses*). The task of the respondent (*respondens*) was to defend the proposed theses. Professors also re-used their material—this means the disputations often represent a compilation of previous ideas and texts.

The structure of early modern disputations adhered to conventions that were already established during medieval period when the practice was foremost an oral exercise.[9] With the advance of the printing press during the sixteenth century it became increasingly common to print the disputations; theses were expanded considerably and the title page came to serve simultaneously as an invitation to the disputation.[10] The title page was usually followed by a dedicatory letter from the respondent to his benefactors and sometimes also by an introductory letter (*prooemium, praeloquium*), often addressed to 'friendly reader' (*benevolo lectori*). The body of

---

[5] Manfred Komorowski, 'Bibliotheken', in Ulrich Rasche (ed.), *Quellen zur frühneuzeitlichen Universitätsgeschichte: Typen, Bestände, Forschungsperspektiven* (Wiesbaden, 2011), 55–81, 56.

[6] 'Nulla autem disputatio aut declamatio proponatur publice, non inspecta a Decano, aut magistris, quorum iudicium probat Decanus': *Leges academiae Witebergensis de studiis et moribus auditorum* (Wittenberg, 1546), *lex sexta de studiis*; [Decani] privatorum publicorumqve exercitiorum curam gerent. Theses inspicient et de iis judicabunt, adhibitis Collegis vel omnibus vel plerisque, si opus fuerit: Vasar, *Tartu Ülikooli ajaloo allikaid*, 51; Daniel Heinrich Arnoldt, *Ausführliche und mit Urkunden versehene Historie der Königsbergischen Universität. Erster Theil* (Königsberg, 1746), Beylage nr. 46, 121.

[7] Hanspeter Marti, 'Dissertationen', in Rasche (ed.), *Quellen zur frühneuzeitlichen Universitätsgeschichte*, 293–312, 293.

[8] Sometimes the page count does not correspond to sheet folding schemas: there are many disputations that have an extra half-sheet of 4° pages appended, thus producing e.g. 20 or 28 pages altogether.

[9] Chang, 'From oral disputation to written text', 144–5.

[10] Marti, 'Dissertationen', 293–4

the disputation *per se* consisted typically of numbered theses (sometimes also called *theoremata*) or paragraphs that were proposed for discussion.

In the first theses of philosophical disputations the authors often occupy themselves with preliminary remarks concerning the topic at hand and also provide definitions of relevant words. The interest of the current article is to follow the practices of nominal definitions, as these were often called. The custom of the nominal definition was a global one (disputations from Scandinavia to Spain often employ some kind of *definitio nominis* at the beginning of the text) but the current article concentrates on the disputations that originate from Protestant universities of the German cultural space[11] and relies mostly on the database *Verzeichnis der im deutschen Sprachraum erschienenen Drucke des 17. Jahrhunderts* (VD17).[12] The focus will be on the philosophical disputations. This does not however automatically mean that all the disputants were from an arts faculty, as there are many cases when professors of theology presided over philosophical disputations or students of theology or medicine were respondents of philosophical disputations. For the purpose of narrowing down the selection, at least five disputations that included some definition about name were selected from every decade of seventeenth century.[13] To this end, the disputations sampled mostly announced a concern with logic (*disputatio logica, dialetica*) or physics (*disputatio physica, disputatio physico-medica*, etc). Furthermore, only one disputation was chosen from any one *praeses*, as the disputations written under the supervision of the same person tended to have repeating elements. The main interest of the article is in the authorities and texts that were cited in the disputations in favour of nominal definitions, thus giving an idea of which kind of authors were deemed to be authoritative or acceptable when dealing with the question of name. The general tendency is that nominal definitions were more important in the early seventeenth century because the authors were operating with an Aristotelian and Platonic view of names, and words were deemed to give us some idea about the essence of things. Nominal definitions however become decisively different during

---

[11] For the list of universities in German cultural space see: William Clark, *Academic Charisma and the Origins of the Research University* (Chicago, 2008), Appendix 6, 509–13; Thomas Ellwein, *Die deutsche Universität: vom Mittelalter bis zur Gegenwart* (Frankfurt am Main, 1992), Anhang 1, 321–3.

[12] As of April, 2015 VD17 lists 60,076 items under the keywords Disputation/Dissertation. See http://www.vd17.de. The database however is far from complete. See: Jürgen Beyer, 'How complete are the German national bibliographies for the sixteenth and seventeenth centuries (VD16 and VD17)?', in Malcolm Walsby & Graeme Kemp (eds), *The Book Triumphant: Print in Transition in the Sixteenth and Seventeenth Centuries* (Leiden, 2011), 57–77.

[13] See Appendix 1.

the shift to Cartesianism, as names lost any connection with the things they denoted, making it impossible to derive any idea about the essence from the name only. Accordingly, at the end of the seventeenth century, disputations that were influenced by Cartesian thinking define words only to clear possible ambiguities and to limit semantic boundaries.

Different practices of *definitio nominalis*

Seventeenth-century disputations typically include at least some discussion of terms or names when introducing a given topic. Paying attention to the origin and content of words is of course not peculiar to early modern thinking; already Homer discusses the significance of names in the *Odyssey*.[14] This kind of thought that stresses the usefulness of an investigation of names continued in the Christian world via the New Testament (e.g. Mt 16:18) where Jesus says to Simon, 'And I tell you that you are Peter ('rock' in Greek) and on this rock I will build my church'. The practice maintained its popularity during the Middle Ages through the works of Isidore of Seville, whose encyclopedic work *Etymologiae seu Origines,* which employed etymology as its principal method, has survived in almost a thousand manuscript copies, and of which 'nearly a dozen printings appeared before the year 1500'.[15] With the development of universities, scholastic logic was also keenly attentive to the question of words and mental concepts.[16]

Thus it is not surprising that we can find disputations from the seventeenth-century German cultural area that discuss the meaning of words from all major universities (Wittenberg, Leipzig, Königsberg, Rostock, Tübingen, Frankfurt an der Oder etc). There does not appear to be any clear distinction between Lutheran or reformed universities in reference to nominal definitions or definitions of names.[17] In the beginning of

[14] For a historical overview of the significance of words and names see: Ernst Robert Curtius, 'Etymologie als Denkform', in id., *Europäische Literatur und lateinisches Mittelalter* (Bern, 1967), 486–90.

[15] Isidore of Seville, *The Etymologies of Isidore of Seville,* trans. Stephen A. Barney (Cambridge, 2007), 3, 24.

[16] For late medieval discussions see: Sten Ebbesen & Russell L. Friedman (eds), *John Buridan and Beyond: Topics in the Language Sciences, 1300–1700* (Copenhagen, 2004); Stephan Meier-Oeser, *Die Spur des Zeichens: Das Zeichen und seine Funktion in der Philosophie des Mittelalters und der frühen Neuzeit* (Berlin, 1997), 114–53.

[17] This tendency has been noted already concerning differences in the teaching of natural philosophy. Howard Hotson, *Commonplace Learning: Ramism and Its German Ramifications, 1543–1630* (Oxford, 2007), 16–25; Jitse M. van der Meer, 'European Calvinists and the Study of Nature: Some Historical Patterns and Problems', in Gijsbert

the century the dividing line seems to be between Platonic and Aristotelian understanding (between understanding words as natural or conventional), but many authors seek also to reconcile these apparently opposing positions.[18] At the end of the century the German universities that were influenced by Cartesian philosophy, at first Calvinist (Duisburg, Frankfurt an der Oder), but later also in Lutheran territories (Giessen, Jena, Halle), display considerable differences from universities which adhered to scholastic tradition.[19]

At the beginning of the century the discussion of names is relatively brief in disputations and tends not to be explicitly titled as such. During the second quarter of the century the activity is gaining in popularity and disputations start to devote more room to nominal definitions. Whole sections appear dealing with onomatology as the practice is sometimes called.[20] Onomatology is understood as an activity that applies not only to proper names but also to names in general.

When discussing the name, the authors of the second half of the seventeenth century regularly mention that this practice is useful, customary or common and thus introduce it most of the time without any lengthy theoretical exposition and without naming any authorities.[21] When some sort of explanation is given as to why the investigation of words is useful, disputants most often single out ambiguity (*homonymia*) as the mother of all errors[22] or simply state that it is disgraceful to

---

van den Brink & Harro M. Höpfl (eds), *Calvinism and the Making of the European Mind* (Leiden, 2014), 101–30, 118–19.

[18] See e.g. Johann Regius, *Commentariorum ac disputationum logicarum libri V*, editio nova, distinctior, emendatior (Witebergae: Bergerus, 1615), lib. 3, prob. 1, 9–10. [The capitalization of Latin titles in this article has been standardized and does not always correspond to the capitalization found on the title page of the cited text. In quotations, the spelling of Greek and Latin has been maintained as it appears in sources.]

[19] On the reception of Cartesianism in German universities see: Francesco Trevisani, *Descartes in Deutschland: die Rezeption des Cartesianismus in den Hochschulen Nordwestdeutschlands* (Münster, 2011); Anton Schindling, *Bildung und Wissenschaft in der frühen Neuzeit 1650–1800* (Munich, 1999), 37–40; 52–3.

[20] E.g. Tobias Bleuel [P], Martin Heidenreich [R], *Physica de natura, disputatio* (Leipzig: Lanckisch, 1640). [Henceforth the *respondens* of the disputation is marked as [R] and *praeses* as [P]].

[21] Hoc vero ut rite id fiat, nomen primo praemittimus rei ipsi. Johann Andreas Schmidt [P], Nicolaus Eberhardi [R], *Disputatio physica de butyro, ut est alimentum* (Jena: Literis Wertherianis, 1680), thes.III; Animus igitur est in hoc primo Capite vocacula ipsa pro rebus supponentia explicare. Christian Krumbholtz [P], Georg Leberecht von Wilke [R], *Disputationem physicam: quod voluntas non necessario determinetur ab ultimo iudicio intellectus practici* (Leipzig: Typis Gözianis, 1687), c. I.1.

[22] Verborum quidem aequivocatio errorum genetrix esse consuevit. Petrus Goetschenius [P], Nicolaus Olai Calmariensis [R], *Dissertatio philosophica et solennis, de mundo in genere* (Dorpat [Tartu]: Pistorius, 1635), thes. 2.

disregard the derivation and origin of words.[23] A typical *definitio nominalis* starts thus along these lines:

As ambiguity is really the most fruitful mother and ancestress of many errors, I think it is worthwhile to dispel immediately in the beginning the ambiguities in the word 'terra', so that we should not be like those wandering in a strange forest and could be considered similar to the blind, as the saying goes, who give judgement about colour.[24]

Here *synonymia* and *etymologia* of the words could be discussed, and *paronymia* is also sometimes mentioned.[25] This means of course following a well-established peripatetic practice what stresses the primacy of definition.[26] Accordingly, when authors see the need to cite authorities, most often different works of Aristotle are cited in favour of nominal definition.[27] During the period between the end of the thirteenth century and the end of seventeenth century, forms of Aristotelianism[28] were the prevalent philosophical current in European universities and the practice of definition was developed further and formalized by different commentators on Aristotle. Of particular importance here is Petrus Hispanus, whose texts were used widely in late-medieval and Renaissance schools as an introduction to Aristotle: even in the early modern period the school discussions about logic were based largely on his work.[29] The widely read commentary of Petrus Hispanus states that 'in acquisition of sciences

---

[23] Turpe enim doctori artis, nominis derivationem et originem ignorare. David Crusius [P], Martin Mylius [R], *Disputatio de definitione, subiecto et fine dialectices* (Erphordiae: Wittelius, 1607), thes. II.

[24] Cum vero ambiguitas errorum multorum mater ac genetrix sit foecundissima, operae pretium existimavi, vocis Terrae ambiguitates in principio statim enodare, ne in ignota quasi sylva versari, et sicut caeci, ut dicitur, de colore judicare videamur. Nicolaus Zapf [P], Heinrich Renis [R], *Disputatio physico-elementaris de terra* (Wittenberg: Hake, 1626), thes. 1.

[25] Cum autem omnis cognitio sit ex praevia cognitione Nominis, igitur ante Definitionem Realem, merito Nominalis est explicanda, ubi tria veniunt observanda, ἐτυμολογία, ὁμονομία et συνωνομία. Johannes Erici Stregnensis [P], Andreas Flojerus [R], *Disputatio philosophica de natura et constitutione scientiae naturalis* (Dorpat: Vogelius, 1651), thes. 4;

[26] Marguerite Deslauriers, *Aristotle on Definition* (Leiden, 2007), 1–2, 115–17.

[27] E.g. Nicolaus Strauch Zapf [P], Aegidius Strauch [R], *Disputatio physica de elementis in genere et in specie* (Wittenberg: Müllerus, 1633), thes 1, cites Posterior Analytics; Johann Balthasar Mathesius [P], Erhard Lindner [R], *Disputatio physica, qua in transitu Israelitarum per Mare Erythraeum non fuisse fluxum et refluxum maris* (Leipzig, c.1700), thes. I, cites Arist. Soph. Elench. 165a.

[28] Charles B. Schmitt, *Aristotle and the Renaissance* (Cambridge, MA, 2013); Christia Mercer, 'The Vitality and Importance of Early Modern Aristotelianism', in Tom Sorell (ed.), *The Rise Of Modern Philosophy: The Tension Between the New and Traditional Philosophies from Machiavelli to Leibniz,* (Oxford, 1993), 33–67.

[29] See: Brian P. Copenhaver, Calvin G. Normore & Terence Parsons, *Peter of Spain: Summaries of logic: text, translation, introduction, and notes* (Oxford, 2013).

dialectics must be the first', and the text also discusses nominal definition and word origins at length.[30] Similarly Philipp Melanchthon, in his works on rhetoric and logic, understands that Aristotelian dialectics is the basis of all deliberation.[31] His *De dialectica libri quattuor* (first published 1528) became one of the most influential textbooks in the Protestant universities of the sixteenth century.[32] Melanchthon states that: 'Dialecticians have made two kind of definitions. The first kind is the definition of name (*definitio nominis*). This is simply the etymology of the word or whichever exposition we use to establish the word and in what sense we plan to use it'.[33]

The task of the nominal definition was thus to remove any possible ambiguity from a word and to say something about the object to be defined—the Aristotelian definition of a name tries to establish *genus* or *differentiae*, which can be more familiar to or observable by us.[34] Most of the disputations of the seventeenth century adhere to this kind of understanding about the definition of names and discuss the common usage of words and what exactly we have in mind when we utilize certain words:

> Due to such difference and variety of opinions, and dispute between the most excellent men, if we are to find out the truth we have to put aside the judgement of men and should methodically examine the thing itself. Firstly it should be noticed, that the word 'somnus' is used in two ways. Mostly it is taken to mean natural privation of sense perception and movement. That's why sleep is called the image and brother of death and is said by Aristotle in the 1st chapter of the 5th book of the *Generation of animals* to be like a boundary between life and death.[35]

---

[30] In acquisitione scientiarum Dialectica debet esse prior. Johannes Versor, *Petri Hispani summulae logicales* (Venetia: Juntas, 1550), 2r.
[31] Nicole Kuropka, *Philipp Melanchthon: Wissenschaft und Gesellschaft : ein Gelehrter im Dienst der Kirche (1526–1532)* (Tübingen, 2002), 31–2.
[32] Peter Mack, *A History of Renaissance Rhetoric 1380–1620* (Oxford, 2011), 107.
[33] Fecerunt igitur dialectici duo genera definitionum. Primum genus, definitio nominis est, ea simpliciter etymologia vocabuli est, seu enarratio qualiscunque, qua de voce constituimus, qua significatione uti velimus. Philipp Melanchthon, *De dialectica libri quattuor* (Straßburg: Mylius, 1545), 6–7.
[34] Deslauriers, *Aristotle on Definition*, 77–8.
[35] In tanta opinionum varietate et discrepantia, et excellentissimorum virorum pugna, si veritatem invenire volumus, auctoritate hominum seposita, Methodo rem ipsam examinare cogimur. Primum igitur scire oportet, nomen somni bifariam usurpari. Nam plerumque pro naturali privatione sensus ac motus sumitur, propter quam somnus imago et frater mortis et ab Arist. 5. de gener. animal. 1. μεθόριον τοῦ ζῆν καὶ τοῦ μὴ ζῆν (Arist. GA 778b 30), vitae mortisque interstitium quoddam dicitur. Fabianus Hippius [P], Thomas Erastus [R], *De somno disputatio* (Witebergae: Bergerus, 1604).

The definition is here methodically[36] established and explained, but the name in itself is not deemed especially useful. There is however a group of disputations that see names as something that could be informative in and of themselves: 'Before we start to cunningly track down the essence of the air, we will assess in the first place carefully the name, since it is the instrument for showing and discerning the substances of things'.[37]

Here the author, understanding words as tools that teach us about the essence of things, departs clearly from the purely Aristotelian tradition. Aristotle explicitly states in *De interpretatione* that 'every sentence is significant (not as a tool but, as we said, by convention)' and asserts that 'spoken sounds are symbols of affections in the soul, and written marks symbols of spoken sounds'.[38] A common interpretation is that words are merely conventional signs that have nothing in common with the things they signify, so the words themselves cannot teach us anything.[39] The position of the predominant part of late mediaeval and early modern commentators of Aristotle regarding the relationship of words with objects and terms can be understood in such a manner. So the most authoritative theologian of the Middle Ages Thomas Aquinas interprets Aristotle to mean that words themselves are not natural but created by the human capacity for interpretation.[40] It is thus necessary to differentiate between natural sounds such as moaning, groaning or blowing and intelligible spoken words. The former sounds are 'the same for all of us' (Arist. *De int.* 16a7) and so can be understood even by animals, who have no rational soul.[41] These moaning or blowing sounds are natural and have a natural form, which makes them natural objects akin to stones, trees or planets. Thomas Aquinas makes this very clear in his comments on how articulate speech differs from natural sounds:

---

[36] About the concept of method see: Neal Ward Gilbert, *Renaissance Concepts of Method* (2nd edn, New York 1963); Giacomo Zabarella, *Über die Methoden*, trans. Rudolf Schicker (Munich, 1995), 34–40.

[37] Priusquam igitur Aeris essentiam solerti investigemus indagine, Nomen, cum rerum substantias docendi discernendique instrumentum sit primo loco perpendemus. Friedrich Moller [P], Balthasar Heintke [R], *De aere, aqua, et terra: physica diaskepsis* (Frankfurt a.d.O: Typis Sciurinis, 1601), thes. III.

[38] *De int.* 16a 3–9; 16b33. English translation: Aristotle, *Categories and De Interpretatione*, trans. J.L. Ackrill (Oxford, 1963), 43, 45.

[39] C.W.A. Whitaker, *Aristotle's* De interpretatione (Oxford, 2002), 12.

[40] Thomas Aquinas, 'In Aristotelis libros Peri hermeneias', in *In Aristotelis libros Peri hermeneias et Posteriorum analyticorum expositio*, ed. R.M. Spiazzi (Turin, 1964), 1.6.8.

[41] See also: Umberto Eco et al., 'On animal language in the medieval classification of signs', in Umberto Eco & Costantino Marmo (eds), *On the Medieval Theory of Signs* (Amsterdam/Philadelphia, 1989), 3–42; R.W. Serjeantson, 'The Passions and Animal Language, 1540–1700', *Journal of the History of Ideas* 62/3 (2001): 425–44.

Vocal sound is something natural. The name and verb, on the other hand, signify by human institution, that is, the signification is added to the natural thing as a form to matter, as the form of a bed is added to wood. Therefore, to designate names and verbs and the other things he [Aristotle] is going to define he says, 'Those that are in vocal sound', in the same way he would say of a bed, 'that which is in wood'.[42]

Therefore forms (*species*) that reach us from natural objects are the same for all creatures—but humans are capable of creating words to symbolize these forms.[43] According to an Aristotelian understanding no perceivable object can exist without some kind of form, where sensible form is understood as a certain likeness (*similitudo*) that objects 'give birth to' and which represents the image of the object to the senses.[44] The interpretative ability of humans[45] however permits us to form sounds in our throat according to our will and assign them to denote things, just as we are able to use our hands to make different objects according to our interpretative ability: e.g. make a bed out of wood or draw a sign that might not bear any resemblance to the item we were meaning to depict. Because of this languages differ and spoken sounds and written characters are not the same for everybody. Thomas Aquinas uses here an example of a trumpet which can symbolize war, although the instrument has no similarity to war whatsoever.[46]

Thus, when understanding words as instruments to unveil the essence of things the authors of the disputations follow a different school of thought. These texts often cite Plato's *Cratylus*,[47] where Socrates states (388a8), that 'a name is also a sort of tool'. In the dialogue the idea is asserted that 'things have natural names' and that the names express the

---

[42] Thomas Aquinas, *In Aristotelis libros Peri hermeneias*, 1.2.4. English translation: *Aristotle: On Interpretation. Commentary by Saint Thomas and Cajetan*, trans. J.T. Oesterle (Milwaukee, WI, 1962), 25.

[43] For the discussion on *species* see: Leen Spruit, *Species intelligibilis—from Perception to Knowledge*, ii: *Renaissance Controversies, Later Scholasticism, and the Elimination of the Intelligible Species in Modern Philosophy* (Leiden, 1995).

[44] Species sensilis nihil aliud est quam similitudo quaedam, quam objectum reale quodvis ex se gignit, quaeque per medium ad sensum delata imaginem objecti repraesentat. Johann Scharf, *Physica, auctior et correctior; in qua methodo Aristotelica in scholis peripatheticorum usitata proponuntur*, ed. sec. (Leipzig: Schürer, 1626), 526.

[45] Johannes Versor, *Petri Hispani summulae logicales*, 4v.

[46] Thomas Aquinas, *In Aristotelis libros Peri hermeneias*, 1.2.9.

[47] E.g. Friedrich Moller [P], Balthasar Heintke [R], *De aere, aqua, et terra: physica diaskepsis* (Frankfurt a.d.O: Typis Sciurinis, 1601); Tobias Tandler [P], Georg Boltzen [R], *Disputationis I. De homine in universum themata* (Wittenberg: Lehmannus, 1601); Zacharias Brendel [P], Wolfgang Ulrich [R], *Disputatio inauguralis de dysenteria* (Jena: Typis Weidnerianis, 1628).

true forms of things in letters and syllables.[48] This understanding is also explicitly referenced in some of the disputations, e.g.: 'Names are in fact signs and symbols of things and are like seals that are pressed upon the margins of things and thus educate us abundantly about themselves'.[49]

When comparing words to seals or reliefs (*sigilla*) the author indicates here that there is a certain type of similarity between words and things. The same idea is expressed by Marsilio Ficino in his preface to the first Latin translation of Plato's *Cratylus*. Ficino stresses that a 'name [...] is nothing other than a certain power of the thing itself',[50] and makes connections too with the *tetragrammaton* and hermetic philosophy.[51] This makes the words themselves useful and an examination of the words etymologically a meaningful exercise. In *Cratylus* the aim of onomastical discussions is to present not what is nowadays called historical etymology but instead the internal etymology of the word—in the hope that it will show the word's true meaning more clearly than a simple definition could do (the Latin word 'etymologia' comes from Greek *etymos* which means 'true, real, actual'). At the same time, it is also useful to note that by describing something etymologically, 'considerations of philosophical profundity and complexity are assumed to outweigh those of philological obviousness'.[52] Petrus Ramus, who became influential and at the same time controversial in Protestant universities at the end of the sixteenth century, also references Plato's *Cratylus* when considering the origin of words.[53] He agrees with Plato that if the name is assigned to a thing prudently, then it becomes a certain type of definition, which reveals something about the nature of the thing (*declaratio quaedam naturae est*), although the name reveals the nature only in a confused and implicit way.[54]

---

[48] *Crat.* 390d–e. English translation: Plato, 'Cratylus', in *Complete works,* ed. John M. Cooper & D.S. Hutchinson, trans. C.D.C. Reeve (Indianapolis, 1997), 101–56, 109.

[49] Nomina namque rerum notae sunt et symbola ac velut sigilla hunc in finem rebus impressa, ut nos de ipsis plenius edoceant. Georg Preuss [P], Georgius Gezelius [R], *Disputatio ethica de fortitudine* (Dorpat: Vogelius, 1656), thes. 1.

[50] Nomen enim uerum [...] nihil aliud est quam rei ipsius uis. Plato, Marsilio Ficino, *Omnia divini Platonis opera tralatione Marsilii Ficini* (Basileae: In officina Frobeniana, 1546), 303.

[51] Richard Marback, *Plato's Dream of Sophistry* (Columbia, 1999), 57–8.

[52] David N. Sedley, *Plato's Cratylus* (Cambridge, 2007), 97.

[53] On Petrus Ramus and his influence see: Walter Ong, *Ramus, Method, and the Decay of Dialogue: From the Art of Discourse to the Art of Reason* (Chicago, 2005); Mordechai Feingold, Wolfgang Rother & Joseph S. Freedman (eds), *The influence of Petrus Ramus: studies in sixteenth and seventeenth century philosophy and sciences* (Basel, 2001); Steven J. Reid & Emma Annette Wilson (eds), *Ramus, Pedagogy and the Liberal Arts: Ramism in Britain and the Wider World* (Aldershot, 2011); Jenny Ingemarsdotter, *Ramism, Rhetoric and Reform: An Intellectual Biography of Johan Skytte (1577–1645)* (Västerås, 2011).

[54] Notatio est nominis interpretatio: que a Graecis symbolum et etymologia nominatur. Si autem nomen (ut in Cratylo sapienter Plato disputat) recte, prudenterque sit impositum:

Plato and Aristotle are thus usually understood as having opposing positions regarding the origins of names, but during the sixteenth and seventeenth centuries many popular authors were trying to reconcile their views. Perhaps the most often cited passage about the definition of name in the disputations comes from Julius Caesar Scaliger's commentary on Cardanus' *De subtilitate* (first published 1557).[55] Scaliger writes: 'At first it is suitable to examine the usage of the word, through what we on many occasions arrive at the perception of the thing. That is shown by Plato in *Cratylus* and by Aristotle in many places'.[56] It is evident here that Scaliger does not see the positions of Plato and Aristotle as radically opposing (though elsewhere he is sceptical about the significance of names).[57] There are also other writers (e.g. Franciscus Toletus, Jacopo Zabarella, Franciscus Sanctius Brocensis, Bartholomäus Keckermann) whose works enjoyed considerable popularity in universities and who considered the positions of Aristotle and Plato to be at least not contradictory. The question of how these viewpoints could be reconciled and why the attitude towards words changed decisively toward the end of the seventeenth century and the beginning of the eighteenth,[58] could be answered by approaching the problem from a general understanding of physics. Or to put it differently, how and what we sense in the world influences how we can understand words and names.

What are names?

In an Aristotelian framework our senses and memory operate with the forms or likenesses of objects we receive from things and every time we contemplate an object we do this with the help of the likeness of the object in our sensitive soul.[59] Our understanding is often compared to a judge, who sits on the tribunal and inspects all the forms of *sensibilia* that are

declaratio quaedam naturae est, sed intexta, atque implicata. [. . .] nomina (sicut dixi) definitiones quaedam sunt. Petrus Ramus, *Petri Rami Veromandui Dialecicae institutiones* (Lugduni: apud Theobaldum Paganum, 1547), 19.

[55] Cited by e.g. Johannes Musaeus [P], Daniel Agricola [R], *Disputatio physica de terra* (Erffurti: Dedekindus, 1636); Johann Caspar Zopff [P], Andreas Lindenmuth [R], *Disputatio physica de homine* (Leipzig: Ritzsch, 1636); Johann Sperling [P], Michael Blume [R], *Disputatio physica de pavone* (Wittenberg: Röhner, 1643).

[56] Oportet igitur prius vocis ipsius usum cognoscere: a quo saepenumero provehimur in rei perceptionem: quemadmodum Plato in Cratylo, multis in locis Aristoteles ostendit. Julius Caesar Scaliger, *Exotericae exercitationes, XV: De subtilitate ad Hieronymum Cardanum* (Lutetiae: Ex officina typographica Michaelis Vascosani, 1557), ex. 1, sect. 1, 1.

[57] Scaliger, *Exotericae exercitationes*, ex. 266, 337v–339r.

[58] Avi Lifschitz, 'The Arbitrariness of the Linguistic Sign: Variations on an Enlightenment Theme', *Journal of the History of Ideas* 73/4 (2012), 537–57.

[59] Scharf, *Physica*, 536–9.

presented to it.[60] In John Versor's commentary on Petrus Hispanus he discusses the question how words are created to signify these forms in the soul.[61] He agrees that the concepts in the soul have similarity (*similitudo*) to the things but the vocal sounds that signify these concepts are not necessarily similar to the concepts.[62] Only sounds that are formed from natural instinct (*ab instinctu naturae*) represent the affects in the soul so that they would be the same for everybody.[63] From here it is possible to argue that the statement of Aristotle, which explained that names are by nature not related to the things they signify, can be interpreted as asserting that they can in some cases be similar according to human will.

This is how names are understood by Franciscus Toletus, whose works became standard textbooks in the sixteenth and seventeenth centuries both in Catholic and in Protestant universities.[64] He writes in *Commentaria una cum quaestionibus in universam Aristotelis logicam* (first published 1572) when commenting upon Aristotle's *De interpretatione*:

> Signification means that the words denote concepts of intellect and things not by nature but arbitrarily or mentally. Plato did not have a different opinion from Aristotle here, I think. Maybe it is the first signification that is referred to here, or like it is well explained by Michael Psellos in the chapter about the name – he [*i.e.* Plato] called it 'natural signification' because he means the best and the most experienced giver of names who gives things such names that suit them by nature. This is why he said 'names signify by nature'. We are used to call the artificial things that very closely imitate the natural, by exaggeration natural, and this may be what the lines in Gn 2 mean: 'and whatever the man called each living creature, that was its name'.[65]

---

[60] Ibid., 537.

[61] John Versor was a fifteenth-century commentator on Aristotle and peripatetic philosophy; his works were reprinted several times and used widely in French and German universities. See Pepijn Rutten, '"Secundum processum et mentem Versoris": John Versor and His Relation to the Schools of Thought Reconsidered', *Vivarium* 43/2 (2005), 292–336.

[62] Johannes Versor, *Petri Hispani summulae logicales*, 4r C.

[63] Ibid., 3v H.

[64] Spruit, *Species intelligibilis*, ii. 282; Roger Ariew, *Descartes among the Scholastics* (Leiden, 2011), 43.

[65] Significatio, qua voces intellectus conceptus, et res manifestant, non a natura, sed ad placitum inest. Haec est secundum mentem Arist. nec oppositum existimauit Plato, quantum existimo: sed forsan loquebatur de priori significatione: vel vt explicat bene Michaël Psellus cap. de nomine, ideo dicebat significationem naturalem, quia loquebatur de optimo, et perito impositore, imponente talia nomina rebus, qualia illarum naturis conveniebant, propter ea vocabat nomina naturaliter significare. Solemus enim artificialia, quae maxime naturam imitantur, naturalia per ex aggerationem vocare et forsan illud est Genesis 2. omne, quod vocauit Adam, ipsum est nomen eius. Franciscus Toletus, *Commentaria, una cum quaestionibus, in universam Aristotelis logicam* (Colonia Agrippina: Birckmannus, 1577), Peri Herm. Arist. lib.1, cap.1, q.1, c.2, 109r.

A giver of names might thus, despite the fact that he gives names according to his own will, nevertheless convey the impression of the concept that the word signifies. Such an interpretation, which is in some respects similar to Epicurus' view about the origin of language,[66] shows that some connection between things and names is possible and names must not be wholly random.[67] Michael Psellos, who is mentioned by Toletus in the passage, was an eleventh-century Byzantine scholar whose Neoplatonicizing expositions on different theological and philosophical subjects were widely read and who was also writing on the symbolic meaning of letters.[68]

Another popular school author, Jacopo Zabarella, who is often cited as an authority regarding names,[69] sees in his *Opera Logica* (first published 1578), that Aristotle and Plato are perhaps not disagreeing here at all and states that words are indeed tools, but not in this sense natural, as Plato had in mind.[70] This is also the view that is supported by the influential Spanish grammarian Franciscus Sanctius in his *Minerva* (first published 1587). Sanctius was also of the opinion that the Aristotle's argument was not wholly dissimilar from that presented by Plato's *Cratylus*.[71] He maintains that names are not assigned casually and 'nobody denies, that names are like tools of things and signs, and for every art a tool is used that is best adapted for that art'.[72] After a long period of everyday use the original form of tools or words might have gone missing and only in reaching the true form do we see the connection between the word and the thing it denotes.

---

[66] John Earl Joseph, *Limiting the Arbitrary: Linguistic Naturalism and Its Opposites in Plato's Cratylus and Modern Theories of Language* (Philadelphia, 2000), 95–100.

[67] Matthew D. Walz, 'The Opening of "On Interpretation": Toward a More Literal Reading', *Phronesis* 51/3 (2006), 230–51, 250–1.

[68] On Psellos see: Stratis Papaioannou, *Michael Psellos: Rhetoric and Authorship in Byzantium* (Cambridge, 2013); Katerina Ierodiakonou, 'The Greek Concept of Sympatheia and Its Byzantine Appropriation in Michael Psellos', in Paul Magdalino & Maria V. Mavroudi (eds), *The Occult Sciences in Byzantium* ed. Paul Magdalino and Maria V. Mavroudi (Geneva, 2006), 97–117, 113–15.

[69] Johann Conrad Schragmüller [P], Wilhelm Scipio [R], *Disputatio physica de monstris* (Marburg: Chemlinus, 1636); Martin Leuschner [P], Johannes Fabinus [R], *Disputatio physica de longa et brevi vita* (Stetini: Goetschius, 1630); Nicolaus Agerius [P], Gregor Hilling [R], *De metallis disputatio physica* (Straßburg: Simon, 1634).

[70] Zabarella notes that words are however not the tools of logic, because method is *habitus* of the soul, and not articulated sound. Giacomo Zabarella, *Jacobi Zabarellae Patavini Opera logica: quorum argumentum, seriem et utilitatem ostendet tum versa pagina, tum affixa praefatio Joannis Ludovici Hawenreuteri doctoris medici, et philosophi, in Argentoratensi Academia professoris*, ed. Johann Ludwig Havenreuter, editio quarta (Coloniae: Zetznerus, 1603), lib. 1. cap. 2, 136; Zabarella, *Über die Methoden*, 83–4.

[71] Franciscus Sanctius Brocensis, *Minerva seu de causis linguae Latinae*. Reprint of the Salamanca edition of 1587, with an introduction by Manuel Breva-Claramonte (Stuttgart-Bad Cannstatt, 1986), xviii–xix; cap. 1, 5–7.

[72] Sed nemo diffitebitur, nomina esse velut insturmenta rerum et notam; instrumentum autem cujuslibet artis ita illi arti accommodatur. Sanctius, *Minerva*, cap. 1, 5v.

This tendency, which has parallels in the syncretistic thought of *philosophia perennis*[73] and the principles of Kabbalah, also remained influential in the seventeenth century.[74] When the arbitrary nature of words was generally recognized, it was also admitted that some languages (such as the language spoken by Adam) could be more suitable for naming.[75] This understanding is expressed by reformed theologian and philosopher Bartholomäus Keckermann and Lutheran scholastic author Friedemann Bechmann, who are both commonly cited authorities in German disputations of the seventeenth century.[76] Keckermann states in *Systema logicae* (first published in 1600) that articulate words may not be indeed natural, but there are some words that are chosen deliberately (ἐκ προαιρέσεως) and respond very closely (*respondeant aptissime*) to the things they denote.[77] Especially in Hebrew there are many such words: far fewer however in other languages. He notices also that languages change over time and words can become corrupted, so that we no longer understand some words that were used by the ancients, referencing here the story of the tower of Babel (Gn 11).[78] Friedemann Bechmann in his *Institutiones logicae* (first published 1667) does not devote much room to this question but directs those interested in the topic to the works of Michael Psellus and Athanasius Kircher. Kircher argues in his *Oedipus Aegyptiacus* (first published 1652) that names were assigned by Adam according to various properties of things, some according to accidents and some according to substances and, as Adam had received language directly from God, these names 'were indeed the definitions of things'.[79] All other languages are however derived from the first language.[80]

---

[73] Wilhelm Schmidt-Biggemann, *Philosophia perennis: Historical Outlines of Western Spirituality in Ancient, Medieval and Early Modern Thought* (Dordrecht, 2007).

[74] Frank L. Borchardt, 'Etymology in Tradition and in the Northern Renaissance', *Journal of the History of Ideas* 29/3 (September 1968), 414–29, 422.

[75] See also: Angus Vine, 'Etymology, Names and the Search for Origins: Deriving the Past in Early Modern England', *Seventeenth Century* 21/1 (Spring 2006), 1–21, 3; Lifschitz, 'The Arbitrariness of the Linguistic Sign', 555–6.

[76] On Keckermann see: Joseph S. Freedman, 'The Career and Writings of Bartholomäus Keckermann (d.1609)', *Proceedings, American Philosophical Society* 141/3 (1997), 305–61.

[77] Bartholomäus Keckermann, *Systema logicae: tribus libris adornatum, pleniore praeceptorum methodo, et commentariis scriptis ad praeceptorum illustrationem et collationem cum doctrina Aristotelis, atq aliorum, tum veterum, tum recentium logicorum sententiis ac disputationibus*, editio secunda, ab authore recognita et emendata (Hanoviae: Antonius, 1603), lib. 1, 12.

[78] Ibid., lib. 1, 11.

[79] Nomina illa veras fuisse rerum definitiones. Athanasius Kircher, *Athanasii Kircheri Oedipus Aegyptiacus hoc est universalis hieroglyphicae veterum doctrinae temporum iniuria abolitae instauratio. Tomus secundus, pars prima* (Romae: Mascardus, 1652), class. 2, cap. 1, disq. 2, 49.

[80] Ibid., class. 2, cap. 1, disq. 2, 50.

This understanding supported the search for the true meaning of words and thus discussions about the significance of names became more popular than they had ever been before,[81] and were conducted with a fervour which Erasmus had already described aptly and ironically.[82]

Understanding words as being somehow connected to things is however only possible in the framework of Aristotelian physics and epistemology. In the latter part of the seventeenth century, when the spread of Cartesian ideas took place, this understanding no longer had theoretical support because Cartesian physics does not take any forms into account.

Cartesian theory of perception and names

From the second part of the seventeenth century, remarks concerning Cartesian philosophy appear in German university disputations (e.g. in Duisburg, Frankfurt an der Oder Marburg, Helmstedt, Wittenberg, Jena, Giessen etc). Mostly the remarks are critical but there are also authors who are supportive of the new philosophy, *e.g.* Johannes Clauberg (Academy of Duisburg) and Johannes Placentinus (Frankfurt an der Oder). Even the works that are critical usually give an overview of important problems concerning the theories of Descartes.[83] In addition to other deviations from traditional physics, Descartes argues against a peripatetic understanding of perception and states that we can give up qualities and forms and clearly explain everything pertaining to sense perception only by local movement. According to Descartes light is nothing more than movement of the substance of *aether* or particles of *aether*; sound is the striking and beating of air against tympanum; pain is nothing but vehement movement in our body.[84] The motion of particles itself lacks any qualitative information and only through the interpretation of movements do perceptions acquire some content. Therefore it is possible to differentiate sharply between perceiving a thing, which is carried out by sense

---

[81] Vine, 'Etymology, Names and the Search for Origins', 3–4; W. Keith Percival, 'Renaissance linguistics: the old and the new', in Theodora Bynon (ed.), *Studies in the History of Western Linguistics: In Honour of R.H. Robins* (Cambridge, 1986), 56–68, 63–4.

[82] Desiderius Erasmus, *The praise of folly*, ed. Helen Mary Allen, trans. John Wilson (Oxford, 1913), 133.

[83] E.g. Georg Caspar Kirchmaier [P], Johann Friedrich Scharf [R], *De origine vitae humanae, et potioribus quibusdam philosophiae Cartesianae speciminibus: additis, a fine, notis apologeticis, ad secunda responsa Placentiniana* (Wittenberg: Hake, 1660).

[84] René Descartes, *Oeuvres de Descartes. VIII.1, Principia philosophiae*, ed. Charles Adam & Paul Tannery (Paris, 1905), 319–20, (*Principles of Philosophy* CXCIV- CXCVI). Henceforth the edition by Adam & Tannery is abbreviated AT, followed by volume number and page number(s).

organs, and understanding a thing, which is done only by the soul, with the help of innate ideas.[85] Normally sensations about external objects arise when some body or matter reaches us from outside. Our sense organs receive no data other than particles of matter, so that we qualities such as colours, tastes, and smells arise in us due to the different sizes and movements of particles, which by bouncing back from materials of different structures change in their rotational motion. This we interpret as tastes, smells or colours, but these do not themselves exist in sensation.[86]

Accordingly, Descartes argues also against the peripatetic understanding that the ideas of qualities and things have to be similar to the perceived objects.[87] In the *Treatise on Man* Descartes describes at length a mechanism through which perceptions encode information in our mind and explains that the encoded information (memory) need not resemble the objects.[88] He gives here the example of an organist who uses keys to produce sounds from the pipes of the organ, where the sounds themselves are very different from the pressing of the keys (AT X 165–6). When ideas thus encoded in our mind do not resemble their objects it is only consistent to argue that the words that humans assign to denote ideas and objects do not resemble concepts in our mind or the things themselves either. Accordingly, in *Treatise on Light* (AT X 4) Descartes states that words 'signify something only through human convention' and in *Dioptrics* (AT VI 509) that words 'do not in any way resemble the things which they signify'. This reasoning was picked up by authors who were influenced by the philosophy of Descartes.[89] Antoine Le Grand published his *Institutio philosophiae* in 1672 to make Cartesian philosophy more accessible for use in education, presenting it in the familiar scholastic form.[90] He argues in the chapter concerning logic that all names should be taken as sounds only, empty of any meaning and used only according to simple definition.[91] Accordingly the definition of the name can never be wrong,

[85] AT X 3.

[86] For Descartes' theory of perception see: Celia Wolf-Devine, *Descartes on Seeing: Epistemology and Visual Perception* (Carbondale, 1993), 18–20, passim.

[87] In *Dioptrics*, AT VI 509. English translation: René Descartes, *Discourse on Method, Optics, Geometry, and Meteorology*, trans. Paul J. Olscamp (Indianapolis, 2001), 89–90.

[88] René Descartes, *The World and Other Writings*, trans. Stephen Gaukroger (Cambridge, 1998), p. xxv.

[89] For Descartes' and his followers' understanding see: Meier-Oeser, *Die Spur des Zeichens*, 354–76.

[90] On the influence of Le Grand see: Gary Hatfield, 'The Cartesian psychology of Antoine Le Grand', in Mihnea Dobre & Tammy Nyden (eds), *Cartesian Empiricisms* (Dordrecht, 2013), 251–74.

[91] Antoine Le Grand, *Antonii Le Grand Institutio philosophiae, secundum principia d. Renati Descartes: nova methodo adornata, et explicata. In usum juventutis academicae* (Norimbergae: Johannis Ziegeri, 1695), I.X Appendix, 52.

as it depends entirely on human institutions, so we cannot infer from the name some kind of definition of the thing itself. Le Grand stresses that in conflating the definition of a name and the definition of a thing the Aristotelians are hallucinating—the words do not explicate in any way either the essence of the things or the ideas that we form about them.[92] This understanding is also supported by Jacques Rohault, whose *Tractatus physicus* (Latin translation from French 1674) became a popular textbook in the latter part of the century and was cited in many disputations.[93] Rohault discusses the signification of names in the preliminary chapters, and concludes that we cannot derive any knowledge about things from the name.[94]

Such an attitude towards words is a frequent occurrence in the disputations that were influenced by Cartesian thinking.[95] Authors feel that it is not beneficial to expend effort on explicating and describing terms at length, as these are often 'familiar, plain and clear enough, so that anyone could understand them easily even from the frontispiece of the disputation'[96] and bemoan the 'waste of good hours' on onomatology.[97] There are some disputations that seek to justify this attitude and bring explicit arguments against the usefulness of lengthy onomatology:

> As a thorough and clever discussion about onomatology, often with long series and lists of equivalent words, tends to make words which are clear and comprehensible enough more confusing and impenetrable, we will try not to delay too long on this point. Words are signs for things on which we have agreed; they have been assigned to things as we know, mainly according to human will, without taking any kind of form into consideration. Therefore it is not suitable to research everything, as some tend to do; neither do we find

---

[92] Ibid., I.X Appendix, 53.

[93] E.g. Gabriel Sjöberg [P], Andreas Westerman [R], *Dissertatio philosophica de erroribus sensuum* (Dorpat: Brendeken, 1692); Johann Balthasar von Wernher [P], Johann Andreas Plohr [R], *Disputationem physicam de saporibus eorumque differentiis* (Leipzig: Literis Brandenburgerianis, 1698).

[94] Simplex enim nominis impositio rei nondum notae, eius notitiam non promouet. Jacques Rohault, *Tractatus physicus, gallice emissus et recens latinitate donatus per Th. Bonetum* (Genevae: Widerhold, 1674), pars 1, cap. 2, xlii, 18.

[95] E.g. Petrus Wolfart [P], Jacob Fabricius [R], *Disputatio physico-medica, de antlia pneumatica* (Gissae-Hassorum: Müllerus, 1697); Johann Christian Lehmann [P], Andreas Bretag [R], *Disputationem physicam de transmutationibus corporum extraordinariis* (Leipzig: Fleischerus, 1697).

[96] Ast non existimamus opus esse, ut in explicanda describendaque hac multiplicationis voce multum desudemus, cum usu satis trita, plana, et perspicua sit, ut unusquisque vel ex frontispicio disputationis facile intelligat. Johann Heinrich Greulinck [P], Peter Berger [R], *De multiplicatione hominis, secundum utramque essentiae partem, disputationem physicam* (Halle: Henckelius, 1697).

[97] Olaus Hermelin [P], Gustav Camitz [R], *Dissertatio politica de transfugis* (Dorpat: Brendeken, 1693), cap. 1, § 1.

it necessary. We will try to be concise and discuss briefly only those that are connected to our undertaking.[98]

Johannes Sperlette's textbook *Logica et metaphysica novae: ad usum academicae iuventutis* (1696), which he wrote for the use of the university in Halle, also echoes the statements of Le Grand when he discusses definition of names in his chapter about logic. He advises against explication of names in an etymological manner, which is for grammarians and states that *definitio nominis* should deal with the usage of names only in a particular situation. We use names through mutual agreement and they cannot be the definition of the thing as sounds signify ideas indiscriminately. Accordingly we always understand words as references to something that we are already familiar with in some other way.

Thus the definition of the name still remains important and continues to be used in disputations. However without the existence of forms it can also be understood how easily disputants might conclude that words and letters have nothing in common with the things they signify. We cannot derive a definition about a thing from a name only because ideas, which pertain to the definition of the thing, are immaterial and words are just material air particles that strike our tympanum. The words cannot thus have any similarity to things, not even that created by the interpretative capacity of humans. Words are simply signs that in themselves do not communicate much information.

Conclusions

As nominal definitions played an important role in schools by preparing the students to think in a logical way, disputations often discussed names and words at the beginning of texts. On the one hand, based on the view presented by Plato in *Cratylus*, and on the other hand, based on the Aristotelian hylomorphic theory, it was possible to argue that words could teach something about the essence of things. These are also the views most often found in German seventeenth-century Protestant disputations which rely on authorities such as Scaliger, Keckermann or Bechmann.

---

[98] Sed cum scrupolosa disputatio circa ὀνοματολογία ingeniis non paucis longa series et enumeratio vocum idem significantium, verbaque satis clara et perspicua interdum obscuriora et magis impedita reddat, idcirco eadem hic nos detineri haud multum patiamur. Verba esse signa rerum, de quibus convenimus, plurimaque ex arbitrio humano, sine respectu formae alicujus, cum sciamus rebus imposita; idcirco omnia inquirere, quae alias adsolent, nec convenit, nec necessarium judicamus, brevitatemque qui affectamus, haec paucis attingere, quae ad institutum nostrum pertinent, contenti erimus. Gabriel Sjöberg [P], Andreas Kiemmer [R], *Exercitium academicum de cura animi* (Dorpat: Brendeken, 1698), sect. 2.

However, at the end of the seventeenth century, in the disputations that display Cartesian influence, the authors start to view nominal definitions differently. In the framework of a mechanistic theory of perception words can no longer be understood as signs that have some connection with things or concepts. This tendency is easily observable in disputations that follow the examples and attitudes presented in new textbooks by Le Grand, Rohault or Sperlette. The questions about whether the ideas which the words refer to are formed in a person's mind only after sensing something in the world, or whether it is also possible to access the ideas altogether without using our sense organs, is continuously under discussion. These questions acquire however a very different character without the theory of forms.[99]

Appendix 1

1.	Moller, Friedrich [P], Balthasar Heintke [R]	*De aere, aqua, et terra: physica diaskepsis; in duas disputationes tributa*	Frankfurt a.d. O: Typis Sciurinis	1601
2.	Tandler, Tobias [P], Georg Boltzen [R]	*Disputationis I. De homine in universum themata*	Wittenberg: Lehmannus	1601
3.	Peter Gottart [P], Johann Rasper [R]	*Disputationum logicarum secunda, de natura logices*	Frankfurt a.d. O: Typis Voltzianis	1601
4.	Heinrich Huberin [P], Bartholomaeus Bargmann [R]	*Logicarum disputatio prima, de philosophia in genere eiusque partibus*	Helmstedt: Lucius	1604
5.	Crusius, David [P], Martin Mylius [R]	*Disputatio de definitione, subiecto et fine dialectices*	Erfurt: Wittelius	1607
6.	Timpler, Clemens [P], Johannes Wirtz [R]	*Theoria physica, de intellectu humano: certis thesibus perspicue, et methodice comprehensa*	Steinfurt: Caesar	1611
7.	Johannes Steuber [P], Johann Christoph Burger [R]	*Disputatio VII physica de loco*	Gießen: Hampelius	1615
8.	Johann Regius	*Commentariorum ac disputationum logicarum libri V*	Wittenberg: Bergerus	1615
9.	Johann Engelbach [P], Justus Wormbser [R]	*Disputatio prima physica, de formarum pluralitate*	Gießen: Chemlinus	1615

[99] Hannah Dawson, *Locke, Language and Early-Modern Philosophy* (Cambridge, 2007), 91–128; Lifschitz, 'The Arbitrariness of the Linguistic Sign'; James J. Bono, *Word Of God & The Languages Of Man: Interpreting Nature In Early Modern Science And Medicine*, i: *Ficino To Descartes* (Madison, Wisc, 1995), 26–8.

10.	Sleker, Johann [P], Reinhold Mittendorp [R]	*De intellectu humano disputatio*	Rostock: Pedanus	1618
11.	Johann Hartranfft [P], Melchior Exner [R]	*Theoremata physica sensibus internis, de potentia appetitiva et locomotiva, nec non de somno, vigilia et somniis*	Leipzig: Lanckisius	1620
12.	Abraham Heinick [P], Gottfried Lehner [R]	*Disputatio de somno*	Wittenberg: Richter	1621
13.	Paul Müller [P], Augustin Neuwirth [R]	*Disputatio physica de animae rationalis essentia deque intellectu et voluntate*	Wittenberg: Gormannus	1621
14.	Gottfried Raspe [P], Nicolaus Wolschendorf [R]	*Disputatio III. De natura, et causis naturalibus externis, tam per se, quam per accidens*	Leipzig: Ritzsch	1625
15.	Scharf, Johann Carpzov [P], Johann Benedict Carpzov [R]	*Hypnologia seu disputatio physiologica de somno et somniis*	Wittenberg: Boreck	1625
16.	Raspe, Gottfried [P], Johann Hess [R]	*De natura et constitutione physicae*	Leipzig: Ritzsch	1626
17.	Zapf, Nicolaus [P], Heinrich Renis [R]	*Disputatio physico-elementaris de terra*	Wittenberg: Hake	1626
18.	Aenetius, Gottlieb [P], Georg Emmerich Pfefferkorn [R]	*Disputatio physica de coelo*	Jena: Typis Viduae Weidnerianae	1628
19.	Brendel, Zacharias [P], Wolfgang Ulrich Amthor [R]	*Disputatio inauguralis de dysenteria*	Jena: Typis Weidnerianis	1628
20.	Nicolaus Agerius [P], Johann Mundler [R]	*Disputatio physiologica. De somno, sentientis facultatis affectione*	Straßburg: Reppius	1629
21.	Johann Heinrich Tonsor [P], Johannes Lucas [R]	*Disputatio physica, de vigilia somno et somniis*	Marburg: Chemlinus	1629
22.	Leuschner, Martin [P], Johannes Fabinus [R]	*Disputatio physica. De longa et brevi vita*	Stettin: Goetschius	1630
23.	Jeremias Metzler [P], Matthaeus Pöllner [R]	*Disputatio physica, de terra*	Leipzig: Lambergius	1632
24.	Olearius, Adam	*Disputatio physica, de natura*	Leipzig: Ritzsch	1632
25.	Zapf, Nicolaus Strauch [P], Aegidius Strauch [R]	*Disputatio physica de elementis in genere et in specie*	Wittenberg: Müllerus	1633
26.	Agerius, Nicolaus [P], Gregor Hilling [R]	*De metallis disputatio physica*	Straßburg: Simon	1634
27.	Daniel Beckher [P], Johann Michaelis [R]	*Disputatio physica de lachrymis*	Königsberg: Segebadius	1634
28.	Petrus Goetschenius [P], Nicolaus Olai Calmariensis [R]	*Dissertatio philosophica et solennis, de mundo in genere*	Dorpat: Pistorius	1635
29.	Musaeus, Johannes [P], Daniel Agricola [R]	*Disputatio physica de terra*	Erfurt: Dedekindus	1636

30.	Schragmüller, Johann Conrad [P], Wilhelm Scipio [R]	*Disputatio physica de monstris*	Marburg: Chemlinus	1636
31.	Johann Sperling [P], Tobias Mezner [R]	*Disputatio physica de homine, cuius brevem delineationem cum quibusdam quaestionibus annexis*	Wittenberg: Röhnerus	1636
32.	Zopff, Johann Caspar [P], Andreas Lindenmuth [R]	*Disputatio physica de homine*	Leipzig: Ritzsch	1636
33.	Peter Lauremberg [P], Philipp-Georgius Ludecus [R]	*Disputatio physica de coelo et stellis*	Rostock: Kilius	1637
34.	Samuel Avenarius [P], Andreas Fuchs [R]	*Disputatio physica de somno, eiusque adiuncto, insomnio, et opposito, vigilia*	Leipzig: Köler	1638
35.	Bleuel, Tobias [P], Martin Heidenreich [R]	*Physica de natura, disputatio*	Leipzig: Lanckisch	1640
36.	Paul Marquard Schlegel [P], Johann Theodor Schenck [R]	*Disputatio physico-medica, de natura lactis*	Jena: Steinmannus	1640
37.	Joachim Crell [P], Martin Holmer [R]	*Disputatio physica de facultatibus animae rationalis primariis, intellectu et voluntate*	Rostock: Kilius	1643
38.	Sperling, Johann [P], Michael Blume [R]	*Disputatio physica de pavone*	Wittenberg: Röhner	1643
39.	Johann Sperling [P], Gabriel Elvering [R]	*Disputatio physica de intellectu*	Wittenberg: Röhner	1649
40.	Johannes Erici Stregnensis [P], Andreas Flojerus [R]	*Disputatio philosophica de natura et constitutione scientiae naturalis*	Dorpat: Vogelius	1651
41.	Johann Conrad Brotbeck [P], Johann Jacob Bavarus [R]	*De somno*	Tübingen: Litteris Werlinianis	1653
42.	Heinrich Bussenius [P], Johann Sturm [R]	*Disputatio philosophica, de sensuum affectionibus, somno, et vigiliis*	Königsberg: Reusnerus	1656
43.	Friedemann Bechmann [P], Johann Hünefeld [R]	*Disputationum logicarum de demonstratione*	Jena: Freyschmid	1658
44.	Johann Conrad Brotbeck [P], Johannes Hafner [R]	*De intellectu humano ἀγώνισμα*	Tübingen: Cellius	1658
45.	Friedrich Rappolt [P], Christian Langenberg [R]	*Disputatio physica de somno*	Leipzig: Hahnius	1659
46.	Johannes Placentinus [P], Reinhold Tinctor [R]	*De origine caloris et motus membrorum naturalis; in humano corpore, adeoq vitae brutae, quae nobis communis est cum bestiis, et nonnullis philosophiae Cartesianae speciminibus*	Frankfurt a.d. O: Eichorn	1660

47.	Georg Caspar Kirchmaier [P], Johann Friedrich Scharf [R]	*De origine vitae humanae, et potioribus quibusdam philosophiae Cartesianae speciminibus: additis, a fine, notis apologeticis, ad secunda responsa Placentiniana*	Wittenberg: Hake	1660
48.	Johann Parpard [P], Erdmann Hoffmann [R]	*Disputatio de fato inprimis physico*	Wittenberg: Wendt	1661
49.	Johann Adam Schertzer [P], Samuel Dögius [R]	*Uranologia h.e. disputatio physica de coelo*	Leipzig: Hahnius	1661
50.	Johann Ernst Hering [P], Johann Christoph Förstel [R]	*De morte*	Wittenberg: Borckardus	1662
51.	Christoph Krahe [P], Johann Gigel [R]	*Exercitatio philologico-physica somniis*	Leipzig: Literis Wittigauianis	1662
52.	Paul Preuser [P], Johannes Schultze [R]	*Disputatio physiologica de odore*	Leipzig: Wittigau	1662
53.	Isaac Thilo [P], Elias Luja [R]	*Disputatio physica de temperamento*	Leipzig: Michael	1662
54.	Georg Wagner, [P], Georg Neukirch [R]	*Disputatio physica de hyeme*	Wittenberg: Borckardus	1670
55.	Johann Christoph Hundeshagen [P], Johannes Dreier [R]	*Disputatio philosophica de fulmine*	Jena: Literis Bauhoferianis	1670
56.	Isaac Schoock	*Dissertatio physica de nive, cum rarissimis adhaerentibus quaestionibus, de meteoris aqueis*	Frankfurt a.d. O: Sumptibus Eichornianis,	1673
57.	Johann Schmidt [P], Johann Michael Bonhöfer [R]	*Disputationum logicarum tertiam de praedicatione*	Jena: Stanno Gollneriano	1675
58.	Lorenz Strauß [P], Johannes Reiche [R]	*Disputatio physica, de iride*	Gießen: Offic. Academ. Kargeriana	1679
59.	Schmidt, Johann Andreas [P], Nicolaus Eberhardi [R]	*Disputatio physica de butyro, ut est alimentum*	Jena: Literis Wertherianis	1680
60.	Johann Jakob Waldschmidt [P], Christian Kursner [R]	*Disputatio physica, de magnete*	Marburg: Kürsnerus,	1683
61.	Georg Wolfgang Wedel [P], Conrad Georg Hartmann [R]	*Disputatio medica inauguralis de somno praeternaturali*	Jena: Literis Krebsianis	1686
62.	Christian Krumbholtz [P], Georg Leberecht von Wilke [R]	*Disputationem physicam: quod voluntas non necessario determinetur ab ultimo iudicio intellectus practici*	Leipzig: Typis Gözianis	1687
63.	Johann Christian Schamberg [P], Gottfried Boenigk [R]	*Disputatio physica de gustu ex recentiorum philosophorum hypothesi explicato*	Leipzig: Typis Wittigauianis	1689

64.	Georg Otho [P], Johann Philipp Elckenbracht [R]	*Disputatio philosophica de meteoris aqueis*	Marburg: Stockius	1690
65.	Abraham Heinrich Deutschmann [P], Johann Lang [R]	*Disputatio pneumatica, ex theologia naturali, de intellectu, voluntate, ac libertate divinae essentiae*	Wittemberg: Schrödterus	1692
66.	Johann Sperlette [P], Charles Goullet [R]	*Disputatio philosophica, de arte cogitandi, deque veris corporum principiis*	Halle: Salfeldius	1695
67.	Mathesius, Johann Balthasar [P], Erhard Lindner [R]	*Disputatio physica, qua in transitu Israelitarum per Mare Erythraeum non fuisse fluxum et refluxum maris*	Leipzig	1696
68.	Johann Heinrich Greulinck [P], Peter Berger [R]	*De multiplicatione hominis, secundum utramque essentiae partem, disputationem physicam*	Halle: Henckelius	1697
69.	Gabriel Sjöberg [P], Andreas Kiemmer [R]	*Exercitium academicum de cura animi*	Dorpat: Brendeken	1698

Scholarship, Politics, and Jewish Identity in Italian Post-Unification Academia

Marco Di Giulio

The emergence of the Italian nation state in the late 1850s coincided with a rapid and radical transformation of its institutions of higher education as these were assembled into a national system.[1,2] The leaders of the embryonic nation state recognized that educational reforms provided an opportunity to integrate figures who had been instrumental in securing the political reform into the university system.[3] Since the campaign for Italian unification had long been identified with the campaign for Jewish emancipation, educational reform also provided a way to begin to introduce Jews as professors into university faculties.[4] In the years leading up to and immediately after Unification, five Jewish intellectuals were appointed

---

[1] This article is based on research I conducted as a fellow participant in the seminar 'On the Word of a Jew: Oaths, Testimonies, and the Nature of Trust' at the Oxford Center for Hebrew and Jewish Studies in the fall of 2013. I wish to thank all the fellow members for engaging in stimulating conversations, as well as L. Scott Lerner for commenting on earlier drafts of this work.

[2] See Ilaria Porciani and Mauro Moretti, 'La creazione del sistema universitario nella nuova Italia', in Gian Paolo Brizzi, Piero Del Negro & Andrea Romano (eds), *Storia delle Università in Italia* (3 vols, Messina, 2007) i. 323–79. The university system of the post-unification period, as Ilaria Porciani and Mauro Moretti have shown, played a key role in the project of nation-building, in so far as it was designed to train the class of teachers of primary and secondary education. On the reform of the university system and its significance for Italian nation-building, see also Alessandra Ferraresi and Elisa Signori (eds), *Le Università e l'Unità d'Italia (1848–1870)* (Bologna, 2012); Ilaria Porciani (ed.), *Università e scienza nazionale* (Naples, 2001).

[3] Marino Raicich, *Scuola, cultura e politica da De Sanctis a Gentile* (Pisa, 1981), 60, 219–20.

[4] On the link between the struggle for Italian independence and Jewish emancipation, see Dan Vittorio Segre, 'The Emancipation of Jews in Italy', in Pierre Birnbaum & Ira Katznelson (eds), *Paths of Emancipation: Jews, States, and Citizenship* (Princeton, 1995), 206–37.

as professors in various fields: Beniamino Sadun (1818–1911) in hygiene (University of Siena, 1859); Alessandro D'Ancona (1835–1914) in Italian literature (University of Pisa, 1860); Graziadio Isaia Ascoli (1829–1907) in Oriental languages and comparative grammar (Accademia Scientifico-Letteraria in Milan, 1861); Salvatore De Benedetti (1818–91) in Hebrew language and literature (University of Pisa, 1862); and Luigi Luzzatti (1841–1927) in statistics and economics (Istituto Tecnico Superiore of Milan, 1863). Their entry into Italian academia marked a signal moment in the history of Italian Jewry. Long excluded from participation in the state, Jews were enlisted to collaborate in the project of nation-building promoted by the new regime through education as barriers to equality fell during political unification.

Two of these Jewish academics, Graziadio Isaia Ascoli and Salvatore De Benedetti, are of special interest because of the connection between their Jewish identity and their fields of specialization. Unlike the other Jewish appointees in the early 1860s, neither was a university-trained scholar. In part, they acquired their positions because their peers believed that they had an innate facility with Hebrew by virtue of their Jewishness. But each man possessed a range of talents, and they both developed remarkable careers: Ascoli raised the profile of Italian linguistics to new heights, shaped academic politics in the late nineteenth century as a secretary of the Council of Public Education (Consiglio Superiore della Pubblica Istruzione), became a senator of the Kingdom in 1889, and was a major figure in the debate over the Italian national language in the years following Unification. De Benedetti contributed to the expansion of Oriental studies, popularized medieval Hebrew literature through intensive activity as a translator and a scholar, and in 1881 was appointed a *Cavaliere* (Knight) of the Order of the Crown of Italy, which was established by King Victor Emmanuel II in 1861 to celebrate Unification. Since Judaism was a salient dimension of both the personal and professional lives of each man, their careers invite a number of questions: How did they understand their roles as academics and as Jews involved in the project of nation building? What impact did their entrance into the newly secularized university system have on their understanding of their identity as Jews? How did they present themselves to a public that was well acquainted with negative stereotypes of Jews and Judaism? How did the rise in anti-Jewish sentiment that began in the 1870s affect their scholarship?

In what follows, I focus on the inception of Ascoli's and De Benedetti's careers in order to explore how they, as Jews and intellectuals, negotiated their rapid transition from 'outsiders' to members of the cultural hegemony. Individual studies have specifically explored Ascoli's and, to a much lesser extent, De Benedetti's biographies in connection with their Jewish background, but these have overlooked the impact that the cultural and political reorientation of the university system had on their recruitment, as well as on the ways they envisioned their role as Jewish intellectuals serving national interests.[5] Recognizing this impact helps us appreciate the variety of factors that sustained and shaped the Jews' experience in their encounters with the secularized cultural institutions of post-Unification Italy—a topic that has become central to recent scholarship on processes of Jewish cultural accommodation to the non-Jewish majority.[6]

Following a review of the historical circumstances that facilitated the admittance of Jews into Italian academia, this paper examines the inaugural addresses delivered by Ascoli and De Benedetti, which reveal how the two men began to construct their public personae as both Jewish scholars and loyal servants of the state. A discussion of these addresses, in which they laid out the trajectory of their academic endeavours, shows how they leveraged their newly acquired positions to incorporate Jewish, and more broadly Semitic, legacies in modern society, at a time when academia was leading the effort to foster a national culture, often based on a notion of 'Italianness'.[7] The last half of the paper reviews the later careers of Ascoli and De Benedetti, when both men witnessed and responded to a rise in anti-Semitic sentiment. The anti-Jewish claims propagated in the last

---

[5] In particular, see Guido Lucchini, 'Il giovane Ascoli e la tradizione ebraica', *Studi di grammatica italiana*, 18 (1999), 329–435; Felice Israel, 'Graziadio Isaia Ascoli: gli studi ebraici in Italia e il suo rapporto con Isacco Samuele Reggio', *Materia Giudaica*, 15–16 (2010–2011), 229–49; Maddalena Del Bianco Cotrozzi, 'Ascoli e l'ebraismo del suo tempo', in Carla Marcato & Federico Vicario (eds), *Il pensiero di Graziadio Isaia Ascoli a cent'anni dalla scomparsa: Convegno internazionale, Gorizia-Udine, 3–5 maggio 2007* (Udine, 2010), 51–72. On De Benedetti, see Alessandro D'Ancona, 'Salvatore De Benedetti', in Alessandro D'Ancona (ed), *Ricordi e affetti* (Milan, 1908), 240–50; references to De Benedetti's biography are contained in Alberto Cavaglion, '*Israele italiano*: Risorgimento, ebrei e vita politica nell'Italia unita – alcuni casi-studio', *Rassegna Mensile di Israel*, 76 (2010), 75–93; Bruno Di Porto, 'L'approdo al crogiuolo risorgimentale', *La Rassegna Mensile di Israel*, 50 (1984), 803–62, esp. 842–52.

[6] See, for example, Elizabeth Schächter, *The Jews of Italy 1848–1915: Between Tradition and Transformation* (London, 2011); Carlotta Ferrara degli Uberti, *Fare gli ebrei italiani: autorappresentazioni di una minoranza (1861–1918)* (Bologna, 2011). While Schächter's work examines the developments of Italian Jewry from the point of view of intellectual history, Ferrara degli Uberti's book embraces a social-historical perspective. The two works also differ in the emphasis placed on the impact of anti-Jewish ideologies in Italy.

[7] The link between academia and the definition of an Italian national culture has been the object of recent studies: Paul Arpaia, 'Constructing a National Identity from a Created Literary Past: Giosuè Carducci and the Development of a National Literature', *Journal of Modern Italian Studies*, 7 (2002), 192–214; Colin Johnson, 'An "Italian Grimm": Domenico Comparetti and the Nationalization of Italian Folktales', *Italica*, 87 (2010), 462–87. A general treatment of this question is offered by Porciani, 'Introduzione', in *Università e scienza nazionale*, pp. xiii–xxix.

third of the nineteenth century threatened to undermine the public personae that they endeavoured to assert at the time of their installation as professors.

The Secular Turn in Italian Education

The belief that political independence could not be fully achieved without the intellectual revitalization of the nation, which in turn required the liberation of academic institutions from church oversight, motivated politicians to promote wide-ranging educational reforms. Already in the late 1840s, Piedmontese officials had devised ways to reduce or eliminate the Catholic Church's control of the local educational system. About a decade later, beginning in 1859, the entire institutional and educational system of the old dynastic states was dismantled and rebuilt as the independent Italian states were assembled into what would become the Kingdom of Italy in 1861.[8]

Francesco De Sanctis (1817–83), the Kingdom of Italy's first minister of education, directed the effort to coordinate educational reforms in the pre-unitarian states.[9] A literary scholar as well as a radical activist who had taken part in the revolt of Naples in 1848, De Sanctis was expelled from the Kingdom of Sicily and found shelter in Piedmont from 1853 to 1856 and later in Zurich, where he taught Italian literature until he returned to Italy in 1860. During his tenure as minister, he combated illiteracy and sought to improve the educational standards of a country that had long been culturally and geographically fragmented. But his principal achievement was to fully secularize the educational system. In addition to hindering clergy from becoming university professors, De Sanctis worked to free education from ecclesiastical influence and bring it under state jurisdiction. At the same time, he used opportunities to reward those who had demonstrated their patriotism in the struggle toward unification. A record of patriotic activity could compensate for a lack of scholarly accomplishments as members of the new class of academics were selected on the basis of their adherence to the ideologies of the Risorgimento.[10]

The entrance of Jews into academia was not an assured outcome of the secularization process. Early in the 1860s, when the cultural policy of the

---

[8] Porciani & Moretti, 'La creazione del sistema universitario', 323–50.

[9] De Sanctis served as a minister of education in 1861–2 and 1878–81. On De Sanctis, see Paolo Jachia, *Introduzione a De Sanctis* (Bari, 1996); Salvatore Valitutti, *La riforma di Francesco De Sanctis* (Naples, 1988).

[10] Raicich, *Scuola, cultura e politica*, 218–25.

Ministry of Education was in the making, it was unclear whether religious difference (even in the wake of legal emancipation) would still disqualify a candidate for a university position. Indeed, in 1860 Alessandro D'Ancona's appointment as chair of Italian literature at Pisa encountered opposition from Catholic moderates who insinuated that, as a Jew, he lacked the knowledge of Christian theology necessary to fully appreciate the symbolism of Dante's literature.[11]

Even in fields without explicitly religious content, Jews were still subject to prejudice. When Luigi Luzzatti decided to compete for the chair of philosophy of law in Urbino in 1863, he was sceptical about his chances of success.[12] Born into a Venetian Jewish mercantile family, Luzzatti graduated in law from the University of Padua in 1863. In that same year he published a groundbreaking and enthusiastically reviewed book, *La diffusione del credito e le banche popolari* (Padua), which he hoped would help him to secure a chair in an Italian university.[13] A non-Jewish friend, Guido Vanzolini, warned Luzzatti how difficult it would be for a Jew to pursue an academic career, especially in a conservative place like Urbino, which had recently been captured from the Papal States.[14] Vanzolini suggested that religious prejudice could effectively bar non-Catholics from an ideologically sensitive field such as education, on which the new state placed great emphasis.

Indeed, there was feeling that religious sentiment could thwart the forces of secularization. Francesco Dini, a former priest, felt that both Luzzatti's Jewishness and his own status as an ex-clergyman were considered 'two tremendous crimes by people, who, though atheist', would nonetheless show reverence for Catholicism and would take religion into account in appointing scholars.[15] Nevertheless, Luzzatti did win the chair in Urbino, despite the fact that his competitor was Eusebio Reali, a priest who had made a name for himself as a liberal intellectual.[16] A few years later, Reali (who eventually assumed the chair when Luzzatti declined it) wrote a bitter denunciation of the cultural politics of the post-unification

---

[11] Mauro Moretti, 'La dimensione ebraica di un maestro pisano: Documenti su Alessandro D'Ancona,' in Michele Luzzati (ed.), *Gli ebrei di Pisa (secoli IX–XX)*(Pisa, 1998), 241–82, at 243.

[12] Luigi Luzzatti, *Memorie autobiografiche e carteggi, 1841–1876* (3 vols, Bologna, 1929–66), i. 128. On Luzzatti see Paolo Pecorari & Pier Luigi Ballini (eds), *Luigi Luzzatti e il suo tempo: atti del Convegno internazionale di studio, Venezia, 7–9 novembre 1991* (Venice, 1994); eid., *Luigi Luzzatti presidente del consiglio* (Venice, 2013).

[13] Luzzatti, *Memorie*, 126.   [14] Ibid., 129.   [15] Ibid., 130.

[16] On Eusebio Reali, see Luigi Rubechi, *Della vita e degli studi del professore Eusebio Reali: memoria* (Siena, 1870).

governments.[17] He criticized the habit of using appointments as a 'reward for patriotism', and the practice of discriminating against 'friars and priests, only because (they were) friars and priests'.[18]

While the process of secularization made it possible for Jews to settle into academic pursuits, it had another consequence that specifically enabled them to hold positions in Hebrew, long the monopoly of clergymen: the reclassification of the study of the biblical tongue as a philological pursuit, rather than a theological one. In 1862, Carlo Matteucci (1811–68), who briefly served as De Sanctis's successor at the Ministry of Education, sent the universities of the Kingdom a questionnaire soliciting opinions on how to improve critical aspects of the educational system; one query explored the prospect of making Hebrew part of the philology curriculum.[19] This move had recently been undertaken in France, which had embarked on a massive effort to equip its institutions of higher learning with the whole spectrum of Oriental languages.[20] Matteucci sought to emulate France, believing that comprehensive coverage of Semitic languages was crucial to a modern university system. But the transfer of Hebrew from the field of theology to philology also took on a political connotation: it allowed the state to gain control over a field that had long been subject to church authority.

While various administrators contributed to the expansion of philological disciplines in Italy,[21] the figure who placed the study of Hebrew, and Semitics in general, on firm ground was Michele Amari (1806–89), a patriot who lived in exile in Paris until 1859 and served as minister of education from 1862 to 1864.[22] His reputation as an Arabist was such

[17] E. Reali, 'Del Riordinamento scolastico nel Regno d'Italia', in *Atti della Reale Accademia de' Fisiocritici di Siena*, Ser. 2, 3 (1868), 71–160.

[18] Reali, 'Del Riordinamento', 98.

[19] *Raccolta dei documenti relativi alla legge sulle tasse universitarie del 31 luglio 1862 e al Regolamento generale delle Università del Regno* (Turin, 1862).

[20] Gabriel Bergounioux, '«Aryen», «indo-Européen», «sémite» dans l'université française (1850–1914)', *Histoire Epistémologie Langage*, 18 (1996), 109–26.

[21] In 1860, the minister of education of the provisional government of Emilia, Luigi Montanari, went to great pains to provide the University of Bologna with a chair in Semitics. The administrative document that established this chair is published in Emmanuele Bollati (ed.), *Fasti Legislativi e Parlamentari delle Rivoluzioni Italiane nel Secolo XIX* (3 parts in 2 vols, Milan, 1865), ii.1 850.

[22] On Michele Amari, see Andrea Borruso, *Michele Amari storico e politico: atti del Seminario di studi* (Palermo, 1990). On the development of the academic study of Hebrew, see Mauro Perani, 'Jewish Studies in the Italian Academic World', in Albert van der Heide and Irene E. Zwiep (eds), *Jewish Studies and the European Academic World* (Paris, 2005), 45–75.

that De Sanctis sought his advice in 1861 when, as a minister, he worked to establish the study of Oriental languages at the newly founded Istituto Superiore di Studi Pratici e Teorici of Florence. In reply, Amari laid out a plan for placing Florence 'in line with the most renowned universities'.[23] Florence needed chairs in Semitics, Arabic, and Hebrew. But while Amari failed to specify any requirements for the scholars who would occupy the chairs of Semitics and Arabic, he had no doubt that the candidate for the Hebrew chair had to be a '*secular* professor and a freethinker'—in other words, a scholar without a confessional affiliation. The search for such a scholar was not an easy one, and fifteen years would elapse before David Castelli (1836–1901), a Jewish Hebraist and freethinker, was chosen by a committee chaired by Amari.[24] The only member on the search committee to express a negative judgement of Castelli's work was Giuseppe Ghiringhello, a Catholic priest who taught Hebrew and scriptural exegesis at the University of Turin. He argued that Castelli's exegesis conflicted with Christian doctrine and therefore represented a 'scandal or a danger for most readers'.[25] Amari not only endorsed Castelli, he also snubbed Ghiringhello, expressing his hope that 'Italy would never have a minister of education who would perceive danger in the critical study of the Hebrew Scriptures'.[26]

Thus, it was a broader tide of secularization of state policies—not simply emancipation itself—that laid the groundwork for the appointment of Ascoli and De Benedetti as professors responsible for teaching subjects with Jewish content. Although each was a '*secular* professor and a freethinker', their relation to their subject matter was coloured by their awareness of their dual identity as Italians and as Jews. In Ascoli's scholarship, this duality is reflected in a concern to illuminate the connections and influences linking Semitic and Indo-European languages and cultures. In De Benedetti's work, his dual identity is more directly represented by his interest in developing parallels between ancient Israel and contemporary Italy. Each of the two scholars responded to the secularizing leanings of the unified state by representing Jewishness as a cultural rather than a religious heritage.

[23] Francesco De Sanctis, *Epistolario (1861–1862)*, ed. Giuseppe Talamo (Turin, 1969), letter 744 (Florence, August 7, 1861), 224.

[24] On Castelli see Cristiana Facchini, *David Castelli: Ebraismo e scienze delle religioni tra otto e novecento* (Brescia, 2005).

[25] Fausto Parente, 'David Castelli', in *Dizionario Biografico degli Italiani*, ed. Istituto dell'Enciclopedia Italiana, 21 (1978), 698–707.

[26] Parente, 700.

Ascoli's and De Benedetti's Appointments

Ascoli was the first Jewish scholar to enter the newly unified country's academia as a professional academic. Born in 1829 into an Italian-speaking family in Habsburg Gorizia, Ascoli did not receive a formal education. Although he was expected to continue the entrepreneurial activity of his family, as a youth he devoted his energy to acquiring an impressive command of languages. The most prominent Jewish scholars of the time, Isaac Samuel Reggio (1784–1850) and Samuel David Luzzatto (1800–65), served as both mentors and intellectual models for Ascoli. He learned Hebrew and secular subjects from his Jewish private tutor, and taught himself Sanskrit, Latin, Greek, Arabic, and other Oriental languages. At the age of seventeen, he published a study contrasting the Friulian and Wallachian dialects, which foreshadowed his career as a comparative linguist.[27]

Ascoli's ambition to pursue a scholarly career became apparent not long thereafter. In 1852, he embarked on a two-month-long journey to establish contacts with prominent Italian scholars who were or would become professional academics.[28] His plan to launch the first Italian journal of Oriental languages as a platform for cutting-edge Italian scholarship impressed them greatly. The first two volumes of *Studi linguistici e Orientali* (Gorizia), which contained groundbreaking research in Oriental philology, Sanskrit, and Indo-European languages, were published in 1854 and 1855. Although this publication failed to live up to expectations—it featured only one essay that was not authored by Ascoli himself—it increased his visibility in the scholarly community. In 1860, endorsed by the scholars he had met eight years earlier, Ascoli was offered the chair in Semitics at the University of Bologna, a city that had just aligned itself with the Kingdom of Sardinia.

Yet the offer did not appeal to Ascoli. Writing on December 25, 1860, he thanked Terenzio Mamiani (1799–1885), secretary of education of the Kingdom of Sardinia, for the offer but stated that his Jewishness had led the minister to overestimate his qualifications as a candidate for a chair in

---

[27] *Sull'idioma Friulano e sulla sua affinità con la Lingua Valacca: Schizzo storico-filologico* (Udine, 1846).

[28] Graziadio Isaia Ascoli, 'Note letterario-artistiche minori durante il viaggio nella Venezia, nella Lombardia, nella Liguria, nel Parmigiano, Modenese e Pontificio—Maggio-giugno 1852', ed. Sebastiano Timpanaro, in *Annali della Scuola Normale Superiore di Pisa*, 28 (1959), 151–91.

Semitics.[29] Instead, he requested an appointment that would allow him to carry out the broad comparative research he had initiated in the *Studi linguistici e Orientali*. Aware of the minister's project to establish a new university in Milan, recently captured from Austria and incorporated into the Kingdom of Sardinia, Ascoli proposed himself as a candidate for its chair in comparative grammar and Oriental languages. Within a fortnight Mamiani sent Ascoli the appointment letter for Milan.[30]

Ascoli was invited to join Italian academia with the express purpose of raising the study of language to new heights. However, the inaugural address that he read on November 25, 1861 at the Accademia Scientifico Letteraria in Milan contained more than a programme for research and teaching. In it, Ascoli emphasized the different components of his identity, as a scholar, an Italian, and a Jew. Presenting himself as an autodidact who had never 'crossed the threshold of a university, neither for studying nor for teaching', Ascoli nevertheless promised to position Italy at the centre of the broader European intellectual discourse. Thus, he announced his intention of replacing the antiquarian approach to the study of language current in Italy with comparative methods, citing Alexander von Humboldt, Heymann Steinthal, Karl W.F. von Schlegel, Franz Bopp, and other giants of nineteenth-century linguistics.

In keeping with this goal, Ascoli devoted the body of his lecture to the much-discussed topic of the relationship between Indo-European and Semitic languages and cultures. Contemporaneous scholarship emphasized the divisions between these two large groups and their civilizations, and conclusions drawn from historical linguistics led to the development of ethnic hierarchies that elevated Aryans over Semites. In the 1850s, for example, Ernest Renan (1823–92) pointed to clear differences between the intellectual and moral predispositions of Aryans and Semites. Based on notions of linguistic determinism, Renan's theory stressed that the Aryans possessed ability, discipline, and a capacity for political independent organization, whereas the Semites were uncreative, voluptuous, and subjective. Ascoli took a different tack. First, he demonstrated the value of 'Semitic-Sanskritic intellectual mixings' (*mistioni intellettuali semitico-sanscritiche*), offering a rich survey of cultural and linguistic exchanges between the East and the West throughout the centuries. His chief example of the harmonious 'intertwining of Sanskritic and Semitic civilizations' was the New Testament: written in Greek that had 'a taste of Hebrew', its doctrines bore the indelible marks of Semitic influence.[31]

[29] Comitato goriziano per le onoranze a Graziadio Isaia Ascoli (ed.), *Graziadio Ascoli, 1860–1861*(Gorizia, 1907), 16.

[30] Raicich, *Scuola, cultura e politica*, 261.   [31] Ascoli, 'Prolusione', 300.

Ascoli went a step further, however, claiming that the Old Testament possessed a greater pureness and aesthetic dignity than the New Testament. Indeed, the Old Testament was a 'pure and noble plant' that had 'spread its roots throughout Europe', entering the 'faith and art of many Indo-European nations'.[32]

Despite this emphasis on the place of the Old Testament in European culture as a whole, Ascoli presented it as the special possession of the Jewish people. He depicted the Jews as jealous guardians of the Old Testament as well as 'infidels' whom the church had sought to 'convert and confute'.[33] A little later in his address, Ascoli presented himself in terms that echoed this depiction:

> [Belonging myself] in the circle of those who are called the *infidels*, I hope that, without causing offence in any respect, I will be given [the opportunity] to show how the coursing of the word of Moses, David, and Isaiah in my blood from childhood on will benefit [the teaching] of such disciplines [i.e., biblical philology and Semitic languages].[34]

Ascoli's terminology is striking: by numbering himself among the 'infidels', Ascoli appropriated a word whose connotations differed sharply from the usual contemporary Italian words for Jews, *ebreo* and *israelita*.[35] The ethno-religious designation *ebreo* also denoted a 'deceitful' individual,[36] whereas the biblically derived word *israelita* indicated an emancipated Jew whose self-definition was based on religious affiliation rather than ethnicity. When referring to themselves, Jews preferred the latter term.[37] The term *infedele*, however, had specific intellectual connotations at the time, for it was often used in Catholic rhetoric as a synonym for 'heretic' in attacks against the advocates of an anti-metaphysical historicism, scientism, and materialism that was gaining currency in Italian cultural discourse.[38] Thus, by referring to himself as an 'infidel', Ascoli not only reminded his audience of his Jewishness but also suggested that he regarded himself as a secular, anticlerical positivist who had been recruited by a university that was replacing religious dogmatism with an unbending faith in science. Ascoli's strategy of self-presentation turned on

---

[32] Ibid.   [33] Ibid., 300–1.   [34] Ibid., 301.

[35] See Giuseppe Manuzzi, *Vocabolario della lingua italiana già compilato dagli Accademici della Crusca ed ora novamente corretto e accresciuto* (2nd edn: 4 vols, Florence, 1859–60), ii. 261.

[36] Ibid.

[37] For a similar distinction between *israélite* and *juif* in the French language, see Phyllis Cohen Albert, 'Israelite and Jew: How did nineteenth-century French Jews understand assimilation?' in Jonathan Frankel & Steven J. Zipperstein (eds), *Assimilation and Community: The Jews in Nineteenth-Century Europe*, (Cambridge, 1992), 88–109.

[38] Guido Verucci, *L'Italia laica prima e dopo l'unità, 1848–1876* (Rome, 1996), 10–15.

his rejection of the ideal of the pious educator in favour of the figure of the intellectual who capitalizes on religious disbelief to build his reputation as a scholar.

At the same time, Ascoli claimed that his Jewishness especially qualified him to teach Semitic languages because 'the word of Moses, David, and Isaiah' had flowed in his blood from a young age. When declining the chair of Semitics in Bologna a few months earlier, Ascoli had stressed that being Jewish did not necessarily guarantee a deep knowledge of the field, but now that he was employed as a comparative linguist he proudly asserted the contrary. Indeed, in a letter written in the following year to Eude Lolli (1826–1904), a close friend of Ascoli and a rabbi of Padua from 1869 until his death, Ascoli made the case that as a Jew, he possessed assets that enabled him to be a linguist in general: 'I believe that our literary talent and taste being second nature to us since childhood, and being simultaneously indigenous to the East and the West, it comes naturally to us to identify ourselves with the genius of extra-European languages and literatures, even non-Semitic'.[39] In suggesting that the Jews were indigenous to both the East and the West, Ascoli endorses a characterization of the Jews as an Oriental people that began to circulate in Europe during the early modern period.[40] Both Jews and Gentiles contributed to the creation of the image of Jews as the 'Asiatics' of Europe. But while some Jews rejected this representation, other emancipated Jews did embrace this view of themselves proudly, in an attempt to develop a new form of Jewish distinctiveness in nation states that were in search of unifying values. As Ivan Kalmar has pointed out, Orientalist representations of the Jews were instrumental in articulating 'the quest for Jewish dignity' as an emerging bourgeoisie dictated standards of morals, ideals, and beliefs that were new to the Jewish cultural, religious, and social space.[41] It is not surprising, however, that Ascoli refrained from using in public a double-edged trope: those who accused the Jews of not being able to fully integrate into society argued that they belonged outside the West; their fundamentally Oriental nature rendered them unable to assimilate Western mores.

Ascoli's concern for the public image of Italian Jews is explicitly laid out in another letter, probably also addressed to Eude Lolli, in which he argued that Jews were unable to make good use of legal emancipation in

---

[39] The 1862 letter is quoted in Rita Peca Conti, 'Per un profilo di Ascoli Indoeuropeista', in Marcato & Vicario (eds), *Il pensiero di Graziadio Isaia Ascoli*, 249–99, at 252.

[40] See Ivan Kalmar, 'Jewish Orientalism', in Judit Targarona Borrás & Angel Sáenz-Badillos (eds), *Jewish Studies at the Turn of the Twentieth Century* (2 vols, Leiden, 1999), ii. 307–15.

[41] Ibid.

order to release themselves from the constraints of the past.[42] Instead of seeking full cultural integration, in Ascoli's view, the Jews used the benefits of emancipation to dominate the world of finance and thus reinforce the long-lived perception of the Jew's devotion to profit. Ascoli's criticism was harsh: 'The emancipated Jew exhibits an ugly arrogance within a society that is justified in calling him a parasite', he maintained. In the remainder of the letter, Ascoli suggested that efforts to forge a positive Jewish identity were disrupted by those Jews who failed to seize the core of the 'regenerative' discourse of emancipation as an opportunity to eradicate negative stereotypes associated with Jews.

Thus it is likely that Ascoli was conscious that in his inaugural address, he was presenting himself as a public representative of other Jews striving to secure social and cultural integration. By emphasizing his identity as an Italian, a scholar, and a Jew, he offered himself as a model intellectual. But his proud assertion of his identity as one of the 'infidels' met with disapproval within his own community after his address was published in the journal *Il Politecnico* in 1862. Eude Lolli felt that Ascoli's declaration of 'religious nationality' was rather provocative;[43] similarly, David Lolli (1825–84), Eude's brother, perceived Ascoli's insistence on his Jewishness in his self-presentation as a sign of arrogance.[44] But while Eude and David may have preferred to see Ascoli deal with his Jewish identity with greater aplomb, others were untroubled by his boldness. Writing in the Austrian Jewish newspaper *Die Neuzeit* of Vienna (January 31, 1862), Adolf Jellinek (1821–93), a rabbi and leading scholar of the *Wissenschaft des Judentums* movement, treated Ascoli's appointment as an impressive success story, quoting in full the passage in which he declared himself an 'infidel'.[45] And an Italian non-Jewish correspondent perceived Ascoli's Jewishness as just one of the paradoxical dimensions of a man of modernity: 'Italian, without exclusivism; cosmopolitan, mindful of his own hometown; Jewish and a man of the nineteenth century at the same time'.[46] This description captured the qualities of the public persona that Ascoli worked to establish, in which commitment to Jewish continuity was coupled with an embrace of modern patterns of thought and sensibilities.

---

[42] Ascoli to Eude Lolli(?), September 12, 1862, Archivio G. I. Ascoli 61.168, Biblioteca Nazionale dei Lincei e Corsiniana (hereafter BNLC).
[43] Conti, 'Per un profilo di Ascoli Indoeuropeista', 252.
[44] David Lolli to Ascoli, February 19, 1862, Archivio G. I. Ascoli 61.201, BNLC.
[45] *Die Neuzeit: Literarische Chronik* (January 31, 1862), 54.
[46] Unnamed writer to Ascoli, April 4, 1862, Archivio G. I. Ascoli 61.40, Biblioteca Nazionale dei Lincei e Corsiniana (hereafter BNLC).

Social acceptance of Jews began later in Italy than in Germany, but proceeded more rapidly. Consequently, the Jewish press north of the Alps was always attentive to developments within a community that was collaborating in the formation of a modern nation state. Shortly after Ascoli's installation as professor, Ludwig Philippson (1811–89), an advocate of the reform movement of Judaism in Germany, informed the readers of *Allgemeine Zeitung des Judenthums* about Ascoli's recent appointment, quoting the controversial lines of his lecture.[47] In the same short note, Philippson reported that another Jewish intellectual, Salvatore De Benedetti, had been appointed to the chair of Hebrew language and literature at the University of Pisa. This achievement must have appeared remarkable to those German Jews who recalled how, over a decade earlier, Leopold Zunz's and Abraham Geiger's attempts to promote the creation of chairs in Jewish studies at German universities had failed. As Alfred Jospe has pointed out, Geiger had not fully realized the 'pervasiveness of anti-Jewish prejudice in [German] government and academic circles which considered the admission not just of Jews but of Judaism into the university' as conflicting with the Christian character of state institutions.[48]

Unlike Ascoli, De Benedetti, when he became a professor, was not yet a scholar. Rather, he was an educator, a journalist, and an intellectual who had committed himself to the ideals of the liberal revolution. Entirely secular in his outlook, De Benedetti possessed an extensive knowledge of Jewish sources gained as a student at the Collegio Foa in Vercelli, a boarding school where Jewish youngsters were educated to loyalty and commitment to the House of Savoy.[49] There he trained as a rabbi, but felt no inclination for the office and soon drifted away from religious observance. After a period in Milan, De Benedetti moved to Tuscany, where he experienced the political ferment that animated Leghorn and connected with the liberal intelligencia who supported Giuseppe Mazzini (1805–72). In Leghorn he served as the superintendent of the local Pie Scuole Israelitiche.[50] When the Austrian army invaded Tuscany to crush the revolts of 1848–9, De Benedetti returned to the Piedmont, where he founded and edited a newspaper, *La Vedetta* (*The Watchtower*), that agitated for the liberation of occupied Lombardy.

[47] *Allgemeine Zeitung des Judenthums* 27, no. 17 (April 22, 1862), 217.

[48] Alfred Jospe, 'The Study of Judaism in German Universities Before 1933', *Leo Baeck Institute Year Book*, 27 (1982), 295–319, at 309.

[49] On the Collegio Foa, see Rossella Bottini Treves, 'Nascita di un'istituzione vercellese: il collegio Foa', *Bollettino Storico Vercellese*, 1 (1994), 99–144.

[50] D'Ancona, 'Salvatore De Benedetti', 222.

Jewish networking and political considerations made De Benedetti's academic career possible. It was Isacco Artom (1829–1900)—former secretary of Count Cavour—who began to arrange for his appointment as professor of Hebrew at the University of Pisa.[51] Traditionally, clergymen were responsible for teaching Hebrew, but the secularization of the university system had opened the way for Jewish candidates; in addition, installing a Jew in the position would make a strong anticlerical statement. On October 21, 1861, Artom wrote to Alessandro D'Ancona, who had succeeded De Sanctis as professor of Italian literature in Pisa the year before, to endorse De Benedetti's candidacy.[52] Artom described De Benedetti as both an expert in Jewish sources and an eloquent writer and orator. Furthermore, he argued, teaching Hebrew was the Jews' 'providential mission', and 'the Ministers of Education should be delighted to find in European dress and speaking Italian, professors as authentic as if they had been born in Palestine or Mesopotamia'.[53] In closing his letter, Artom told D'Ancona that he was hopeful of obtaining the favour as long as the appointment depended on De Sanctis, who at that time was the minister of education.

One week later, no doubt acting upon Artom's advice, De Benedetti wrote to De Sanctis to apply for the Hebrew position at Pisa.[54] Although he was not a university-trained scholar, he could cite his early experience teaching literature and history, as well as his seven years as a superintendent of the Jewish secondary schools (Le scuole pie Israelitiche) in Leghorn. He pointed with pride to his work as a private tutor who successfully prepared candidates for state offices. De Benedetti made extensive reference to his own political background, demonstrating that both his civic engagement and journalistic career were in line with the cultural policy of the new state. The application was successful.

In March 1862, De Benedetti began his university career by reading an inaugural address entitled 'On the Study of Hebrew in Relation to Science and Civility'.[55] Unlike Ascoli, De Benedetti made no explicit reference to

---

[51] On Artom, see Aldo A. Mola (ed.), *Isacco Artom e gli ebrei italiani dai risorgimenti al Fascismo* (Foggia, 2002).

[52] Artom to D'Ancona, October 21, 1861, Carteggio Alessandro D'Ancona 2.38, Biblioteca della Scuola Normale Superiore, Pisa. The letter is partially transcribed in Moretti, 'La dimensione ebraica di un maestro pisano: Documenti su Alessandro D'Ancona', in Michele Luzzati (ed.), *Gli ebrei di Pisa (secoli IX–XX)*, (Pisa, 1998), 241–82, at 252.

[53] Artom to D'Ancona, October 21, 1861.

[54] Salvatore De Benedetti to De Sanctis, October 29, 1861. 698.45, Fondi del Ministero della Pubblica Istruzione—Personale, Archivio Centrale dello Stato, Rome.

[55] The inaugural address ('Dello stato della lingua ebraica in relazione alla scienza e alla civiltà') is published in *Annali delle Università Toscane*, 7/1 (1862), 19–33.

his personal identity as a Jew. Instead, he expanded on a common motif in Risorgimento rhetoric, the analogy between the struggle of the Israelites to become a nation and the labours of the Italians to achieve independence.[56] Both peoples were driven by patriotic sentiments that enabled them to rise from disgrace and fight for liberty. De Benedetti's description of Israel as a people with 'powerful religious, moral, and civil ideals' and 'formidable institutions' built upon the same set of ideas that Vincenzo Gioberti had used some twenty years earlier to define the mission of the Italians among the European nations in his seminal *Del Primato Morale e Civile degli Italiani [The moral and civil primacy of the Italians]* (Brussels, 1843). De Benedetti's determination to connect the two national histories led him to imagine an Italy that bore Semitic traces even in its landscape. Pisa was described as a crucible of Semitic and Italian elements: 'Your memories, oh Pisa, your monuments, your trophies, your squares speak to us about the Semitic Orient ... Isn't the sand that covers your illustrious fallen men the sand of Palestine?' De Benedetti's reference to the 'sand of Palestine' that covers the graves of the heroes of Pisa alludes to recent historical events in Italy, but it also suggests the physical, cultural, and historical continuity between ethnic communities whose shores are washed by the same sea.

In his discussion of Israel's literary heritage, De Benedetti promoted a reading of the Bible in line with contemporary concerns, linking the past to the present. The Old Testament, stripped of its theological resonance, was understood as a historical document that recounted the past of a 'very ancient people', replete with examples of heroism. It was precisely the political dimension of the Old Testament on which De Benedetti placed the highest premium.

> The pages of the Bible are soaked with a love of the nation [and] inflamed by patriotism: for this reason the Bible should be the religious work dearest to Italian youth. Whether bewailing the defeat of their kingdom or praising its redemption, the prophets of Israel used powerful language and affectionate eloquence that resonate with anyone among us who is moved by the same feelings of love, hope, resentment, sorrow for his homeland.[57]

Speaking to those who had upheld the principles of the Risorgimento, De Benedetti argued that the Old Testament lessons of civility and heroism that had inspired the great figures of Italy should now be used to stimulate its youth. De Benedetti's understanding of the biblical text resembled the

---

[56] On the Jewish appropriation of Risorgimento rhetoric, see Francesca Sofia, 'La nazione degli ebrei risorgimentali', *Rassegna Mensile di Israel*, 76 (2010), 95–112.

[57] De Benedetti, 'Dello stato della lingua ebraica', 30–1.

reading proposed by the venerated advocate of Italian unification Giuseppe Mazzini, who regarded the Old Testament as a source of civic passion and imitated the rhetoric of the biblical prophets in his political writings.[58] In praising the beauty of the ancient idiom of the Bible, De Benedetti stressed the need for a translation of the Old Testament into Italian that would express the power of the Hebrew language. In his view, such a translation had to become part of the literary canon that Italian authors were constructing. De Benedetti's call could be understood as a response to the ban that the church had long maintained on Italian translations of the Bible that did not adhere to traditional Catholic exegesis.[59]

In keeping with the reclassification of Hebrew as a matter of philological rather than theological inquiry, the theme of De Benedetti's address was the scientific approach to the study of religion. He proposed to study the 'Bible in its literal and philological signification' according to the principles of a 'science' that was 'a modern and free daughter of experience' (*moderna libera figliuola dell'esperienza*).[60] Only a positivistic approach, he maintained, could rectify rooted misinterpretations of religion. De Benedetti's rational understanding of the scriptural text and religious legacy of Israel was nowhere more evident than in his exegesis of the unpronounceable name of God. He turned it into an object of philological scrutiny, arguing that the divine name was nothing but a simple predicate—'he is' or 'he will be'—that signified the immanent character of God.[61]

In closing his address, De Benedetti shifted the discussion from the rarefied field of philology to the practical benefits of the study of Hebrew. He addressed himself directly to his future students:

> The work of the scholar will ... appear more fruitful than war and politics. You, the young generation that has restored Italy to her ancient honour and reclaimed the glory of arms and government, will also reclaim the glory of wisdom and knowledge by pursuing this study [i.e., philology], which is highly valued in modern society. Through conscientious inquiries, we hope to obtain seeds for a fertile future through investigating the ancient tongues, so as to enhance knowledge, to fight horrors, to glorify our beloved motherland, to benefit universal brotherhood![62]

---

[58] See Samuele Colombo, 'Il pensiero religioso di Giuseppe Mazzini', *La Rassegna Mensile di Israel*, 38 (1972), 469–76.

[59] On the history of the ban on vernacular translations of Scripture, see Gigliola Fragnito, *La Bibbia al rogo: La censura ecclesiastica e i volgarizzamenti della scrittura (1471–1605)* (Bologna, 1997).

[60] De Benedetti, 'Dello stato della lingua ebraica', 19.

[61] Ibid., 24.   [62] Ibid., 32.

Noteworthy is De Benedetti's proposition that the 'work of the scholar' would 'appear more fruitful than war and politics'. This assertion undid the close linkage that, as Porciani has reminded us, existed between war and 'science' in the rhetoric of post-unification Italy.[63] It is significant that De Benedetti invited youths to withdraw from activism and pursue a life of scholarship at a university whose students had distinguished themselves by their military participation in the struggle toward political unification.[64] Here he seems to suggest that students should redirect their energies toward a programme of cultural unification that would be nourished by philology.

De Benedetti's application of positivism to traditional religious texts and concepts was doubtless one of the reasons why the university chose him to lead a ceremony honouring the tercentenary of Galileo's birth in 1564.[65] Indeed, this was a landmark in De Benedetti's career. The commemoration of Galileo—who had trained and taught in Pisa—carried national, cultural, and scientific significance: it celebrated the birth of the Italian physicist, as well as the recent birth of the Italian nation state, in the presence of the academic representatives of other European countries. This event was fraught with anticlerical implications, and thus it was highly symbolic that De Benedetti, a Jewish proponent of a rational reading of the Bible, was charged with honouring an Italian scientist who had been forced to abjure a theory with heretical implications. In an address that gave full expression to the culture of positivism, De Benedetti depicted Galileo as a 'hero, a myth—to say it in a modern fashion—of the invincible resistance of free thinking against the violence of the unreasonable authority'.[66] But Galileo—who had been 'condemned in the name of the biblical texts'—understood such texts 'better than his judges, before whom he set forth in vain the correct interpretation'.[67] De Benedetti used the occasion to defend the independence of critical inquiry and promote a philologically oriented understanding of Scripture, thereby reaffirming the secular values that the newly reformed university chose to celebrate.

---

[63] Porciani, 'Introduzione', in *Università e scienza nazionale*, pp. xxvi–xxvii.

[64] On the activism of the students and faculty members at the University of Pisa, see Ersilio Michel, *Maestri e Scolari dell'Università di Pisa negli avvenimenti del 1848* (Pisa, 1948).

[65] De Benedetti, *Il terzo centenario di Galileo: Narrazione istorica del prof. Salvatore De Benedetti* (Pisa, 1864); idem, *Del metodo di Galileo nella filologia* (Turin, 1864).

[66] De Benedetti, *Del metodo di Galileo*, 5.

[67] Ibid., 11.

Defending the Gains of Emancipation

During the first decade or so of Ascoli's and De Benedetti's academic careers, Italian institutions remained immune to anti-Jewish influence, and most Jews regarded any opposition to Jewish participation in institutional life as a minor inconvenience in the process of social integration following emancipation. In their later years, however, both scholars witnessed a rise in anti-Jewish sentiment that they resisted and combated in different ways.

When laying out his scholarly programme in 1861, Ascoli had focused on both the Semitic and Aryan components of ancient and modern cultures. In the years that followed, the discourse on Aryans and Semites quickly acquired racist overtones. Perhaps in an attempt to counter this shift, Ascoli continued his research on the philological and linguistic underpinnings of the anthropological claims being made about the superiority of the Aryan race. He published a series of three studies arguing that the Semitic and Indo-European lexicons contained words derived from a set of roots common to both language families.[68] Ascoli may have reasoned that by proving the primeval unity of these linguistic groups, he would undermine anthropological claims about racial hierarchies.[69] Nevertheless, in Italy, Aryanism would soon become a source for national self-understanding while the term 'Semite' was applied to those deemed to be 'outsiders'.[70]

After a few years Ascoli's research focus shifted from Semitics to the study of Italian dialects, a choice that strengthened the link between his own research and the cultural life of the nation. Some twenty years after his last comparative study of the Semitic and Indo-European lexicons, however, he returned to investigating the relationships between Semites and Aryans, this time specifically on Italian territory. In work that challenged the idea that 'Semites' were outsiders, Ascoli sought historical traces of interactions between Aryans and Semites in the land of Italy, in the hope of establishing that Semitic—notably Jewish—cultures were

---

[68] 'Del nesso ario-semitico: Lettera al professore Adalberto Kuhn di Berlino', *Il Politecnico*, 21 (1864), 190–216; 'Del nesso ario-semitico: Lettera seconda al professore Francesco Bopp', *Il Politecnico*, 22 (1864), 121–51; 'Studi ario-semitici', *Memorie del Reale Istituto Lombardo*, 10 (1867), 1–36.

[69] Sebastiano Timpanaro, 'Ritratti critici di contemporanei: Graziadio Isaia Ascoli', *Belfagor*, 27 (1972), 149–76, at 153.

[70] Mauro Raspanti, 'Il mito ariano nella cultura italiana fra Otto e Novecento', in Alberto Burgio (ed.), *Nel nome della Razza: Il razzismo nella storia d'Italia, 1870–1945* (Bologna, 1999), 75–85.

deeply rooted in Italian soil. Through a painstaking philological study of Latin, Greek, and Hebrew sepulchral inscriptions, he documented the flourishing of Jewish settlements from the fourth to the eleventh century in southern Italy, shedding light on a period of the Middle Ages previously known, for the most part, only from Christian sources.[71]

While much of Ascoli's scholarship implicitly challenged anti-Jewish and anti-Semitic sentiments, in 1891 he confronted an acute attack on the Jews mounted by the *Osservatore Cattolico*, a newspaper published in Milan. The paper issued a challenge to any scholar who believed he could refute the 'blood libel', namely the allegation of ritual murder of Christians by Jews that was gaining widespread ascendancy in the second half of the nineteenth century: submissions to the journal would be evaluated by a jury of experts. The proposal attracted the attention of the Protestant Orientalist Hermann Leberecht Strack (1848–1922) in Berlin, who wrote to Ascoli for further information.[72] Strack took up the challenge but he refused to submit his work to the experts appointed by the editor of the *Osservatore Cattolico*, David Albertario (1846–1902), who had selected three judges known for their anti-Jewish positions, including August Rohling (1839–1931), the author of *Der Talmudjude* (Münster, 1871).[73] Likewise, Ascoli was determined to rebut the arguments being propagated in his own city, but unwilling to participate in the *Osservatore Cattolico*'s rigged contest. He published his reply in a journal of progressive views, *Il Secolo*.[74] 'As a Jew, I am unable to refrain from taking part in any discussion of this despicable slander', wrote Ascoli, before embarking on a meticulous philological analysis of the errors in the newspaper's interpretation of an edict issued in 1247 by Innocent IV, in which the pope rejected the blood libel. Ascoli accused the *Osservatore Cattolico* of intentionally misrepresenting the document in order to encourage popular belief in the practice of ritual murder.

---

[71] Ascoli, 'Iscrizioni inedite o mal note greche, latine, ebraiche di antichi sepolcri giudaici del Napolitano', in *Atti del quarto congresso internazionale degli orientalisti tenuto in Firenze nel settembre 1878* (2 vols, Florence, 1880), i. 239–354.

[72] H.L. Strack to Ascoli, July 26, 1892, Archivio G. I. Ascoli 85.17, BNLC. On the *Osservatore Cattolico*'s campaign, see Annalisa Di Fant, 'Don Davide Albertario propagandista antiebraico: L'accusa di omicidio rituale', *Storicamente* 7 (2011): article 21: <http://www.storicamente.org/07_dossier/antisemitismo/difant_davide_albertario.htm> [accessed on 25 June 2014].

[73] Strack's refutation was published separately under the title *Der Blutaberglaube in der Menschheit, Blutmorde und Blutritus* (Munich, 1891), an extensive investigation of the blood libel intended to counter the rise in child murder accusations against the Jews.

[74] 'La Pasqua degli Ebrei: A proposito della calunnia del rito nel sangue degli Ebrei', *Il Secolo*, August 14, 1892.

De Benedetti also reacted to Catholic hostility toward Jews, although in a less public fashion than Ascoli did. He felt exposed to the antagonism of Italy's influential moderate Catholic intellectuals. In September 1867, commenting on rumours of a plan to move the Scuola Normale (where he also taught) from Pisa to Florence, De Benedetti wrote to D'Ancona:

> Good Catholics, such as Father Giuliani, Lambruschini, Tommaseo, and Conti, who piously deplore that the Scuola Normale is marred by Jews and rationalists, have something to do with this plan. If the Normale is moved from Pisa to Florence, I am confident that somebody in that gang will take it over, with the hope of kicking the heretics out of the university.[75]

The 'good Catholics' to whom De Benedetti referred were those who exerted an influence on the public sphere under the banner of political moderation. More broadly, De Benedetti's concern that 'good Catholics' would work to marginalize rationalists, 'heretics', and Jews pointed to the tension between anticlerical forces and the church that intensified in the post-unification period.[76] In 1864, Pius IX had issued his *Syllabus of Errors*, in which he attacked the main tenets of liberalism. The syllabus prompted an enduring debate over the influence that rationalists exerted on public education. In a series of articles that appeared in the journal *La scuola cattolica* between 1880 and 1883, Pietro Rota (1805–90), archbishop of Cartagine and a staunch defender of Pius' syllabus, expressed concern about the growing influence of rationalist teachings on public education.[77] Rota attacked 'the atheist governments' that 'encouraged libertinage' with the intent of 'corrupting the masses' with their 'artful schemes' (*arti*).[78] It is clear that Rota voiced the anxiety of a church that felt increasingly deprived of power in the public sphere. Government policy makers, faithful to the anticlericalism of the Risorgimento, had no qualms about blocking the entry of ecclesiastics into the university system and secularizing its curriculum. Thus, Rota went on to argue that the sole interest of the state was to '[appoint] heretics, unbelievers, and religious apostates to chairs so as to exert its tyrannical despotism against the Catholic Church, its teachings, and its schools'. In another article Rota waxed ironic on the consequences for Catholics of admitting Jews,

---

[75] Moretti, 'La dimensione ebraica di un maestro pisano', 241.

[76] See Manuel Borutta, 'Anti-Catholicism and the Culture War in Risorgimento Italy', in Silvana Patriarca & Lucy Riall (eds), *Risorgimento Revisited: Nationalism and Culture in Nineteenth-Century Italy* (New York, 2012), 191–213; Giovanni Miccoli, 'Santa Sede, questione ebraica e antisemitismo fra Otto e Novecento', in Corrado Vivanti (ed.), *Storia d'Italia. Annali 11. Gli ebrei in Italia*, (2 vols, Turin, 1996–7), ii. 1369–574.

[77] Rota's publications are collected in his *Il Sillabo di Pio IX commentato da Monsig. Pietro Rota* (Milan, 1884).

[78] Ibid., 261.

atheists, and freemasons to teaching posts of state universities. Fearing the interference of the state in the affairs of Vatican controlled theological institutions too, he wondered, 'What would happen if a Jew, who does not believe in Jesus, an atheist, who does not admit God, and a freemason, who is an enemy of God, had to examine catholic students of theological disciplines?'[79]

Not all Catholics shared Rota's animosity toward Jews, however. In an 1880 article, De Benedetti wrote that in Italy 'some isolated voices spoke out against the public offices bestowed upon the Jews, repeating the usual sophistic arguments. Not only were these voices not heeded, but eminent voices within Catholicism imposed silence on them'.[80] Most likely, De Benedetti was referring to an incident that occurred in 1873: a liberal deputy, Francesco Pasqualigo (1821–92), opposed the appointment of a Jewish candidate, Isacco Pesaro Maurogonato (1817–92) to the Ministry of Finance, but Pasqualigo was soon condemned in the press by the Catholic deputy, Francesco Musio (1796–1876).[81] In the meantime, friction between reactionaries and the state, viewed as the sponsor of secularized institutions and education, became more frequent and took on a sharper edge. In 1879, Raffaele Mariano (1840–1912), a professor of the history of Christianity at Naples, published a study of the relation between church and state that included a long chapter on the *Kulturkampf* containing sharply worded judgements of German Jews.[82] Mariano also made reference to Italian Jews who engaged in politics and journalism, attributing to them a disproportionate and anti-religious role in the shaping of relations between state and church.[83] Mariano described the Jews as the cause of the weakening and corruption of state institutions insofar as they undermined their fundamentally Catholic values. Distressed by these pronouncements, De Benedetti wrote in 1880 or 1881 to a colleague in Germany, Heinrich Graetz (1817–91), to inquire about the reception of Mariano's anti-Jewish positions there. Graetz—the head of the

---

[79] Ibid., 188.

[80] '. . . si levò qualche voce solitaria a ripetere contro gli Israeliti, cioè contro gli uffici pubblici conferiti contro gli Israeliti, i soliti argomenti sofistici. Ma non soltanto non ebbe eco, ma ritrovò in seno al cattolicesimo autorevoli voci che le imposero silenzio'. S. De Benedetti, 'Una voce autorevole sopra questione d'attualità,' *Il Vessillo Israelitico*, 28 (1880), 208–10. The piece announced the publication of Adolf Jellinek's *Franzosen über Juden* (Vienna, 1880), a collection of short essays that French intellectuals had written in defence of the Jews and Judaism. This pamphlet was intended as a response to Germany's growing anti-Semitism.

[81] See Andrew M. Canepa, 'Emancipazione, integrazione e antisemitismo liberale in Italia: Il caso Pasqualigo', *Comunità*, 174 (1975), 166–203.

[82] *Cristianesimo, Cattolicismo, e Civiltà* (Bologna, 1879).

[83] Mariano, *Cristianesimo*, 455–6.

rabbinical seminary in Breslau and a practitioner of the *Wissenschaft des Judentums*—was the target of a harsh anti-Semitic campaign launched by the leading professor of Christianity in Berlin, Heinrich von Treitschke, in 1879–80.[84] Graetz reassured De Benedetti that 'the anti-Semite [i.e., Mariano] already [had] lost his identity' and that his 'attacks had already gone under in the flood'.[85]

In the 1880s, a growing number of anti-Jewish publications were propagating negative images of the Jews to show that they were incapable of complete integration.[86] One of De Benedetti's late scholarly projects may have been designed to counter that trend. Over the course of his career, De Benedetti devoted much effort to translating medieval Hebrew literature into Italian, working to create the literary symbiosis between Jewish and Italian cultures that he had first proposed in his inaugural address.[87] In the last years of his life, he undertook a translation of the Talmudic tractate *Derekh Eretz Rabbah*, a Jewish code of behaviour for various branches of life, probably written in the second century CE[88] De Benedetti hoped to legitimize the role of the Jews in Italian society by demonstrating that the notion of civility had long been entrenched in the history of Judaism. He chose for his translation a title that would have resonated with an Italian readership: *Il Galateo Giudaico* (Jewish rules of polite behaviour). The title was an explicit allusion to *Il Galateo [Rules of polite behaviour]* (1558), a work in which Giovanni Della Casa envisioned a community of gentlemen citizens who espoused the highest standards of social behaviour and decorum. Unfortunately, De Benedetti never published what he probably considered the final testament to his mission as an educator and Jewish-Italian citizen.[89]

---

[84] George Y. Kohler, 'German Spirit and Holy Ghost—Treitschke's Call for Conversion of German Jewry: The Debate Revisited', *Modern Judaism*, 30 (2010), 172–95.

[85] H. Graetz to S. De Benedetti, March 16, 1881, Fondo Salvatore De Benedetti, unnumbered manuscript, Biblioteca Universitaria di Pisa.

[86] Andrew M. Canepa, 'The Image of the Jew in the Folklore and Literature of the Postrisorgimento', *Journal of European Studies*, 9 (1979), 260–73; Elizabeth Schächter, 'Perspectives of Nineteenth-Century Italian Jewry', *Journal of European Studies*, 31 (2001), 29–69, esp. 45–59.

[87] De Benedetti completed translations of post-biblical works that were published in several journals. Translations that appeared as independent works are *Vita e morte di Mosè* (Pisa, 1879), a collection of Muslim, Christian, and Jewish texts concerning the life of Moses; and *Canzoniere Sacro di Giuda Levita* (Pisa, 1871), a collection of Yehuda ha-Levi's poems intended to acquaint an Italian readership with the Hebrew poetry of the Middle Ages.

[88] On the date of composition of *Derekh Eretz Rabbah*, see *The Ways of the Sages and the Way of the World: the Minor Tractates of the Babylonian Talmud: Derekh 'Eretz Rabbah, Derekh 'Eretz Zuta, Pereq ha-Shalom*, ed. Marcus van Loopik (Tübingen, 1991), 10–18.

[89] The 240-page manuscript is held by the Biblioteca Universitaria di Pisa, Fondo Salvatore De Benedetti (Galateo Giudaico, ms. 857). The manuscript is a partial translation of *Derekh Eretz Rabbah*.

Conclusion

After successfully negotiating their entry into academia, Ascoli and De Benedetti carried on their work for several decades: De Benedetti taught in Pisa until his death in 1891, and Ascoli retired in 1902. During their careers they played central roles in the expansion of Oriental disciplines in Italy. They were both involved in the development of the Società Italiana per gli Studi Orientali, founded in 1872, which helped to organize the fourth International Conference of Orientalists (Quarto Congresso Internazionale degli Orientalisti) in Florence in 1878.[90] The event was intended to place Italy at the centre of European discourse on Orientalism. On that occasion, Ascoli presented preliminary work on his research on the Jewish sepulchral inscriptions in southern Italy, whereas De Benedetti discussed how to produce a faithful translation of the Talmud that might satisfy modern literary tastes.[91] Some time later, on November 10, 1878, Ascoli sent De Benedetti a personal note containing words that echoed the ideas of his lecture of 1861 in Milan. In referring to the event which was held in Florence, he described their scholarly efforts as 'creating links between the West and the East'.[92] Although Ascoli did not explain this remark further, it indicates that he, at least, saw himself and De Benedetti engaged in similar projects, using Western methods of inquiry to investigate and explain Eastern modes of thought.

The careers of Ascoli and De Benedetti illustrate how academia provided Jews with an opportunity to break with established patterns of Jewish life: Ascoli did not take a hand in the family business, and De Benedetti rejected the rabbinate. In a cultural and political climate imbued with anti-Catholicism and anticlericalism, both scholars were able to sustain secularized identities while retaining traits of Jewish particularism. Unlike other Jewish academics who confined the expression of their ethnic identity for the most part to the private sphere, Ascoli and De Benedetti participated in the secular state while openly maintaining a connection,

---

[90] On the Fourth Conference of Orientalists, see Filipa Lowndes Vicente, *Altri orientalismi: l'India a Firenze 1860–1900* (Florence, 2012), 53–75. On the development of the Società Italiana per gli Studi Orientali, Rita Peca Conti, 'Dal carteggio Ascoli–Lasinio (1862–1890)', *Quaderni giuliani di storia*, 7 (1986), 273–96.

[91] Ascoli, 'Iscrizioni inedite o mal note greche, latine, ebraiche di antichi sepolcri giudaici del Napolitano', in *Atti del quarto congresso internazionale degli orientalisti tenuto in Firenze nel settembre 1878* (Florence, 1880), i. 239–354; De Benedetti, 'Dei presenti studi sul Talmud e specialmente sull'Aggadà', ibid., 175–87.

[92] Ascoli to De Benedetti, November 10, 1878, Fondo Salvatore De Benedetti (ms. 189.49), Biblioteca Universitaria di Pisa.

through their academic positions, to their cultural heritage. Indeed, the academic study of traditionally Jewish subjects allowed them to reconcile their dual cultural legacies. Nonetheless, their public statements as well as their correspondence reveal the efforts they made to assume a persona that integrated their Jewishness and their role as scholars. In public, Ascoli flaunted his 'infidel' status as a badge that admitted him into the intellectual hegemony. Similarly, De Benedetti cast himself as a 'heretical' figure; his Jewish identity, rather than being a political liability, allowed him to distance himself from Catholic values and thus qualify for roles in public life. Their efforts to navigate between secularism and their Jewish background are worthy of attention not only for what they tell us about the individual stories of these two scholars, but for the insights they provide into the tensions between citizenship and ethnic distinctiveness faced by those making the transition from the Jewish sphere to the state.

Program of Judaic Studies & Italian Department
Franklin & Marshall College
Lancaster, PA 17604-3003
United States

Disciplinary Histories of Classics

Christopher Stray

The phrase 'disciplinary histories' could be taken to refer to three different things. First, published histories of classical scholarship like those of J.E. Sandys (1903–8), U. von Wilamowitz–Moellendorff (1921), C.O. Brink (1986), and R. Pfeiffer (1968–76), which are discussed below.[1] Second, the stories we might tell of the emergence of Classics as a modern field of study, from the early nineteenth century onwards. Third, histories of Classics as a means to the confirmation of scholarly identity: that is, histories which themselves possess a disciplining function. In this paper I shall discuss all three, before focusing on the role of journals in disciplinary identity.

The notion of disciplinary identity was highlighted between the two world wars by the emergence of the term 'interdisciplinary'. The *Oxford English Dictionary*'s first citation is from 1937, from the *Journal of Educational Sociology*. It is perhaps significant that the citation comes from the field of education, and from an American journal. Education was a long-established but academically not very prestigious field, an accessible setting for efforts at definitional (self-) promotion. The term 'disciplinarity' emerged later in the twentieth century; the earliest occurrence I know of is from 1972, where it was defined in a discussion of interdisciplinarity.[2] Its emergence in academic discourse was probably a product of the US culture wars of the 1980s and 1990s, when the traditional disciplines were challenged by an aggressive and ambitious newcomer, Cultural Studies,

---

[1] J.E. Sandys, *A History of Classical Scholarship* (3 vols, Cambridge, 1903–8); U. von Wilamowitz–Moellendorff, *Geschichte der Philologie* (Berlin, 1921), translated as *History of Classical Scholarship*, trans. A. Harris, ed. H. Lloyd-Jones (London, 1982); R. Pfeiffer, *History of Classical Scholarship from the Beginnings to the End of the Hellenistic Age* (Oxford, 1968); id., *History of Classical Scholarship 1300–1850* (Oxford, 1976). C.O. Brink, *English Classical Scholarship: Historical Reflections on Bentley, Porson and Housman* (Cambridge, 1986).

[2] OECD, *Interdisciplinarity: Problems of Teaching and Research in Universities* (Paris, 1972), 75–139. Cf. the analysis in J.T. Klein, *Interdisciplinarity: History, Theory and Practice* (Detroit, 1990). 'Disciplinarity' is not recorded in *OED*, but a file has just been opened in anticipation of a future listing.

whose practitioners' writings often defined disciplines as an old order to be overcome. C. Telson and D. Gaonkar's *Disciplinarity and Dissent in Cultural Studies* (1996) belongs to this movement. The power struggle involved in getting Cultural Studies onto the academic map generated arguments and strategies which resembled those employed by supporters of other insurgent areas; for example, the study of English literature in late nineteenth- and early twentieth-century Britain; Modern Greek Studies, from the 1970s, on both sides of the Atlantic; and Classical Reception Studies more recently.

Where does Classics figure in this literature? A look at the subject coverage of the literature on disciplinarity shows, perhaps not surprisingly, that it hardly figures in post-Foucauldian studies of disciplinary history. It is not mentioned, for example, in Messer-Davidow et al., *Knowledges: Historical and Critical Studies of Disciplinarity* (1993), nor in Anderson & Valente's *Disciplinarity at the Fin de Siècle* (2002). Nor is it dealt with in Bender and Schorske's *American Academic Culture in Transformation: Fifty Years, Four Disciplines* (1997), even though the editors restricted themselves to the humanities.

In the USA, the influence of Foucault led to the foundation in 1983 of the Group for Research into the Institutionalisation and Professionalisation of Literary Study (mercifully acronymized as GRIP). This was a project developed by the Society for Critical Exchange, founded in 1975 to promote the theoretical discussion of literature; its discussions continue online at its bulletin board, the Electronic College of Theory. Among the SCE's projects was an encyclopaedic dictionary of modern critical terminology; this never got off the ground because its funding from the National Endowment for the Humanities, after being approved, was cancelled by the NEH's then chair, Lynne Cheney. Cheney, a right-wing ideologue, and wife of Dick Cheney, had succeeded William Bennett, who had notoriously declared that 'Humanities are in the past'. Like many similar projects, GRIP arose from the fortuitous coming together of individuals in specific places: in this case, Jim Sosnoski, Jim Fanto, Steve Nimis, and David Shumway at Miami University, Ohio, to which SCE had moved its institutional base in 1982.[3] Of the founding members of GRIP, Steve Nimis was the only classicist; he contributed several papers to GRIP meetings, but the only one he published was a paper entitled 'Fussnoten: der Fundament des Wissenschaft', which appeared in 1984 in an issue of the progressive classical journal *Arethusa* devoted to critical and theoretical

[3] See S. Nimis, 'The Society for Critical Exchange at Miami University', *Works and Days* 25/1–2 (2007), 135–6.

studies.[4] Readers of the journal had been prepared for the critical orientation of Nimis's article by the journal's editor John Peradotto's frontal assault of 1983 on the conservatism of classical scholars.[5]

Nimis's paper investigates the history, nature, and rhetoric of what he calls, from its exemplary manifestation, the Wilamowitz footnote, after the famous German classical scholar Ulrich von Wilamowitz-Moellendorff (1848–1931), the 'Prince of Hellenists'. In his words, 'The Wilamowitz footnote is an institutional function... an inevitable concomitant of a discipline which continues to reproduce, without self-reflection and without any clearly-defined goals, its own discourse' (117). Nimis is referring to the kind of footnote, often a very long one, which situates and authorizes a stance taken in a main text by retailing the history of previous discussion: 'Wilamowitz in 1913... but Busolt already in 1879... and even before him, Boeckh in 1823'. As a young man, in 1872, Wilamowitz launched an attack on his ex-schoolfellow Nietzsche's *Birth of Tragedy*, in a pamphlet entitled *Zukunftsphilologie!* (*The philology of the future*). Nietzsche's friend Erwin Rohde replied with a pamphlet entitled *After-philologie* (*Philology my backside*).[6]

The history of the footnote has attracted a considerable amount of attention since Nimis wrote. In his *The Footnote: A Curious History*, Anthony Grafton traces the fashion for using footnotes to Pierre Bayle's *Critical Dictionary* of 1697.[7] The Oxford English Dictionary's first citation of the word dates only from 1841, when William Savage, in his *Dictionary of Printing*, declared that 'Bottom Notes are also termed Foot Notes'; and Charles Darwin used it in a letter of 14 April that year: 'I have sent two or three foot notes on separate pages' (C. Darwin, *Correspondence* (1986), ii. 289). But the term had in fact appeared in 1711 in a posthumous edition of the works of the poet William Drummond, edited by John Sage and Thomas Ruddiman: 'And in the very Bosom of the Declaration 'tis solemnly declar'd, that *John's* right is not asserted as if it had been dubious, but *ex abundanti, &c*, As you may see in the Foot-Note *(i)*'. This is

---

[4] 'Fussnoten: der Fundament des Wissenschaft', *Arethusa* 17 (1984), 105–34. Despite the German title, the article is in English.

[5] J. Peradotto, 'Texts and unrefracted facts: philology, hermeneutics, and semiotics', *Arethusa* 16 (1983), 15–33. Repr. in P. Culham & L. Edmunds (eds), *Classics: A Profession in Crisis?* (Lanham MD, 1989).

[6] This might seem to bring us back to Nimis's paper, but its author has denied that the word 'fundament' in his own title is a reference to Rohde's pamphlet.

[7] A.T. Grafton, *The Footnote: A Curious History* (London, 1997), 191–200. Cf. R.J. Connors, 'The Rhetoric of Citation Systems, Part I: The Development of Annotation Structures from the Renaissance to 1900', *Rhetoric Review* 17/1 (1998), 6–48; 'Part II: Competing Epistemic Values in Citation', 17/2 (1999), 219–45.

keyed to a long Latin footnote.[8] The dating locates it just where one might expect, not long after the publication of Bayle's *Dictionary*.

Histories of Scholarship

What is a disciplinary history? Most obviously, it is the history of a discipline. I think we expect, and certainly hope, such a history to bear the marks of disciplinary identification. Yet for a long time looking into the history of one's subject was seen as an amateur activity: what one did on Sundays, or in retirement. If you were a Livy scholar, you might publish on the nineteenth-century German scholar Wilhelm Weissenborn, or on Niccoló Machiavelli, both of whom wrote on the Roman historian. If you lived in Warrington, you might write about the eccentric scholar and radical Gilbert Wakefield, who taught there in the 1780s. But the subjects of this kind of work were not disciplines, but books, or individuals, or episodes.

The histories of classical scholarship by Sandys (1903–8), Wilamowitz (1921), Pfeiffer (1968–76), and Brink (1986) offer a variety of approaches and styles. Sandys's and Pfeiffer's books were written in English; Wilamowitz's book was published in an English translation in 1982. Between them they indicate in different ways the relationship between English scholarship and the once-dominant German tradition of *Altertumswissenschaft*. Sandys's history draws heavily on (some would say plagiarizes) German reference works like Konrad Bursian's *Geschichte der klassischen Philologie in Deutschland* (1883). Its overall structure is national and chronological, its detailed organisation biographical. A reviewer, Charles Gulick of Harvard, complained that

> ... though the biographical method has the advantage of including in their proper place many interesting and instructive personal details, these are sometimes so disconnected that one is apt to miss the perspective. We should have liked to have a clearer account of the tendencies of thought that marked each important epoch ... Moreover, a separate survey of the progress of learning in the several departments of classical philology and archaeology would have been welcome. Here and there we get incidentally sections on the rise of the English colleges, on the pronunciation of Greek, on the founding of the national academies, and the like. By means of the

---

[8] J. Sage & T. Ruddiman (eds), *The Works of William Drummond, of Hawthornden* (Edinburgh, 1711), p. xxxiv. I learn from Edmund Weiner that this citation is now in the *OED* files.

index a student may piece together an account of the study of Homer or of Lucretius; but it will be piecework.

C.B. Gulick, *Classical Philology* 5/1 (1910), 105–6.

Another reviewer was the American-born German Jew Alfred Gudeman, whose own brief history of classical philology (1892) had been enlarged in later editions, and was enlarged again in a German edition published by Teubner in 1907.[9] Gudeman thought Sandys's account of American scholarship undeservedly flattering, but then his American career had been cut short by anti-Semitism, and he had left for Germany in 1904.[10] Sandys and Gudeman however had in common an interest in the use of visual evidence. Sandys's editions of Euripides' *Bacchae* and Cicero's *Orator* had both included engravings from ancient gems, and in correspondence with his publisher, Cambridge University Press, he specified that the *History of Classical Scholarship* should include portraits of scholars. Gudeman built up a large collection of portraits of classical scholars ('Imagines Philologorum'), which was sent to Columbia University in the 1930s.[11]

Wilamowitz's *Geschichte der Philologie* provided a short running survey (the English translation's main text runs to 189 pages), an eagle's eye view from a personal viewpoint, with some curious omissions. Wilamowitz's only reference to American scholarship is the statement that 'America too is beginning to set up museums and to furnish its quota of energetic workers in many fields' (156). He made no mention of the work of W.W. Goodwin or B.L. Gildersleeve, German-trained American scholars whose work was internationally recognized; but the book was published not long after the end of the First World War, which the USA had joined on the side of the Allies in 1917, and Wilamowitz was an aggressive German nationalist.[12] In addition, we can assume that Wilamowitz will not have forgotten the aggressive American Platonist Paul Shorey's dismissive remarks about German scholarship in 1911, nor their bruising encounters while Shorey was teaching at Berlin just before the war in

---

[9] Gudeman's review of Sandys's first volume appeared in *Classical Review* 18 (1904), 271–6, 316–21; his review of vols 2–3 in *Classical Review* 23 (1909), 112–16.

[10] Gudeman fared no better there, failed to retrieve his US citizenship, and died in Theresienstadt in 1942. See Donna W. Hurley, 'Alfred Gudeman, Atlanta, Georgia, 1862 - Theresienstadt, 1942', *Transactions of the American Philological Association* 120 (1990), 355–81.

[11] A current project to assemble an international online database of biographies of classical scholars, led by Roger Bagnall (New York), is planned to include these images.

[12] On his role in the publication of the notorious 'professors' manifesto' of October 1914, see R.E. Norton, 'Wilamowitz at war', *International Journal of the Classical Tradition* 15 (2008), 74–97.

1912–13.[13] One might suspect that Wilamowitz shared a widespread European view of the US as a young upstart, not worthy of serious attention; but he also left out of his account the British scholars J.E.B. Mayor and R.C. Jebb, famous for their editions of Juvenal and Sophocles respectively. Sandys, by contrast, devoted his final chapter to the United States (Sandys, *History*, iii. 451–76). As with Sandys, Wilamowitz's text moves from one biography to another. The English version of 1982, translated by Alan Harris, was annotated by the Oxford classical scholar Hugh Lloyd-Jones. Lloyd-Jones's annotations were extensive, but some rather strange statements were left to speak for themselves. The paragraph on the nineteenth-century German scholar Gottfried Hermann, for example, begins, 'Gottfried Hermann remained all his life a typical Leipziger, with the unmistakable rationality of the Saxon' (109). A British or American reader in 1982 deserved to have this unpacked; perhaps some German readers would also have been glad of elucidation, even if they were Leipzigers themselves.

Rudolf Pfeiffer's two volumes appeared in 1968 and 1976; both were products of his retirement. The first volume stopped at the end of the Hellenistic age; the second, a collection of sketches, covered the period 1300–1850. Pfeiffer was temperamentally akin to Sandys, and a more eirenic character than Wilamowitz. A Catholic himself, he was married to a Jew, and because of this emigrated to England in 1937.[14] His text is more expansive and detailed than Wilamowitz's, and broader perspectives are employed but, as with Sandys, the text is basically a series of discussions of individual scholars, grouped by national tradition.

Charles Brink's *English Classical Scholarship* (1986) was also written by a German refugee, one who unlike Pfeiffer did not return to Germany after the war. Brink in fact went native: he changed his name (he had been born Karl Levy in Berlin), joined the Church of England, and married an Englishwoman. In 1950, when Brink applied for a post at King's College London, the Oxford Greek scholar E.R. Dodds wrote as follows in a letter of recommendation:

---

[13] Paul Shorey 'American scholarship' *The Nation* 92 (1911), 466–9. When Shorey arrived in Berlin as Roosevelt Professor in 1912, Wilamowitz blocked his first two choices of topic for a seminar.

[14] On Pfeiffer, see A.T. Grafton, 'The origins of scholarship', *The American Scholar* 48 (1979), 236, 238, 240, 242, 244, 246, 256–8, 260–1; C. Kaesser, 'Rudolf Pfeiffer. A Catholic classicist in the age of Protestant Altertumswissenschaft', https://www.princeton.edu/~pswpc/pdfs/kaesser/090906.pdf (Sep. 2009). J. Elsner, 'Pfeiffer, Fraenkel and Refugee Scholarship in Oxford during and after the Second World War', in S. Crawford, J. Elsner & K. Ulmschneider (eds), *Ark of Civilization: Oxford and Refugee Academics in the Arts during World War II* (Oxford, forthcoming 2015).

Too many Germans have proved incapable of adapting themselves to English ways, and in particular have failed to understand the purposes and methods of English education. But I should like to say with emphasis that these objections do not apply to Brink. He came to this country while his mind was still flexible, and being free from the usual German arrogance he deliberately set about knowing how to be an Englishman, with no arrière pensée. His attitude shows itself in the disappearance from his speech of almost all traces of German accent, and in the more important fact that he has married an English wife.[15]

Brink's book follows this Anglicization process, as its title suggests, in focusing on English scholarship; it largely consists of studies of three English scholars, Richard Bentley, Richard Porson, and A.E. Housman, whom he saw as the main exemplars of 'critical scholarship', something he never formally defines, though refers to it as equivalent to 'true scholarship'(1). Brink does however devote a chapter to Victorian classical education, in an attempt to explain why this kind of scholarship he respected was hardly in evidence between about 1825 and 1865. This is a gallant attempt at stepping outside his comfort zone, but not in the end a very successful chapter. It is sprinkled with factual errors, and Brink's views of social structure and social change were very primitive: for example, 'The public wanted reasonably educated and civilized men and it got what it wanted . . . it stands to reason that the public did not get what it did not want' (119).[16] Brink lived through the time in the 1960s when classical recruitment in British schools almost collapsed,[17] and when Cambridge University, where he had held the chair of Latin since 1954, sponsored a new Latin course that rejected traditional grammatical terminology—a project that he himself supported. That is the kind of lived present which might well encourage a scholar to look back to the past for comfort or example, and to act on Housman's injunction that we should look to the past of scholarship rather than its present.

The weaknesses of the biographical approach are fairly clear: classical culture may always be transmitted, in some sense, through individuals, but its transmission is modulated and shaped by national traditions and by institutions: schools, universities, academies, and more informal groupings or 'schools'. Nevertheless biography is an important tool in looking at

---

[15] E.R. Dodds to unnamed recipient, 14 May 1950; Dodds papers, Bodleian Library, Oxford, box 4, ff. 94–5.

[16] The chapter prompted me to write a mini-review: C.A. Stray, 'England, culture and the nineteenth century', *Liverpool Classical Monthly* 13/6 (1988), 85–90.

[17] M. Forrest, *Modernising the Classics: A Study in Curriculum Development* (Exeter, 1996); C.A. Stray, *Classics Transformed: Schools, Universities, and Society in England, 1830–1960* (Oxford, 1998).

the history of disciplines, for at least two reasons. First, it throws light on the micro-structure of transmission, the way transmission takes place at the level of detail and of everyday life. It thus enables us to look for the initiation of change by individuals working within traditions. Second, it offers a different perspective on the structures and changes of social relationship and patterns of knowledge within disciplines and their institutional contexts.

Some biographies of scholars have played down their social and emotional life, in favour of their scholarship. In some cases, this is hardly avoidable: in his biography of Sir James Frazer, Robert Ackerman remarks that his subject's inner life was 'somewhat thin and remote' and that he 'was not given to introspection' (*J.G. Frazer: His Life and Work*, Cambridge, 1987, 4). In some cases, however, biographers have been obliged to seek help to evaluate academic work which lay beyond their power to evaluate. The biography of the Hellenist Sir Richard Jebb (1841–1905) by his widow includes an essay by his pupil Arthur Verrall, commissioned after Lady Jebb failed to find a scholar willing to write the book.[18] The book follows a conventional Victorian memoir tradition in avoiding mention of Jebb's drinking, and his friends' belief that he was violent toward his wife, but breaks new ground in relegating discussion of his scholarship to Verrall's essay.[19] The English literary critic Norman Page's biography of Housman imports long quotations from Housman's protégé A.S.F. Gow to deal with his scholarship, in a sense following Caroline Jebb's strategy.[20] Leslie Mitchell's biography of Maurice Bowra, a Greek scholar who became a well-connected figure in literary and social circles, largely ignores his scholarly work.[21] A resolution of the problem can be seen in the genre of autobiography, where the account of scholarship is provided by a writer who is both author and subject. Examples include the autobiographies of two Oxford Hellenists of the twentieth century. A straightforward though unfinished narrative was provided by Gilbert Murray; a fuller but controversial account by Kenneth Dover, who was unafraid to admit to masturbation, extra-marital temptations, and

---

[18] Her preferred candidate was the litterateur Arthur Benson, who had in 1899 brought out a substantial biography of his father Edward Benson, Archbishop of Canterbury.

[19] C. Jebb (ed.), *Life and Letters of Sir Richard Claverhouse Jebb* (Cambridge, 1907). Verrall's essay is at 427–67. For the suppressed topics, see C.A. Stray, *Sophocles' Jebb: A Life in Letters* (Cambridge, 2013), 84.

[20] N. Page, *A.E. Housman: A Critical Biography* (London, 1983).

[21] L. Mitchell, *Maurice Bowra* (Oxford, 2009). The Wadham College group which commissioned the book was prepared to provide advice on Bowra's scholarship, but was not consulted on this aspect of his life.

planning to secure the death of a difficult colleague.[22] The opposite tendency can be seen in Crosbie Smith and Norton Wise's 800-page biography of the physicist William Thomson, Lord Kelvin (*Energy and Empire: A Biographical Study of Lord Kelvin*, Cambridge, 1989), which is almost entirely devoted to Kelvin's scientific work. The authors break off for less than a page to deal with his complicated series of betrothals, rejections, and a rebound marriage, and then plunge back into physics.

Methodological reflections on the forms and functions of biography are more common in the historiography of science than in the humanities: an example is M. Shortland and R. Yeo's edited collection *Telling Lives in Science: Essays on Scientific Biography* (Cambridge, 1996). As this suggests, intellectual production and institutional organisation in this field is significantly in advance of the historiography of the humanities. I mention this to point out that historians of humanistic scholarship will benefit from reading across into that field; but it is also the case that some aspects of the history of classical scholarship cannot be properly understood without looking at the interaction between humanities and science. A clear example comes from the history of nineteenth-century Cambridge, where mathematics had been dominant since the early eighteenth century and Classics at first (from the 1820s) a struggling add-on in the university examinations. The price paid for the establishment of a classical examination was that candidates were obliged to pass the mathematical honours examination first. This led to the lowest places being targeted by classicists aiming to slip through with minimal marks before escaping to the classical examination. In 1841 what was locally described as a 'slaughter' took place, in which two dozen men who were confidently expected to pass in mathematics were failed. Some of them later took pass examinations; one migrated to Oxford, where Classics dominated, and took a first-class degree. The slaughter was commented on and complained about in the local and national press. The story behind this incident is a complicated one, and in any case not relevant here: the point is that it belongs to an institutional context which cannot be understood in terms of the history of Classics alone. The form of Classics, and the lives of its teachers and learners, can be understood in this case only in relation to other knowledge, and to the institutional context which shaped them both. Classics as taught and examined in Cambridge was local knowledge.

---

[22] G. Murray, *An Unfinished Autobiography* (London, 1960); K.J. Dover, *Marginal Comment: A Memoir* (London, 1994). Dover's autobiography was initially offered to Oxford University Press, which refused to publish it.

Bases of Disciplinarity

Disciplinary history can be seen not just as the history of disciplines, but also as a history that disciplines the members the members of an academic community, creating identity based on a shared past. From this point of view, the biographically based histories make sense as accounts of exemplary individuals, the founding heroes of a discipline. To think back to the heroes is to make contact with a life which represents scholarly achievement. Oxford's first professor of Latin, John Conington, elected to his chair in 1854, read Richard Bentley's 1697 exposure of the 'Epistles of Phalaris' as forgeries once a year to keep in touch with a prime example of scholarship. Writing for the GRIP project in 1984, the American literary theorist Jonathan Arac asked, 'Is history of scholarship a counterdisciplinary practice?', and answered, 'Sometimes'. One of the cases he discussed was that of the New Criticism. Its approach was established in universities by Cleanth Brooks and Robert Warren's *Understanding Poetry* (1938), and theorized in 1949 in Rene Wellek and Robert Warren's *Theory of Literature*. Finally, in 1957 William K. Wimsatt and Cleanth Brooks published their *Literary Criticism: A Short History*, which as Arac observed, 'completed possession of the intellectual field, and in the very area in which the New Criticism was understood as most deficient' (that is, in historical understanding).[23] The irony sharpens the point Arac is making, that New Criticism was established by publication at the level of theory and pedagogy, making it both thinkable and teachable, and then confirmed through disciplinary historiography.[24]

Classics as Discipline/s

The interaction with German scholarship I mentioned in relation to histories of the discipline also played a crucial role in the history of the discipline in Britain. The characteristic pedagogic institution of the nineteenth-century German university, the seminar, had begun as doubly pedagogic, a device for training teachers, but was taken over by philologists, scientists, and historians from the late eighteenth century. This could be seen as belonging to the contemporary romantic reaction against

---

[23] J. Arac, 'Is history of scholarship a counterdisciplinary practice?', *The GRIP Report, Second Draft*, II (1984). The *Report* is not easy to find; I am grateful to Jonathan Arac for sending me a copy of his own paper.

[24] One might compare the history of linguistics courses at MIT in the days of Noam Chomsky's dominance, apparently known locally as 'The Bad Guys' since they dealt with pre-Chomskyan linguistics.

Enlightenment rationalism in Germany.[25] Its first appearance in Britain, as far as I know, was in Oxford in 1879, when the professor of Latin, Henry Nettleship, ran what he called a 'class' on textual criticism. Nettleship had been to lectures and seminars in Berlin in 1865, and had been impressed by the teaching of Theodor Mommsen, Emil Hubner, Jacob Bernays, and Moriz Haupt. Other German-style seminars in Oxford similarly came from individual initiative. The theologian William Sanday ran a New Testament text-criticism seminar from 1894, and in the following decade a law seminar was founded by Paul Vinogradoff, who established a supporting library and a publication series. Vinogradoff came to Oxford from Moscow, but as with Nettleship the inspiration for his seminar came from Berlin, where he had attended the seminars of Mommsen and others in 1875. The only classical seminar of this period other than Nettleship's was run for three years just before the First World War by the classical archaeologist Sir William Ramsay, who had retired from the chair of humanity at Aberdeen to Oxford in 1911. Oxford remained in essence, as is it did up to the Second World War and beyond, a university dominated by the humanities and by college tutors. The first doctoral degree in Classics to be awarded, to the (female) archaeologist Jocelyn Toynbee, came only in 1931.[26] In 1936 there were only two students working at graduate level in Classics; the Oxford scholar Robin Nisbet, in reporting this, commented that he was surprised there were so many.[27] But it was in the 1930s that German Jewish scholars arrived in Oxford, bringing with them the ideals, history, and methods of *Altertumswissenschaft*. The first to arrive was Eduard Fraenkel in 1934; he ran seminars from 1936 till his death in 1970, the seminar on the *Agamemnon* (1936 to 1942) being the first one of its kind in Britain.[28] The vast edition

---

[25] See A. La Vopa, 'Specialists against specialization: Hellenism as professional ideology in German classical studies', in G. Cocks & K.H. Jarausch (eds), *German Professions 1800–1950* (Oxford, 1990), 27–45.

[26] This is usually (as in her ODNB entry) dated to 1930, but though Toynbee submitted her thesis, 'The Revival of Greek Art under Hadrian', on 6 June 1930, the degree was not conferred on her until 14 February 1931. Doctoral degrees (called 'DPhil' to avoid the perceived German associations of 'PhD') had been introduced in Oxford in 1917. The first DPhil was awarded in 1920; the first woman to receive it was the English literary scholar Evelyn Simpson, in 1922. The first classical doctorate in Cambridge was awarded in 1926.

[27] R.G.M. Nisbet, 'Half a century of classical research at Oxford', in C.A. Stray (ed.), *Oxford Classics: Teaching and Learning 1800–2000* (London, 2007), 219–25, 219.

[28] On Fraenkel, see C.A. Stray, 'Eduard Fraenkel: an exploration', *Syllecta Classica* 25 (2015), 113–72, and 'Eduard Fraenkel (1888–1970)', in Crawford, Elsner & Ulmschneider (eds), *Ark of Civilization*. On his *Agamemnon* edition, Stray, 'A Teutonic monster in Oxford: the making of Fraenkel's *Agamemnon*', in C.S. Kraus & C.A. Stray (eds), *Classical Commentaries: Studies in the History of an Academic Genre* (Oxford, 2015), 39–57.

which resulted, published in 1950, is a treasure-house not only of scholarship, but also of Wilamowitz footnotes. Wilamowitz had been Fraenkel's most inspiring teacher in Berlin, and it has been said that even after
the master's death in 1931, it was always for Wilamowitz that Fraenkel
wrote. It was this tradition, a massive and inspiring disciplinary formation,
that Fraenkel's pupils observed in action. One of them, Martin West,
conjured it up vividly:

> Here we saw German philology in action; we felt it reverberate through us as
> Fraenkel patrolled the room behind our chairs, discoursing in forceful
> accents. As he spoke of his old teachers and past colleagues—Leo and
> Norden, Wilamowitz and Wackernagel—it was like an *apparition de l'Église
> éternelle*. We knew, and could not doubt, that this was what Classical
> Scholarship was, and that it was for us to learn to carry it on.[29]

Journals

The next carrier of disciplinary identity I want to consider is the scholarly
journal. This section concentrates on nineteenth-century journals, dealing
mainly with England but bringing in Germany and the USA to some
extent. As I shall suggest, some of them are the products and reflections of
communities, while others have created communities. I have chosen
journals as a focus because they seem to me important and neglected: an
important communication medium and basis for disciplinary solidarity
which we now take for granted. The first scholarly journal was the *Journal
des scavans*, whose first issue appeared in 1665, just two months before the
first of the *Philosophical Transactions of the Royal Society*. The former aimed
to create a community of scholars; the latter derived from an existing
community. I give below a list of British and American classical journals of
the nineteenth century, a period which begins with fairly short-lived
journals, and also with failed attempts to revive them or to found new
journals. These attempts are included in the belief that the history of
failure is as important as the history of success: if we want to understand
what the scholars of the period were trying to achieve, we need to recover
evidence of projects that failed. Apart from anything else, this helps to
make sense of relationships between journals, since some of these failed
projects constituted attempts either to compete with existing journals, or
more commonly to continue those that had collapsed.

---

[29] M.L. West, quoted by S. West, 'Eduard Fraenkel recalled', in C.A. Stray (ed.), *Oxford
Classics: Teaching and Learning 1800–2000* (London, 2007), 203–18, 211.

Nineteenth-Century English-Language Classical Journals, Actual and Projected

Locations of journals: C[ambridge], L[ondon], O[xford]. Failed
   projects are in [brackets]. American titles are in **bold**.
Classical Journal 1810–29. 20 vols, 40 issues. L
Museum Criticum 1813–26. 2 vols, 8 issues. C
[H. J. Rose 1826–7] C
[G. C. Lewis 1830] O
Philological Museum 1831–3. 2 vols, 6 issues. C
['Museum Academicum': B. Jowett, H.G. Liddell, R. Scott,
   A. P. Stanley 1841–2] O
Classical Museum 1843–9. 7 vols, 28 issues. L
*Terminalia; or Notes on the Subjects of the Literae Humaniores and
   Moderation Schools* 1851–2. 2 issues. O
Journal of Classical and Sacred Philology 1854–9. 4 vols, 12 issues. C
Journal of Philology 1868–1921. 35 vols, 70 issues. C (O)
Transactions of the American Philological Association 1870–
Transactions of the Oxford Philological Society 1879–90. 11 issues. O
Journal of Hellenic Studies 1880– Annual. L
American Journal of Philology 1880–
Proceedings of the Cambridge Philological Society 1882–. Annual.
   (*Memoranda* 1872–9, *Transactions* 1881–) C
Classical Review 1887– 10 issues annually. C/O/L
Harvard Studies in Classical Philology 1890–

The *Classical Journal*, the earliest journal listed, was also one of the longest-lasting; a striking exception to the pattern which dominates the list as a whole, of a succession of short-lived publications. The reason is that it was run by the London publisher Abraham Valpy, whose ambition was to be a printer-scholar in the manner of Aldus Manutius. The dilemma faced by the founders of several other journals, of retaining the support of a printer or publisher, was solved by Valpy's filling both roles himself. Valpy's brother and father were classicists, and his monogram, a claim to up-to-date scholarship derided by others, was a large digamma, which appeared on his title pages and also, apparently, on his horse-drawn coach. (The digamma resembled a gibbet, and Valpy's enemies suggested he should be hanged from it.) Another of Valpy's grand projects was a large-scale version of Henri Estienne's Greek thesaurus (1816–26). Edmund Barker, an alumnus of Trinity College Cambridge, was associated with both publications, and there was constant rivalry with the *Museum Criticum* of James Monk and Charles Blomfield, fellows of Barker's old college, who probably began it as a riposte to the *Classical*

Journal. The variable quality and omnium-gatherum antiquarianism of the *Classical Journal* contrasted with the hard-nosed textual criticism of the Cambridge dons, who saw themselves as more professional than the learned but uncontrolled Barker.[30] They denounced his books, and he responded by planting favourable reviews of them under a variety of names, even at one point under Monk's initials.

The *Museum Criticum* closed down after its editors gained ecclesiastical preferment, and after failed attempts to revive it by Hugh Rose and by George Cornewall Lewis, was succeeded by the *Philological Museum*. This was edited by two younger Trinity dons, Julius Hare and Connop Thirl-wall, who had read widely in German scholarship and promoted a broad conception of philology. This too closed down when the editors left Cambridge for church positions. An Oxford attempt to revive it by Hare's nephew Arthur Stanley and his friends Henry Liddell, Robert Scott, and Benjamin Jowett broke down when their printer discovered just how much money the Cambridge printer of the *Philological Museum* had lost. The Germanic tinge of the project was reflected in Stanley's letters, where he referred to it as 'Blatt' [leaf, paper, hence a journal].[31] He and his friends stepped aside for William Smith of London and Leonhard Schmidt of Edinburgh, who were also proposing a journal, and who then founded the *Classical Museum*, bringing in contributors from the continent. This journal was notable for being founded and run outside Oxbridge. Smith was a product of the University of London who edited a series of classical dictionaries; Schmidt was a pupil of Niebuhr who married an Englishwoman and became headmaster of a school in Edinburgh. Space does not permit a consideration of the German classical journals which provided exemplars for several of the English publications I am discussing, so I refer the reader to Graham Whitaker's recent article on the topic, which focuses on *Zeitschrift für die Alterthumswissenschaft* (1834–57), but also discusses earlier and later nineteenth-century journals.[32]

The next contender, the *Journal of Classical and Sacred Philology*, was founded by three Cambridge scholars; two of them, A.F. Hort and J.B. Lightfoot, went on to become well-known biblical scholars, the

---

[30] Their hero was Richard Porson, fellow of Trinity and professor of Greek in the university from 1782 till his death in 1808. See C. Stray, 'The rise and fall of Porsoniasm', *Cambridge Classical Journal* 53 (2007), 40–71.

[31] Stanley's letter of 2 May 1842 to his uncle Julius Hare informing him of the collapse of the project was annotated by him 'Death of Blatt owing to loss of Phil. Mus.'. A.P. Stanley papers, Pusey College Library, Oxford.

[32] G. Whitaker, 'Alterthumswissenschaft at mid-century', in C.A. Stray and G. Whitaker (eds), *Classics in Practice: Studies in the History of Scholarship, Bulletin of the Institute of Classical Studies* Supp.128 (2015), 129–69.

third was J.E.B. Mayor, professor of Latin 1872–1910. Mayor later recalled that the journal was closed down because of a lack of high-quality submissions. The *Journal of Philology*, which picked up the baton in 1868, was seen locally as a continuation of *JCSP*—the bound volumes of which had had 'Journal of Philology' printed on their spines. This time Mayor was joined by two new co-editors, again Cambridge men. With the *Journal of Philology* we witness a transition from classics and divinity to classics and comparative philology (a chair of Sanskrit had just been founded in Cambridge). This was just at the point, in the 1860s, when bright graduates were increasingly turning away from clerical ordination toward academic or school teaching careers.[33] Three years after the *Journal* was founded, the University Test Acts were repealed, so most academic positions could be held without ordination. Here we have the makings of a disciplinary community; and indeed in 1871 the Cambridge Philological Society was founded, probably provoked by the founding of the Oxford Philological Society in the previous year. How was this related to the *Journal of Philology*, which predated both societies? The *Journal* was published by Macmillan and had no formal connection with any academic body, but in 1872 the Cambridge society decided to buy it in bulk and send copies to its members. Five years later, however, the journal was on the point of financial collapse; it was rescued by recruiting an Oxford editor, Ingram Bywater, who brought with him several dozen subscriptions from his colleagues. In the 1890s publication of issues became very erratic. Philological Society members outside Cambridge received only the *Journal* in exchange for their subscription, so there was widespread resentment when publication was late or non-existent in a given year. Macmillan, the journal's publisher, raised the price during the First World War and yet at times did not supply an issue; nor did they respond to a call for a cumulative index to be produced. In 1920 the Cambridge society cancelled its group subscription and switched to the new *Classical Quarterly*, founded in 1909. *The Journal of Philology* promptly collapsed.

It can be seen from the list above that the Cambridge society also published reports of its meetings, but evidently these were not seen as competition for the *Journal of Philology*, and of course they did not include reviews as the *Classical Review* did. Something similar could be said of the *Transactions of the Oxford Philological Society*, which were circulated to members but never morphed into a full-blown journal. An earlier Oxford periodical, *Terminalia*, had been set up in 1851 to support the newly reformed classical syllabus, but only lasted for two years. In its second year

---

[33] A.G.L. Haig, 'The church, universities and learning in later Victorian England', *Historical Journal* 29 (1986), 187–201.

its editors appealed for contributors from outside Oxford to gain additional subscribers, but the response was insufficient to save it.

The *Journal of Philology* had an austere format and carried no reviews; the policy may have been a deliberate attempt to distance the journal from existing general periodicals which included classical reviews, such as the quarterly *Contemporary Review* and *Quarterly Review*, the monthly *Academy* and the weekly *Athenaeum*.[34] In the 1880s this prompted Mayor's younger brother Joseph to organise a new journal, the *Classical Review*, whose first issue appeared in 1887. Mayor's main concern was to provide information about continental, especially German, books and journals. He was probably inspired by the founding in 1881 of the *Berliner Philologische Wochenschrift*, whose editors defected to another publisher in 1884 to found *Wochenschrift für klassische Philologie*. In order to understand the importance of the proposal, we need to remember how hard it was to keep abreast of journal publishing in Classics. In London the only serious depository was the British Museum Library, but it was not easy to gain access to recent accessions, and accessioning was a slow process. While Richard Jebb, professor of Greek at Cambridge, was working on his edition of Bacchylides he more than once wrote to Frederic Kenyon, of the British Museum, to ask for news of recent articles relevant to his project. In 1898 A.E. Housman, than at University College London, wrote to William Hale, professor of Latin at Chicago, that he had not seen his paper on the Vatican MS of Catullus:

> Nor have I seen Schulze's paper. In Chicago no doubt you see all the periodicals as they appear: in London there is no place of the sort. This College takes in eight or nine, but Hermes is not among them: the British Museum tries hard and with some success to withhold from readers everything less than a year old. (Housman to Hale, 21 November 1898; A. Burnett (ed.), *Letters of A.E.Housman* (Oxford, 2007), i. 113–14)

This difficulty also led to proposals to set up reading rooms stocked with periodical literature. For example, the library set up by the Cambridge Philological Society (founded in 1871) formed the basis of the present Classics Faculty library (1926), while that formed by the Hellenic Society

---

[34] In 1868, when the Journal of Philology was founded, the *Quarterly Review* carried two classical articles out of a total of 43—less than 0.5 per cent; the *Edinburgh Review* had none at all. During the editorship of William Gifford, 1809–24, the *Quarterly* had published 50 classical articles out of 733 (14.5 per cent); in the same period the *Edinburgh* had published 20 classical articles out of 613 (3.5 per cent). For these figures and the variations which lie beneath them, see C.A. Stray, 'Politics, Culture, and Scholarship: Classics in the *Quarterly Review*', in J. Cutmore (ed.), *Conservatism and the Quarterly Review* (London, 2007), 87–106, notes at pp. 233–8, where an incorrect percentage is given at p. 98, the correct one at p. 103.

(1879), later merged with that set up by the Roman Society (1910), and still later became the Joint Library at the Institute of Classical Studies in London (1953).[35] In the case of other libraries, surviving records are often inadequate to determine when journal subscriptions were taken out.[36] Another solution to the problem of sharing the contents of journals was adopted in Vassar College in the USA. In 1902 John Leverett Moore, head of the Latin Department, founded a Latin Journal Club to keep members abreast of the latest articles on Latin literature and Roman culture published in classical journals. Each member was assigned several journals and asked to present periodic reports at the group's weekly meetings. Surviving minutes record 382 meetings of the club from 1902 to 1935, when the name was officially changed to the Classical Journal Club, presenting a fascinating picture of the evolution of an unusual and innovative volunteer organization of classicists within a liberal arts college.[37]

Joseph Mayor's campaign to found the *Classical Review* began in 1884, when he sent a circular to scholars in British universities. He gained enough support to send out a prospectus in 1886; this gave a list of over thirty men who had promised to contribute, but he had by then secured undertakings from more than eighty scholars. Soon after the *Review* began to appear, Mayor tried to negotiate an American connection, collecting support from several scholars, including W.W. Goodwin of Harvard. By September 1887 the New York publisher Putnam was being invited to co-publish, with a commitment to take 150 copies for American sale; an extra sheet was to be added, to be edited by a US scholar. In the end Ginn of Boston became the US co-publishers and Thomas D. Seymour (Yale), John Wright (Harvard), and William Hale (Chicago) joined the editorial board. They had control of a substantial section, which enlarged the issues considerably; the *Review*'s size leapt from 336 pages in 1888 to 482 pages in the following year.

The editorial of February 1889 announced the new US link, concluding that 'for a fruitful study of Greek and Roman antiquity the practical

[35] This had and still maintains a close link with journals, since books sent to the societies' journals (*Journal of Hellenic Studies*, *Journal of Roman Studies*) are deposited in the library after being reviewed. See below for the foundation of these journals.

[36] This is the case with Trinity College Library, Cambridge, one of four Cambridge libraries with complete runs of *Hermes*; the others are St John's College library, the Classical Faculty Library and the University Library. In Oxford, runs are held at the Bodleian Library and the Sackler (classical) library. This last succeeds the Ashmolean library, which like the Classical Faculty Library at Cambridge was not in existence when *Hermes* was founded in 1866.

[37] Vassar College Archives, Multiple Collections, box 1: VC Latin Journal Club. I owe my knowledge of the Club to my late and much lamented friend, Barbara F. McManus.

judgment of the English is no less needful than the unwearied research and the daring speculation of the Germans, or the lucidity and mental vivacity of the French'. This invocation of national stereotypes was a topos that was to reappear during the first world war in the writing of Gilbert Murray in Britain and Paul Shorey in the USA. Note that in 1889 'the English' (commonly used as a synonym for 'British' in this period) appears also to include the Americans.

The remaining journal to be mentioned is the *Journal of Hellenic Studies*, founded in 1880, devoted to art and archaeology, setting an example followed by the *Journal of Roman Studies* in 1911. This was a new kind of journal in two ways. First, it was set up by a new society, the Society for the Promotion of Hellenic Studies, founded in 1879, as a house journal, the first classical journal of this kind in Britain. Second, it was explicitly devoted to a specialized field within Classics. In the late 1880s it began to carry reviews, presumably provoked by the example of the *Classical Review*, which had at the end of its first volume begun to publish archaeological reviews. *JHS* exemplified a common modern pattern, the learned society with its own journal, but as I have suggested, earlier journals had created their own communities, of contributors, readers or both—though rarely, as we have seen, with much success. It was when professional academic career structures began to emerge in the later nineteenth century that the social and institutional bases for viable journals began to be laid down. The life and death of the *Journal of Philology*, which covers this whole period, offers an instructive illustration.

Comparing the *Classical Review* and *Journal of Hellenic Studies*, we can see that both were attached to scholarly communities, but in fact the attachments were of different kinds. Mayor assembled a community which constituted a core of both writers and readers of the journal. Only in 1909, when the *Review* was bought by the Classical Association, did it become attached to a separate institution. *JHS* was founded as the organ of a society, a community that was already in place. What the two journals had in common was the problematic nature of their communities. One source of difficulty for *JHS* was that the Hellenic was a fashionable as well as a scholarly field. Within what was known as South Kensington Hellenism, rich patrons held soirees in which they and their guests dressed up in flowing robes to perform scenes from Greek drama. At some of the Hellenic Society's public meetings, naive questions were addressed from the floor to learned foreign speakers, causing embarrassment to the Society's academic leaders. Even within the academic community, however, embarrassment could occur, when rivalries and enmities played out in membership of committees and in the pages of journals. The best-documented struggles were those between Richard Jebb, professor of

Greek at Cambridge, and his arch-enemy John Pentland Mahaffy of Trinity College Dublin. The two men were temperamentally incompatible, and Jebb was convinced that Mahaffy and his allies were conducting a campaign of denigration against him in unsigned reviews. One reason why he supported Joseph Mayor's proposal for a Classical Review so strongly was that reviews were to be signed. Using his position as a major supporter of the project, he insisted that Mahaffy and his allies should be kept away from the journal. Similarly, in the counsels of the Hellenic Society, he worked to marginalize Mahaffy. These struggles even affected another journal, the *Academy*, since Mahaffy and his allies were on good terms with its editor and tended to publish there. Mayor wrote to Jebb in 1886, 'I quite agree with you as to the necessity of keeping clear of the Academy clique' (Mayor to Jebb, 17 August 1886; Jebb papers, Trinity College Library, Cambridge).

In order to understand the history of these journals, we need to remember that they co-existed with an array of general periodicals like the liberal *Edinburgh Review* (1802), its conservative rival the *Quarterly Review* (1809), and many others.[38] Most of these periodicals published reviews of classical works, though such reviews became less common in the second half of the century. But just after the foundation of the *Journal of Philology*, in 1869, an Oxford society founded to promote the endowment of research set up a new monthly journal, *The Academy*, designed as a home for articles and discussions in all academic subjects. The society represented the germanizing party in Oxford which favoured the expansion of the professoriate and the transformation of the university into a more centralized body in which colleges and tutors would be marginalized. The journal prospered at first, but ran into financial difficulties, and by 1890s had become a conventional literary journal. In its early years, however, it symbolized the new world of disciplines, and university curricula in which traditional subjects like classics and mathematics had been joined by history, law, and economics. In this role its main rival was the weekly *The Athenaeum*, founded in 1828.

By this time the United States had journals of its own, the *Transactions of the American Philological Association* (1870) and the *American Journal of Philology* (1880); and they were soon to be joined by *Harvard Studies in Classical Philology* (1890). Of these three, only *AJP* published reviews, as it had from its inception. The *Classical Review*'s focus on reviews soon made an impact on *AJP*, especially after the Anglo-American alliance was

---

[38] See Stray, 'Politics, Culture, and Scholarship'.

established in 1889. In 1890 its editor Basil Gildersleeve wrote to Herbert Weir Smyth of Harvard:

> Have you anything for me?...A review would be especially welcome—as the supply of that department of the Journal has been somewhat interfered with by the transfer of so much work to the Classical Review.[39]

AJP was one of several journals edited from within departments at Johns Hopkins, founded in 1876 as the first American university consciously designed on the model of the German research university. Gildersleeve made it clear that it was not to be a house journal, but to be open to the whole classical community.[40] This inclusivity was of course good for business, and he was privately dismayed, though publicly welcoming, when a new journal, *Classical Philology* was founded in Chicago in 1906. The new journal was published by the University of Chicago Press, which had become a division of the university in the mid-1890s. The histories of both the *Journal of Philology* and the *Classical Review* had shown signs of rivalry between Oxford and Cambridge; similar rivalries were to be expected as Chicago grew in strength as an independent centre of academic activity in the Mid-West after its foundation in 1890, asserting itself against the Ivy League universities of New England.

Similar patterns of rivalry operated in a later generation in the case of the upstart field of sociology, which became one of Chicago's great strengths. The earliest journal in this field was the *American Journal of Sociology*, founded in Chicago in 1895, and published by the University of Chicago Press, a division of the University, as *Classical Philology* was to be in 1906. Its early years were financially fragile, but in 1905 the newly founded American Sociological Society adopted it as its own journal and its fortunes improved. (When acronyms became popular, the ASS changed its name to the ASA to avoid embarrassment.) Chicago sociology became a dominant force in the USA, but this created resentment in other universities, and in 1935 the Association founded a new journal, the *American Sociological Review*, in order to counteract Chicago's influence.[41]

These are not the only sociological journals whose history offers instructive comparisons with classical journals. The origins and early years of the most famous of all sociological journals, *L'Année sociologique*, followed

[39] Gildersleeve to Weir Smyth, 16 Oct. 1890 (Harvard University archives).
[40] Ward W. Briggs jr, 'Basil L. Gildersleeve and *The American Journal of Philology*, in Stray & Whitaker (eds), *Classics in Practice*, 3–15.
[41] Patricia M. Lengermann, 'The founding of the American Sociological Review: the anatomy of a rebellion', *American Sociological Review* 44 (1979), 185–98. Lengermann's analysis of this rebellion is an interesting exercise in historiography, as she situates previous accounts of the rebellion in relation to competing views of scientific change.

a pattern in some ways very like that of the *Classical Review*. In the mid-1890s Emile Durkheim and his collaborators planned a journal that would help them to insert sociology into the French university world. The first issue of the journal appeared in 1898, after a recruitment drive for contributors very like that conducted a few years earlier by Joseph Mayor. The newness of the subject meant that the core group was much smaller than Mayor's, and Durkheim soon found that he had to write a lot of the articles himself. The journal survived Durkheim's premature death in 1917 but closed down in 1925, though it was revived in the 1930s, and again after the Second World War. Its founding and early history can be followed in detail in the biography of Durkheim by Marcel Fournier.[42]

The list of English journals given above shows a clear pattern of development, from a series of short-lived publications, through the long-lived but mortal *Journal of Philology*, to the still-published *Journal of Hellenic Studies, Classical Review*, and *Classical Quarterly*. This fits neatly with the chronology of the emergence of a modern academic discipline and professional community, encouraged by several changes in the second half of the century: reforms at Oxford and Cambridge after the Royal Commissions of the 1850s and 1870s, the declining intake of graduates into Anglican orders and the concomitant growth of an academic profession, and the expansion of provincial universities. A theme evident from the 1870s, as we have seen, is the relationship between journals and scholarly societies, for whom journals are both functional communication media and sources of pride and prestige.

To return, finally, to disciplinary histories and their making. Histories are both what happened and what sense we make of that. Of any histories, in the first sense, we can construct many stories, but as Arnaldo Momigliano once remarked, they must be true stories.[43] We all begin with ideas about our subject—if we did not, we would be in danger of being overwhelmed by its multiplicity. But after that beginning, those ideas should engage in a dialectic with the available evidence. If not, we are in the position of a writer on the history of Classics whose draft text I suggested was evidentially very thin. The reply, delivered with confidence: this was intended not as a historical narrative, but as an ideological intervention. We may be happy to listen to such interventions, but if their authors choose to adduce historical evidence in support, they must submit

[42] M. Fournier, *Emile Durkheim* (Paris 2007; English translation, London 2013).

[43] A.D. Momigliano, 'The rhetoric of history and the history of rhetoric: on Hayden White's tropes', *Settimo Contributo alla storia degli studi classici e del mondo antico* (Rome, 1984), 49–56.

to evaluation according to traditional criteria. Is the evidence strong? Is it accurately referred to? Is it relevant? These questions apply to any period, but the nature of the available evidence varies. For the nineteenth and early twentieth centuries, a radical expansion in some kinds of evidence has been brought about by the expansion of web-based resources. As Patrick Leary pointed out in 2005 in an article on 'Googling the Victorians', we can now locate a word, a name or a phrase buried deep in books and journals, which we simply could not have found before the appearance of such resources as Google Books, the Times Archive, British Newspapers, and British Periodicals.[44] This access however is usually dependent on subscription, and, for example, no British library subscribes to the ProQuest database American Periodicals Online. Yet this increased access to original texts is often mediated not only by familiar processes of selection, but also by technological weaknesses such as inaccurate optical character recognition. A recently publicized example is the consistent misreading of 'arms' as 'anus', producing in one case a text that read, 'she threw her anus around his neck'.[45] With nineteenth-century newspaper evidence, such problems can be compounded by original errors in transmission, through the garbling of syndicated or pirated material. A nice example, recently encountered, is the mistransmission of the Latin phrase 'foemineum sexum', the female sex, as 'foemineum saxum'. The receiving newspaper, a provincial journal whose readers must have been mostly without Latin, helpfully translated this as 'a woman as hard as a stone'.[46] Such texts are not just data hanging in mid-air on our screens; they are the products of complex historical processes of composition, editing, transmission, and distribution even before they come under the fallible gaze of the scanner and its OCR software.

Conclusion

In this paper I have tried to tease out some of the varieties of disciplinary history, to look at some of the sources and forms of disciplinary communities in Classics, and to explore some aspects of the history of classical

---

[44] P. Leary, 'Googling the Victorians', *Journal of Victorian Culture* 10/1 (2005), 72–86.
[45] A. Flood, 'Scanner for ebook cannot tell its "arms" from its "anus"', *The Guardian (online)*, 1 May 2014. http://www.theguardian.com/books/booksblog/2014/may/01/scanner-ebook-arms-anus-optical-character-recognition, accessed 12 Sept 2015.
[46] Reported in *Notes and Queries* 4th Series 8 (1871), 440–1.

scholarship in enough detail to present the fine texture, the micropolitics, of the structures and processes involved. There is much that I have not touched on, including the emergence of the term 'Classics' to denote an academic subject rather than the literature of the ancients ('the classics'). But I hope that what has been surveyed in this paper is enough to offer a basis for discussion.

Review Essays
Oxford College Histories: Fresh Contributions

Robin Darwall-Smith

Jeremy Catto (ed.), *Oriel College: A History* (Oxford: Oxford University Press, 2013), xx + 850 pp. ISBN: 9780199595723; John Maddicott, *Founders and Fellowship: The Early History of Exeter College, Oxford 1314–1592* (Oxford: Oxford University Press, 2014), xxii + 362 pp. ISBN: 9780199689514.

In 2007 I wrote a review article for *History of Universities* called 'Oxford and Cambridge College Histories: an endangered genre?'.[1] As it turned out, my concern was misplaced. It is true that some Colleges then as now have continued to consider that they have done their duty towards the study of their past history by publishing elegant coffee-table books. Such works are certainly fully researched, with contributions from Fellows and other members of the Colleges, but they tend to place greater emphasis on lavish illustrations and cheerful presentation than on scholarly ambition, and they seem intended almost exclusively for an audience of alumni, without attempting to contribute to a wider discussion on the history of Oxford and its Colleges.

On the other hand, more than a few Colleges have continued to consider that they deserve better than this. Among the full-length College histories that have emerged since 2007 have been ones of University, Magdalen, Brasenose, and Christ Church for Oxford, and St John's for Cambridge, and there hints of others in preparation. It is only fair to admit that I have contributed to this pile myself, as the author of the University College history and as a contributor to the history of Magdalen.

---

[1] Robin Darwall Smith, 'Oxford and Cambridge College Histories: an endangered genre?', *History of Universities* 22/1 (2007), 21–9.

These Colleges, at least, have shown themselves willing to commission institutional histories with scholarly ambitions, and their standard has generally been high: the 'traditional' College history—strong on buildings, the boat club, and great Old Members, and weak on any serious engagement with the original sources (especially those before 1500) or any sense of a wider context—has largely been superseded. It is now clear how influential the histories of Lincoln College by Vivian Green and of Balliol College by John Jones have been in setting an example for books which need to appeal both to members of the College and to academics.[2]

There remains room for variety: some of these recent histories are the work of one author (as with University, Brasenose and Christ Church) and others the work of several (as with Magdalen and St John's). Their lengths have likewise varied, with those for Magdalen and St John's running into almost a thousand pages, although it is true that these are among the largest Colleges in either Oxford or Cambridge, with correspondingly complex histories. Some Colleges have even commissioned both types of history: Christ Church, for example, has balanced the popular *A Portrait of the House* with the scholarly history by Judith Curthoys.[3]

Into this field now appear books on Oriel College and Exeter College, Oxford. Of these books, Oriel's history is akin to the histories of Magdalen College and St John's, in being a hefty work, over eight hundred pages long, written by several hands. The editor is Jeremy Catto, an Emeritus Fellow of the College, who is also a leading authority on medieval Oxford, having edited the first two volumes of the *History of the University of Oxford*.

Exeter College has taken a rather different approach. To mark its 700th anniversary, the College produced both a coffee-table history, co-edited by its then Rector Frances Cairncross,[4] and a scholarly history of its first 278 years, written solely by its Emeritus History Fellow, John Maddicott.

Both Colleges are somewhat anomalous, at least in Oxford terms. The 'typical' medieval Oxford College foundation was intended for Masters and Bachelors of Arts who were studying theology, or sometimes law or medicine. Fellowships at such Colleges were normally open only to applicants from specified counties or dioceses, schools, or kinsmen of the founder. University College, giving preference to Masters from the

---

[2] V.H.H. Green, *The Commonwealth of Lincoln College 1427–1977* (Oxford, 1979); John Jones, *Balliol College. A History (1263–1939)* (Oxford, 1988).
[3] Christopher Butler, *Christ Church Oxford—a Portrait of the House* (London, 2006); Judith Curthoys, *The Cardinal's College: Christ Church, Chapter and Verse* (London, 2012).
[4] Frances Cairncross with Hannah Parham (ed.), *Exeter College: the First 700 Years* (London, 2013)

dioceses of York and Durham studying theology, is a good example of this kind of College.

While Exeter was certainly typical in that most of its Fellowships were restricted to candidates from the diocese of Exeter, those Fellows were elected as younger scholars studying in the Faculty of Arts, who were expected to move on soon after graduating as MAs, rather than stay on to study theology. This meant that Exeter would have had a significantly younger population than other Colleges. In addition, the head of Exeter, the Rector, could only hold office for one year (although this term was sometimes renewed), so that it was not possible for a Rector of Exeter to acquire the authority and seniority which could accrue to a long-serving head of another College. Exeter is also unusual in that, in the 1560s it was effectively refounded by Sir William Petre, with greatly revised statutes and a fresh endowment. Only Gonville and Caius College at Cambridge is similar among Oxbridge College in having such a double foundation.

The Fellows of Oriel, on the other hand, were expected to study theology, but there were absolutely no geographical restrictions placed on candidates for vacant Fellowships, a situation unique in Oxford. Furthermore, it was not until the eighteenth century that Oriel was given an endowment to create its first scholarships for undergraduates, even though undergraduates had been members of the College at least three centuries beforehand. On the other hand, it maintained a very close relationship with St. Mary Hall to the north, an institution filled with undergraduates, until the College finally took it over in 1902.

The history of Oriel contains a mixture of chronological and thematic chapters. Chapters 1–3, by Jeremy Catto himself, cover the first two hundred and fifty years of the College's history, up to 1574. Kenneth Fincham then takes up the baton for Chapters 4–5, for the years from 1574 to 1660. Paul Seaward discusses Oriel's long eighteenth century in Chapters 6–8, while Ernest Nicholson, in Chapter 9, tells the story of its rise to eminence under Provosts Eveleigh and Copleston. Peter Nockles examines the early nineteenth century, mainly with reference to the Noetics and the Tractarians, in Chapters 10–11, while Simon Skinner, in Chapter 12, covers the same period, but less from a theological than a social and economic perspective. Ernest Nicholson reappears for Chapter 13 to consider the vicissitudes of Oriel during the great reforms of the nineteenth century.

So far the book has followed a fairly clear narrative thread, but this is now interrupted by six thematic chapters, respectively on Oriel and the wider world (by Alexander Morrison), Oriel's estates (by Ralph Evans and J.P.D. Dunbabin), Oriel's finances in the twentieth century (by Wilf Stephenson), its buildings (by Matthew Bool), its sports (by Clive

Cheesman—this chapter being an essential part of the history of a College famous or infamous for its rowing prowess), and its scientists (by Robert Fox). This approach has the advantage with such topics as finance and architecture: they are not easily slotted into a narrative, and it makes the life of the specialist researcher easier to have a complete chapter devoted solely to their topic.

John Stevenson then covers the history of Oriel in the twentieth century in Chapters 20–23, before Jeremy Catto returns with a brief epilogue to discuss the last twenty years. Writing about the recent past of an Oxford College is always a tricky matter, as there may be too many sensitivities to take account of (and too many people still alive): in the first edition of his history of Balliol, for example, John Jones decided to stop outright in 1939. Catto handles his brief here tactfully and efficiently. Four appendices list respectively the College's Provosts, Vice-Provosts, Deans, and Treasurers.

Catto has assembled an eminent team under his editorship.[5] His own chapters on the early history of the College are as magisterial as one would expect from the doyen of historians of medieval Oxford. In particular, Catto does excellent justice both to the politics surrounding the creation of Oriel, and to the intellectual life of the early College. Likewise Kenneth Fincham and Peter Nockles are among the leading authorities for the periods which they cover, while Robert Fox has written extensively on the study of science at Oxford.

Particular emphasis (one fifth of the main body of the text) is given to the period c.1780–1855, but this is appropriate, for this is the period when Oriel, having until now been only a moderately wealthy and moderately distinguished College, burst into prominence under the Provostship of John Eveleigh, to become the leading College in Oxford, distinguished for its academic excellence and for the intellectual brilliance of its Senior Common Room. This brilliance produced two theological movements of great significance for the Anglican Church, namely the Noetics, under the leadership of Edward Copleston and Richard Whateley, and the Tractarians, led by John Keble and John Henry Newman. While the Noetics believed in the value of reason in the study of theology, the Tractarians wished to rekindle a greater sense of the numinous in worship. Such brilliance, however, would also prove self-destructive: Newman began his career enjoying the support of Copleston and Whateley, and even voted against Keble in the election for a new Provost in 1828, but under that new Provost, Edward Hawkins, relations deteriorated

---

[5] It is a shame that space could not be found to introduce the contributors to a non-Oriel audience.

between the two men, as Hawkins began to distrust the direction in which Newman's spiritual journey was taking him. The energies generated by this brilliant Senior Common Room which had once been used to such creative effect were dissipated in a poisonous atmosphere of faction and civil war. As a result, Oriel lost its pre-eminence among the Colleges to pretenders like Balliol. Nockles rightly calls the chapter describing this period 'A House Divided'.

Many smaller Oxbridge Colleges have similarly enjoyed such a moment in the sun—University College enjoyed a similar pre-eminence in the 1760s and 1770s—but the effects of Oriel's moment of glory could be felt far beyond the College. On the one hand, the Noetic Thomas Arnold became Headmaster of Rugby, and through his colleagues and pupils there transformed Victorian education, and inspired a generation of liberal theologians like Arthur Stanley; on the other, Newman and his follows, like Hurrell Froude, in turn inspired a whole movement of spiritual regeneration within the High Church wing of the Church of England. There can be no doubt that, for many non-Orielenses who pick up this volume, these are the chapters which will be most frequently read.

It is therefore valuable that this period is discussed by two contributors, Peter Nockles and Simon Skinner. Nockles provides two splendid chapters in which he analyses the philosophy of both the Noetics and the Tractarians, keeping himself strictly within the bounds of Oriel College and thus avoiding the temptation merely to retell the stories of the Noetics and the Oxford Movement once again. Meanwhile, Skinner covers the same period in order to discuss the interest shown by the Noetics in social and economic theory likewise, to the point that their writings had a considerable influence on the 1834 Poor Law so excoriated by Charles Dickens.

The juxtaposition does yield some unsettling results. Richard Whateley, Fellow of Oriel and later Archbishop of Dublin, emerges from Nockles's chapters as a burly, rumbustious figure, fond of a good philosophical tussle, but essentially benign. It is a shock to turn to Skinner to find that, in the later 1840s, when confronted by the Irish famine, all he could suggest was that the population was too large, and that emigration was the ideal solution (390–1).

Another character seen to interesting effect from different perspectives is Edward Hawkins, Provost from 1828–82. Hawkins appears in the contributions of Nockles, Skinner, and Nicholson, and the resulting portrait is in many ways a tragic one. Hawkins was clearly possessed of great abilities, and eager to keep Oriel's academic reputation high, but he found himself unable to deal with John Henry Newman. Nockles certainly shows that Newman could be a difficult person to handle, but one cannot but suspect that someone with better interpersonal skills than Hawkins, like Martin Routh at Magdalen, could have handled the situation better. It was also Hawkins's ill luck to be Provost at the very moment when reform was enforced on Oxford in the 1850s. Hawkins had not been alone in supporting gradual reform in his College (even if some other institutions, like Balliol or University, had gone further down this road), but it was not enough to please a wider world, and during his long Provostship Hawkins had to endure seeing his world crashing in around his head as he vainly opposed government intervention.

The risk of a multi-authored work is that some contributions may well be better than others, and also that some contributors may have less material to work with than others, with slightly tendentious results. For example, in his chapter on Oriel and the wider world, when Alexander Morison discusses Goldwin Smith, Regius Professor of Modern History from 1858–65, he is very enthusiastic to claim Smith as an Oriel man. It is true that Smith was made a member of the Senior Common Room there, but for the whole of his time as Professor he was also a Fellow of University College—a fact barely alluded to here—and it is not clear from the chapter just how close his relationship was with Oriel. Another example is Robert Fox's chapter on Oriel and Science. It turns out that, until the early twentieth century there was very little actual science taking place in the College: instead, Fox musters evidence from various members of St. Mary Hall, or has to make do with figures like Gilbert White whose scientific work was carried out in his curacy of Selborne. Of the 33 pages of his chapter, it is not until after the first 24 that the first science Fellow is elected to Oriel.

Nevertheless, this history of Oriel is a distinguished addition to the roster of new College histories; in particular, no future historian of the Noetics or the Oxford Movement can safely ignore the chapters which cover this period. John Maddicott's history of the early years of Exeter proves no less distinguished, albeit in a different way. If the history of Oriel is generous in scale sometimes to the point of diffuseness, this history of the early years of Exeter is more of a highly concentrated monograph, stopping in 1592 at the point when the effects of the refoundation by Sir William Petre had taken full effect. Only A.B. Emden, with his history of the early years of St. Edmund Hall, has taken a similar approach with an Oxford College history.

Maddicott's book is divided into four sizeable chapters. Chapter 1 is devoted to Walter de Stapeldon and the foundation of his College. Chapter 2, which occupies one-third of the whole volume, is arguably the meatiest: titled 'Anatomy of a College', this is a detailed analysis of the College from 1327–1500. Chapter 3 then takes us through the early sixteenth century and the Reformation, up to 1560, while Chapter 4 covers the refounding of the College by Sir William Petre and its consequences.

Chapter 1 has a dramatic story to tell, for Stapeldon resembles Henry VI in being one of the few founders of an Oxbridge College to suffer a violent death. Having been drawn close into the regime of Edward II, and appointed the king's treasurer in 1322, Stapeldon acquired a not unjustified reputation for avarice, and was effectively lynched in 1326 when his king's power crumbled. Maddicott gives Stapeldon a fair hearing, looking to his administrative acumen, and his concern for learning. Indeed it is very clear from Stapeldon's foundation statutes and its idiosyncratic regulations created to ensure a fast turnover of Fellows and Rectors, that he gave the creation of his College a great deal of careful thought.

Chapter 2 has no such drama, but is perhaps the most splendid part of the book. For many years, Exeter College has been something of a dark horse among Oxford College archives: it was among the last Colleges to employ a professional archivist, and little was known of its archives. Maddicott's book now reveals the remarkable riches of Exeter's medieval records, and in particular its sequence of detailed early accounts. Thanks to them, he is able to create a remarkably detailed analysis of the medieval College. It is fair to say that very few other Colleges have received such attention with regard to their early histories, but then few of them have as rich a quantity of source material as Exeter.

Maddicott's task is not an easy one: medieval Exeter was singularly poor and ill-funded. It did not even have a quadrangle until the seventeenth century, and there are few eminent Old Members available to be scattered like gold dust through the narrative. Yet Maddicott is able to show how a medieval College really worked, pointing to its finances, its personnel, and its administration. Archivists and historians of other medieval Colleges can only look on with envy at the amount of detail upon which Maddicott can draw for the portrait of his College. At the same time—and this is one of the book's strengths—Maddicott is careful to place Exeter in its Oxford context, regularly comparing and contrasting it with the other Colleges then established in Oxford.

Chapters 3 and 4 take the narrative in another direction. Exeter shared in the common troubles of the religious upheavals of the mid-sixteenth century, but in addition it suffered from considerable financial difficulties, as its income proved ever less able to keep up with the inflation then afflicting the country. The intervention of Sir William Petre in the 1560s, who bestowed upon the College fresh endowments, more Fellowships, and a new set of statutes, could not have been better timed to save the College.

The reasons for Petre's refounding of Exeter are something of a mystery. It is true that Petre was a Devon man, and that he did study at Oxford, but there is no evidence linking him with Exeter College. On the other hand, when, towards the end of his life, he had enjoyed a successful career in public life, somehow remaining in royal favour through successive changes of regime, and he now decided to use part of his wealth to support an existing College rather than, as Sir Thomas White and Sir Thomas Pope had previously done in 1555 with St. John's and Trinity, found a new one, it was Exeter which was the object of his generosity.

Regional loyalty might have inspired Petre in part; but there may well have been other reasons. In public, at least, he was prepared to conform to every change in religion, but there is evidence that in private he remained committed to Catholicism, as did many members of his family. Meanwhile, early Elizabethan Exeter had become something of a centre of recusancy in Elizabethan Oxford, akin to St. John's College. Maddicott suggests that this recusancy attracted Petre's attention and that he hoped, by supporting it so generously, to help preserve a Catholic enclave within Oxford. He also makes the interesting observation that Petre encouraged the Fellows elected on his new endowment to travel abroad to study medicine or civil law. Many did indeed travel—only to train as Catholic priests, which may well have been Petre's secret hope. After Petre's death, however, his plans came to nothing, and by 1592, when Maddicott ends his narrative, the College had become unambiguously Protestant.

Maddicott's concentration on a particular period in Exeter's history does make his book resemble an academic monograph more than the average College history, and it may therefore not be as immediately attractive to an alumnus audience, who may need some persuading that a three-hundred-page analysis of the medieval and early modern College is worth reading. I can only encourage the Exeter alumni to be brave and give Maddicott a go, as they will find it very rewarding.

It is interesting, therefore, to compare Maddicott's book with Cairncross's 'popular' history of Exeter. This despatches the whole period covered in his book in a mere twenty pages out of 200, and has already reached the twentieth century by page 80. There is much to enjoy in this book, not least because it hints at what could be done in the future. It is clear that since 1592 Exeter's history has been an interesting one: indeed, there are times when it enjoyed a prominence within the University never seen in medieval times, and there are Provosts such as John Prideaux in the early seventeenth century and Lewis Farnell in the early twentieth who are deserving of further investigation. Those in search of 'Great Old Members' will encounter such remarkable figures as the artists Edward Burne-Jones and William Morris, the composer Hubert Parry, and the author and scholar J.R.R. Tolkien. There also remains the complicated architectural history of Exeter to follow, not least its remarkable Chapel, one of the finest buildings created by George Gilbert Scott in Oxford. One earnestly hopes that the Governing Body will not assume that the 'popular' history of Exeter does full justice to its later history, but will instead encourage another scholar or scholars to write a 'sequel' to Maddicott's volume.

University and Magdalen Colleges, Oxford

Whose Space Is It Anyhow?

Sheldon Rothblatt

Paul Temple (ed.), *The Physical University, Contours of Space and Place in Higher Education* (London/New York, Routledge, 2014), 248 pp. ISBN: 9780415662314.

Collections of essays by diverse hands, as any editor understands, are always open to standard criticisms. The contributions vary in quality and presentation. They differ greatly in style, language, empirical strength, conceptual and methodological underpinnings, and objectivity. The absence of a coherent argument moving through prodigious amounts of material interrupts a natural (possibly lazy) desire for summary and focus. A tendency for some of the contributors to this volume to rely upon academic and technical jargon—not so much the occasional apt phrase but whole pages—is a drawback. Another irritant is the presence of ideologically driven analysis and advocacy, if by no means equally across the chapters. But all is hardly lost. Ideological presuppositions notwithstanding, we are at least learning how to ask sophisticated questions.

With a few exceptions, this collection focuses on the United Kingdom. But with so many new institutions arising everywhere in the world, the discussions in the volume are relevant to colleges and universities outside Britain.

As the global expansion of higher education opportunities, to include its virtual dimension, is almost impossible to fathom in its entirety, we cannot be surprised if much of the scholarship on reading spaces is similarly difficult to sort through and absorb. Some of it circles around the subject of spaces and how to make sense of their use; and establishing a direct connection between space and learning eludes heuristic inquiry. Teaching and research relationships are primarily social. They are difficult to describe more precisely because relationships are themselves determined by personality, practice, and culture. The task of the student of the physical university is to calculate how space also affects the acquisition and quality of knowledge.

The subject of the 'physical university' is so comprehensive and so wide-ranging that approaches to it diverge even more than is customary in collections. Taking hold of its complexity virtually requires the use of those disciplines that we can associate with the 'human sciences', every method of analysis and empirical investigation now available to scholars, or for that matter, to professional architects and designers. The strength of the contributions lies precisely in the use of ideas generated by semiotics, art and architectural as well as cultural criticism, city and campus planning, demography, sociology, or geography. By contrast, historical analysis is largely lacking, except in passing. This is unfortunate for any number of reasons, but one in particular. Insofar as a particular aspect of how space is used is to determine how learning can be improved or facilitated—the exact word is elusive—without history we are also without a baseline. How can we measure changes in learning without knowing much about its past? One inadvertent hint of a standard is a brief reference to work on the physiology of the brain. Research on mammals suggests that visual, aural, and tactile stimuli have a beneficial effect on learning (73). The point is so different from the general thrust of the volume as to leave the reader wishing for more.

The virtues of the collection, and of other writings now appearing in considerable profusion in the form of books and articles, and forming the subject of conferences, are that they examine one of the most important of all subjects in history. How lives are led within ever-changing built environments is not exactly a neglected subject, but, as the editor states, its importance for the university has been understated. Aristotle concentrated precisely on this theme when he said that men (ignoring women as an ancient Greek was wont to do) were most themselves and achieved their highest realization when collected in cities. For an ancient Greek, ostracism was almost the ultimate punishment, for it led to a decline in a sense of self. In short, to be with others is life-affirming. To live alone is denaturing. But living together also depended on the spaces in which human interaction occurred, the agora for example. The theme was sounded many times in the Age of the Enlightenment as thinkers constantly explored the vital importance of sociability and civility.

From its inception in the twelfth century, the university has been an important institution, important even when it served only a handful of students, since they were destined to occupy leading positions in church and state. But the life led in common and in common spaces was always critical and remains so. That is why the university of today is a special institution, containing what the late Harold Perkin called the 'key profession', the academic one that trains all the others.

One of the contributors is certain that the university of today instills and conveys a managerial and entrepreneurial mindset which leads to ambivalences (29). A broader view, not so one-sided, is to recall the original analysis of a multiversity as defined by Clark Kerr of the University of California. Today's university is a collection of all that has gone before and daily accrues. Much is added and almost nothing shed.[1] The fact is that not one mindset exists but many, struggling to co-exist. All the while the university hopes to achieve a modicum of internal balance and even collegiality in the hope of preserving its distinct identity. By now this is a twice-told tale. The medieval university acquired functions, structures (faculties, colleges, nations), missions, disciplines, styles, student populations, supporters, detractors, each pressing for attention. Given its numerous constituents ('stakeholders' as some now say), small wonder that most of the contributors repeatedly find so many instances of ambiguity and contradiction. But this is hardly a discovery. It is by now a platitude.

The physical university, the 'campus', as Paul Turner demonstrated in a seminal work,[2] is an American planning tradition commencing in the late eighteenth century, the word applied to the greensward at Princeton University. Although dating from the late Enlightenment, in subsequent development it owes more to the Romantic period and the revolution in sensibility associated with the early nineteenth century. An attachment to place and space is well expressed in the poetry of famous young generations, and novelists, as mentioned in the introduction to the collection. They made location into a familiar theme. One might almost say that the particular and ongoing appeal of Oxford and Cambridge, despite its earlier role in socializing a governing elite, is particularly rooted in the Romantic period. The coming of age, or the 'discovery of adolescence', a subject that attracted historical and sociological attention after the 1960s, especially because of the work of Philippe Ariès,[3] broadly coincides with the 'discovery of the campus', particularly the campus as the locus of undergraduate instruction. If campus planning is a special American contribution to the idea of a university, the 're-discovery' of the pageantry of Oxbridge was nevertheless a transatlantic influence.[4] At the very least, the senior

---

[1] A recent re-statement of this understanding is offered by Neil J. Smelser, *Dynamics of the Contemporary University: Growth, Accretion, and Conflict* (Berkeley, 2012).

[2] Paul Venable Turner, *Campus, an American Planning Tradition* (Cambridge, MA, 1984)

[3] Philippe Ariès, *Centuries of Childhood: a Social History of Family Life* (New York, 1962).

[4] For thoughts along these lines, see Sheldon Rothblatt, Chapter 2 of *The Modern University and Its Discontents: the Fate of Newman's Legacies in Britain and America* (Cambridge, 1997).

universities of England supplied the magic that other universities envied or sought to emulate.

Plentiful land, a plural religious inheritance leading to the foundation of sectarian colleges and the college as a perceived 'outpost' of civilization in a young nation extending both its frontier and its domination over native populations, allowed the American campus idea to take on a larger spatial dimension than the English one. Eventually, however, many sometime American colleges developed into universities, and thereafter into multiversities. Urban ideas of scale and proportion became important, necessary for embracing the expansion in student numbers and proliferation of academic missions characteristic of the half century now passed.

Many of the Romantic generation implicitly disagreed with Aristotle's discussion of *homo politicus*. Cities were dangerous and anonymous, artificial rather than natural, but the cities that they knew were not the manageable city-states of Greek antiquity. For a time the campus idea partook of this anti-urban sentiment, favouring low-rise structures within parks, a kindergarten for adolescents. One of the objections to the founding of London University in the 1820s was a fear that the metropolis was dangerous and unsettling. The adequate supervision of students could not be assured. But numbers have played havoc with the Romantic inheritance, however appealing it remains. Urbanist as well as Romantic ideas of space and structure sit side-by-side in campus settings.

In fact, the university of today is in many respects a city, a circumscribed territory sometimes with gates but elsewhere, as in the American contribution, possessed of weak outer membranes permitting continual border and inner movement, intermixing public and private spaces. It is pre-eminently a collection of people of all ages and backgrounds gathered into landscapes and hardscapes, greenfields and now even reclaimed wasteland, locations 'vacated' as Jill Stoner would say in her plea for a 'minor architecture'.[5]

There is overlap between city and campus. Campus planning is akin to urban planning. Many of the objectives are therefore similar: diverse interests have to be accommodated, space provided for single or communal activities, and traffic to be managed (one English solution as described by Stefan Muthesius was to separate vehicular and pedestrian campus traffic).[6] Other aims are to improve dining facilities, allow for vistas and generally enhance the beauty of the environment. The Modernist Movement in architecture was not friendly to the stylistic flourishes of an earlier

---

[5] See Jill Stoner, *Toward a Minor Architecture* (Cambridge, 2012).
[6] Stefan Muthesius, *The Post-War University, Utopianist Campus and College* (New Haven, 2001).

generation, finding them fussy, frivolous, and wasteful. Viewed through a particular ideological lens, the older neo-historical styles were accused of contributing to social class distinctions. But several decades of post-1945 'Brutalism', bland facades, and unadorned concrete surfaces (easily stained in damp climates) induced the next generation of architects to return to more varied expressions of architectural forms by whatever name we choose to call them (e.g. 'Memphis', 'Postmodern').

The city is a learning experience. Moving about urban space, especially space planned or evolved with human needs foremost, provides plentiful opportunities for sampling the heritage of a built environment. As more and more of the campus folds into a neighbouring city, or is within reach of it, critics of the university as privileged space demand a closer association. That sentiment is also to be found in this volume.

But cities, while they contain universities and colleges and are more connected to universities than ever before because of the digital revolution, are not colleges and universities. They are not places for the systematic and concentrated acquisition and dissemination of knowledge. The goals of campus planning, while they incorporate design features associated with urban development, must in a final reckoning be significantly associated with teaching and learning. A straightforward functionalism is possible. Laboratories and libraries can certainly be designed for instrumental use. But in the traditions of campus planning, we aim to go beyond a barebones functionalism, clinging to an ideal of the campus as a total humanizing experience supporting direct and indirect learning.

A built environment is filled with symbols, historical references, inheritances—all of which, as in architecture or painting or any of the visual arts—can be read differently. The editor, Paul Temple, states, using current postmodern phrasing, that a building is a 'text' to be read. No one disputes this, but the temptation is to reach for a normative reading. Criticisms are frequently offered from a present-day perspective, suggesting a major deficiency that may not have been relevant in the past. One example of this occurs in the chapter by Brett Bligh on learning space design. His reference is to a volume by other authors (themselves apparently influenced by Pierre Bourdieu) where Enlightenment conceptions of learning are regarded as 'neutralising the body'. The mind is engaged while the physical environment is ignored. The sin committed here is that 'authentic learning' is neglected. What follows as a remedy is mention of 'activity-scapes', defined as the 'supportive experiential, spatial, equipmental and service environment immediate to the performance of a particular activity' (47).

The prose is not appealing, but the chief difficulty is a parade of assumptions about learning past and present that seem more idiosyncratic than demonstrable. What is 'authentic learning' in any case? And just exactly what kind of learning are we referring to? Is it certain that Enlightenment educators appealed only to mind and not to body? If so, why build so many attractive spaces only to ignore them? Why insist that a public life led within spaces such as open squares serve human needs best if nothing is to be gained from such planning? Or, speaking of the body in a more conventional manner, is learning more 'authentic' or the body less 'neutralised' when sitting bolt upright or sprawled on an armchair? I may prefer the latter, but unless I am unbearably uncomfortable, whether I learn or work better because of how I sit is problematical. Comfort was, incidentally, virtually an Enlightenment contribution to civilization. Bligh himself questions whether 'activity-scapes' do result in behaviour that carries over into later life, especially within a 'democratic society' (48).

Education for democracy, that is, for participating as a citizen in a democratic society, is a theme congenial to Americans, extending back to the Founders, and now embraced by all western societies. For Jefferson and others of that generation, not to mention later thinkers like John Dewey, himself more concerned with schooling than university, the purpose of higher education is citizenship, and citizenship as the result of a liberal education. Many iterations of liberal exist (I am tempted to use the past tense), but as the university of today has many missions— professional, technical, vocational, research—not all of them are easily aligned to a democratic polity or citizenship model. It is therefore easier to discuss space from the perspective of ordinary use. No one can possibly quarrel with the authors who mention the importance of sanitation, ventilation, adequate heating and light, or building a sustainable environment, all of which I know are ingredients that today's architects and planners already take into account. From the standpoint of reducing carbon emissions, the logic of the argument (to cite the chapter by Marcella Ucci) is more distance and part-time instruction, which leads to the unstated but perverse deduction that worries about physical space would be consequently irrelevant.

No harm is done by identifying virtues that one might imagine as part of any architect's ambitions: wide corridors instead of narrow ones, privacy in changing rooms, adequate storage facilities, durable finishes, and cheerful colours. In noting these, Alexi Marmot also notes the conflicts over them that occur between facilities management personnel and academic staff. Coordination is often lacking. She mentions disputes over furniture and space for internet access. The review is useful. The lecture hall and the classroom as inherited from the past are being reconsidered (and reconfigured) from the perspective of electronic use. Obviously forms of teaching depending upon computer projections or online teaching are handicapped by the absence of proper spatial and technical outlets. 'Talk and chalk' rooms mix social interaction and the sharing of ideas. In older buildings significant lags in upgrades occur as the result of disagreements over priorities. Retrofitting existing structures is also a more challenging and costly undertaking. It is the case that more equipment-dependent learning requires alterations in space appropriation. One result, according to Marmot, is that 'university effectiveness' is enhanced and 'improved learning' results, if merely because of fewer distractions (70). Perhaps. But technology has also increased distractions because of software and hardware failings and because every campus needs to have a host of specialists on call. None of this is cheap. All of it is time-consuming.

New forms of technology in teaching offer new opportunities; and in many disciplines, particularly scientific and technical subjects, cutting edge research and teaching for defined careers are inconceivable without the innovations. But that is merely to say that the technology is forcing adaptations. Whether this means that in some larger sense learning is 'improving' rather than just being different, or that university 'effectiveness' is boosted remains a question seeking an answer. Perhaps it is not true that the best form of education, as in the image of the 'Log Cabin' view of American liberal teaching, is a student on one end of a teeter-totter and a fine teacher on the other, but that simple image remains compelling. With all the sophistication now available to us, many graduates recall that single teacher who made all the difference.

Those contributors who wish to go beyond how space is used to prescribe how it may be used to improve learning are, as already mentioned, handicapped by the absence of pertinent historical comparisons. The possible transformative effects are being discussed in a vacuum, producing a running assumption that attention to the physical university can lead to a radical understanding of how learning takes place. Beyond that, we abound in theories regarding cognition. Keeping abreast of learning theory with so much speculation available, so many partisans of this view or that, while bearing in mind that different age groups and different student populations learn differently because of upbringing, the culture of the home or, where relevant, social class values, is a real stretch. Those contributors to the collection who seek a consensus about how the physical campus can somehow provide a united and superior learning culture have an uphill fight.

The essay in the volume where an element of historical attention is most evident and advocacy less apparent is Chapter 8 by Anthony Ossa-Richardson. Free of the lexical overreaching present in some chapters, he tells us what architects, planners, or thinkers hoped to achieve rather than what they ought to have achieved. He notes, with proper reference to Anglo-American educational ideals—Cardinal Newman et al.—that ideas about liberal education seem to recur despite the present-day emphasis on vocational or instrumental education. He appreciates the attempts of the university builders of the 1960s and beyond to capture the surviving spirit of the Victorian idea of a university: space meant for self-exploration. Basil Spence, in his design for Sussex University, revived quadrangles and cloisters. In Spence's view, the campus must never be complete because the ideal of a liberal education requires ongoing self-understanding, unencumbered by dogma and preconceptions. A spatial vision thus coincides with an educational vision. For Sir Andrew Derbyshire, the principal architect of York and one to whom the volume is dedicated, the open campus flirts with (democratic) socialism since the arrangement of structures eschews a sense of hierarchic centralization.

In reaction to the open campus, and to a conception of liberal education that values contemplation and introspection, we find one school of architects whose aim is to 'counteract the loneliness of modern man' (137). That modern man is lonely is one of those large generalizations well-embedded in the sociological literature. David Riesman's discussions of the historical shift from 'tradition-directed' and 'inner-directed' man to 'outer-directed' is already sixty years old. Of the three ideal-types, it is the last that is most in need of company,[7] or as the contributors would say, most in need of social space.

More recently, Riesman's larger point is captured in a different metaphor in Robert D. Putnam's essay and book of some fifteen years ago. Modern man, he wrote, increasingly bowls alone instead of in leagues. But in revisiting his former thesis, challenged by others, Putnam puts a more positive emphasis on 'civil society', the arena of social activity that lies outside the boundaries of government. He finds many examples of communities voluntarily pulling together to achieve social and political goals. Even Craigslist, the online source for exchanging goods and services, performs a valuable social function.[8]

Planning ideas can be exciting. But do they work as intended? The York campus, states Ossa-Richardson, has been criticized for being open to the point of confusing pedestrians, or, paradoxically, even too coercive in its celebrated freedoms, meaning, I suppose, too insistent on being open without landmark beacons—'hierarchical' structures—and thus defeating

---

[7] David Riesman et al., *The Lonely Crowd* (New Haven, CT, 1950).
[8] Robert D. Putnam, *Bowling Alone: the Collapse and Revival of American Community* (New York, 2000); Putnam & Lewis M. Feldstein, *Better Together: Restoring the American Community* (New York, 2003).

political planning intentions. Hierarchical they may be, but the Campanile at Berkeley and the Hoover Tower at Stanford function well as orientation points. What would one do without the ability to meet under the clock at Waterloo Station in London? Criticisms of open spaces in other new universities in Britain focus on their exposure to the vagaries of the English climate.

Brett Bligh distinguishes between two types of campus dwellers. Some are 'denizens' who are only 'partly enfranchised' while others, fully enfranchised, are 'citizens' because their opinions matter (35). The first group, lacking influence in space use, cannot fully enjoy the benefits of campus life. Are we then to assume that the others acquire a sense of spatial belonging that enhances their capacity for thinking and understanding? How can one ever know? In re-telling the story of the aspirations of the architects of new greenfields universities, Ossa-Richardson hesitates. He makes the salient point that while architecture provides spaces for social contacts, intellectual contacts are not so readily assured.

Flattering remarks about a particular educational experience can always be found. Histories of student groups are filled with accounts of circles and lasting friendships that began at college or university. Such friendships are often as important for learning, to include learning about oneself, as the tutorial and the classroom, the lecture hall and the laboratory. It is however true that the experiences tend to merge, and memories survive in a blur. Yet the general question asked in the volume about how to evaluate the merits of space is worth asking repeatedly. How have spatial arrangements contributed to the formation of vital circles of influence? Does the wide corridor, to take an instance already cited, facilitate learning and social interaction more than the narrow one? And what about spaces that were not planned, or seem not to be planned with social interaction in mind (or maybe were?) but have been praised by graduates? The Oxford and Cambridge college staircases, for example, creaky, winding, even precarious, are often recalled with special affection. If spaces are texts that need to be read, the staircases have certainly been read by the generations using them.

The staircase is the opposite of open. It is closed, confined space, restricting the numbers of users. Possibly it contains an element of mystery, much as the celebrated 'S'-curve pattern of eighteenth-century theorists could be transformed into garden paths whose turns were concealed by shrubbery, adding an element of agreeable surprise to a walk.

Or perhaps the creaky staircases, a planning device almost never to be found in American institutions, simply suggest antiquity. Antiquity in turn suggests prestige, ancient colleges and universities that got into the field before competitors arose. Prestige attracts applicants. One contributor notes as much. Often enough, the glorious facades of brand-name institutions contrast with dark, tattered, and draughty interiors. Famous and expensive American universities seem to have a plentiful supply of disagreeable student residence halls. How much does this matter? Accounts of friendships gained at university are most often associated with institutions of high selection, those that are now full players in the global ranking game. It may well be the case that selection itself is the dominant variable, bringing together students whose backgrounds and abilities make mutual and fruitful interaction possible. They find spaces and turn them into places. Because they have been selected, competitively or not, deserving or not, the privileged students acquire a sense of confidence which is a certain handmaiden to learning.

We are on safer empirical ground when we consider space as territory for collecting research talent. Eugene Trani, for example, discusses the effect of scientific research on campus design. As a prime example, he provides the new gigantic medical complex of the University of California, San Francisco Mission Bay, the largest biomedical construction project in the world. The evidence seems to establish that space design can certainly improve collaboration. Insofar as research is heavily interdisciplinary, I can well believe that minimizing the physical barriers between academic units is a benefit. In fact, the history of what in some institutions are called Organized Research Units or centres that draw participants from many relevant disciplines is evidence of their success. Visitors contribute to the energy of such units. Insofar as postgraduate students, or even some undergraduates, are allowed to share in the facilities and conversations of the centres, an expanded view of specialized research is gained. However, this is not the world of liberal education as handed down in many forms through the centuries, although indirect influences may exist.

For the potential Nobel laureate, what makes a difference are talented colleagues and disciples. The Nobel Museum in Stockholm has a display that shows the exact locations where scientific talent was bunched. We know that 'centres of excellence' advance discovery and application. We know that spatial features that allow for the fullest interaction at top levels are successful. Tea-time at the Cavendish Laboratory at Cambridge remains a much-praised ritual for scientific exchange. Within the high-tech communities of Silicon Valley or elsewhere, the concentration of talent is a commanding object. These communities, science parks in a sense, have borrowed from campus planners. But as parts of Silicon Valley have also moved north into the downtown area of San Francisco, the city replaces the campus while the principle of congregating ability remains foremost.

Insofar as selection suggests inequalities, some planners and thinkers are all the more keen on designs that favour a more egalitarian exploration of space, Derbyshire's bits of socialism. Since the end of the Second World War, as provision for higher education expanded beyond any historical precedent, access issues attracted design attention. Conceptions about social class, many drawn from left-wing political views and manifested in 'reproduction' theory—universities merely reflect the hierarchies in society and 'reproduce' them—found their way into the literature of campus planning. Such ideas were and are at variance with older democratic beliefs in the university as a medium for individual upward social mobility. They are also at variance with the idea of competition for place. Inclusion often means exclusion.

The most straightforward ideological interpretation of space is Mike Neary's chapter on the university and the city. He begins with large generalizations, such as 'The continuing assault on universities by governments of capitalist nation states around the world', and he notes with approval what he terms 'the emergence of radical alternative models of higher education created by academic and student activists' (203). Neary mentions the authoritarian nature of the modern state, the practice of 'state violence', 'the militarization of higher education', the 'aggressive control of student marches and punitive prosecutions against students'. Student marches there may be, but to omit how many of these end in the destruction of property and persons and draw in idle bystanders and street people seeking thrills is hardly faithful to history. Shall we argue about the cause of this? Predictably Neary deplores the market orientation of current government policies, but in truth he is not alone. This is a criticism widely shared without Neary's ideological commitments. But the criticism also depends upon one's understanding of markets, how they function and how they are used or not used by governments. Students are 'consumers' (Riesman placed his lonely man in the world of markets). The financing of higher education has created a 'pedagogy of debt' and a 'poverty of student life'. He alludes to a 'resurgence of Marxist social theory' and confidently proclaims a 'current crisis' of higher education. In support of these encompassing and shopworn views, sadly in need of nuance, perspective, and qualification, he cites a number of allies. These are old quarrels, and it is rather surprising to encounter them again in such naked form. But if past debates are any guide, parties to the disagreements will not be shaken in their primary beliefs.

The entré to Neary's presentation (and several others in the volume) is the work of the French thinker, Henri Lefebvre. A translation of his massive and formidable treatise under the English title *The Production of Space* appeared in 1991 and is often reprinted. As is typical of schools of twentieth-century French scholarship and philosophy, Lefebvre's analysis of space has a staggering range. It draws from almost every imaginable source: thinkers like Hegel, Marx, Nietzsche and Freud, Sartre and Foucault; movements such as Surrealism, Dada, or existentialism; and more recent ideas associated with semiotics, deconstruction, and critical theory. Popular culture, poetry, song, and the carnival attracted Lefebvre's attention. He applied his understanding of space to the sociology of urban life, gaining insight into it from two years spent as a taxi driver in Paris. Risking his life in the French Resistance, he was also a communist but broke from the Party in 1956 after Nikita Kruschev revealed the magnitude of Stalin's crimes.

As is typical of thinkers of great breadth, an immense number of sources and observations, hypotheses and speculations tumble out upon one another. Although connected, they can also be applied discretely. Readers are therefore free to borrow one part while ignoring the whole. However, Lefebvre's basic premises, and the conclusions issuing from them, are clear enough. The neo-marxist element is the strongest paradigm in a work many-layered, ponderous, and convoluted. Lefebvre starts by mentioning the historical journey from mathematical to mental space and criticizes previous philosophers for failing to realize how space is never just mental, or as he puts it, 'extra-ideological'. It is social. It is never empty but a code that must be decoded. Furthermore, space is controlled by the dominant class in society which, as a marxist, Lefebvre associates with capitalists who determine the forces of production and turn them into social relations.

The capitalist control of space is deliberately undefined, insists Lefebvre, in order to conceal its real meaning, which is actually 'violent', that is to say, synonymous with 'power'. Euphemisms such as civic peace, consensus, or non-violence conceal the truth of space use. The urban dweller merely thinks that trees, squares, or town parks are meant for his or her enjoyment; and while this appears to be true, the issue of who pays for the enjoyment is ignored. Space is non-productive consumption since all it yields is pleasure (as if pleasure has no fundamental value of its own). And then there is space that is obviously of benefit to someone but not everyone, space that is private for garages or space that is given over to fast roads, space that is taken from the city at large. Insofar as space is also used for knowledge production, it follows that whoever controls the space also controls the knowledge that takes place within it. That knowledge is the possession of the dominant class. As David Harvey concludes in an Afterword, *The Production of Space* is 'an intensely political document'.[9]

---

[9] Henri Lefebvre, *The Production of Space*, trans. David Nicholson Smith (Oxford, 1991), 1–11, 358–9, 415, 425–31.

The utopian element in this greatly abbreviated summary, and the policy direction explicit within it, is that city space needs to be taken from the dominant class and broadly shared. When that happens, knowledge becomes the possession of all. One other feature is that as capitalist space use is inherently divisive, the knowledge associated with it is also divided into disciplines. As Neary frames the argument, Lefebvre believes that the present-day stress on interdisciplinary studies is both 'dogmatic' and 'authoritarian'. A true convergence of all the sciences cannot occur until the city has been returned to those with rights to it. A city that is inclusive must have a knowledge base that is itself inclusive. Radical alternatives are required.

We need to proceed from abstract theory to practice, and Neary provides an example. The radical educational alternative that he recounts is in fact one that exists and one to which he is connected. It is the Social Science Centre (SSC) at Lincoln in the United Kingdom established in 2010 as a response, says Neary, to government policies that led to an increase in student debt. The Centre is opposed to market discipline and aspires to be a home for academics 'for whom a critique of capitalist modernity is the substance of their academic discipline', that is to say, 'subversive knowledge' (210). The Centre is non-profit, supported by 70 members, who, if able, pay a nominal subscription fee. Donors are welcome, and no one is compensated for working with the Centre. Ten leaders manage the Centre, their occupations varying from school leaver, a banker, and those already teaching in schools. The principles guiding the Centre are regarded as cooperative, 'democratic', and 'non-hierarchical'. Courses are designed in common. They draw from all the disciplines, while embodying 'the controversialist constructivist theme that all sciences are essentially social' (211). The relevant spatial element is that the Centre is part of Lincoln. Space is shared with the city, as are sites and offices used for other programmes. Museums, cafés, galleries, even homeless shelters interconnect with the Centre.

SSC is a tiny outpost of radical fervour. Its founders are at war with society as they understand it. The United States has a long history of breakaway colleges and educational experiments, but by contrast these are ideals well supported by American history and culture. They were closer in tone and style to past understandings of a humanistic education; they were meant to be restorative rather than radical alternatives drawing their inspiration from what might be regarded as alien influences. Well-known are Rollins in Florida, which gave rise to Black Mountain College in North Carolina, and the two colleges of St. John's, one in Annapolis, Maryland, the other in Santa Fe, New Mexico. The experimental colleges incorporated ideas of community and breadth in learning in contradistinction to the specialized trends that were to dominate higher education. One underlying assumption amongst their founders I am fairly certain was that America was losing its way, moving in directions away from its roots, and that past values had to be regained through the handful of students whom the colleges would educate. Gerald Grant and David Riesman referred to this trend in American higher education as a 'perpetual dream'.[10] One of its most ambitious manifestations, unique because public rather than private, are the colleges of the University of California at Santa Cruz. The hopes of President Clark Kerr who inspired the conception, and was himself influenced by the Quaker ideals of Swarthmore College in Pennsylvania, have not been realized as he wished.

The neo-marxist or heterodox-marxist agenda of Neary, or the SSC, declares allegiance to a different intellectual and theoretical heritage, but one of its aspiration fits loosely with the American experimental colleges. These colleges, small and relatively isolated, nevertheless thought of themselves as outposts of a true educational narrative and one that might influence undertakings elsewhere. Similarly, Neary hopes that the model of cooperative learning taking place within the city whose streets have been reclaimed from the domination of money might inspire undertakings elsewhere in the British higher education landscape. How he can entertain this wish in light of his depiction of capitalist society is puzzling. I would not be especially optimistic in any case. Black Mountain College disappeared after a short period, and Rollins became more conventional. The two St. John's Colleges, small but steady, carry on, but their version of liberal education is the 'perpetual dream' long accepted in American history.

It is conceivably possible for a small educational initiative that is not dependent upon substantial sums for survival to literally find space for itself, but let us note the irony that it is within the context of a society and a culture identified as the enemy that even a soi-disant revolutionary initiative can find a haven. The contradictions of capitalism? Lefebvre refers to the 'contradictions of space' implicit in capitalism, an argument repeated by marxist thinkers as if it were a major breakthrough in thought. All of lived human experience is contradictory at some level, and there cannot be cultural or economic change that is not disruptive. It is true that non-marxist economists refer to the creative destruction of technological innovation driven by capital. How one regards this is indeed moral or political, but one would hope for some objectivity in making the judgments.

---

[10] Gerald Grant & David Riesman, *The Perpetual Dream: Reform and Experiment in the American College* (Chicago, 1978).

But the larger narrative is far more interesting, or to quote from the chapter by Paul Benneworth, 'late capitalist society is immensely complex'. Lefebvre would agree. Capitalism wants it that way, and he himself favours simplicity as utopians are wont to do. Benneworth's remark is an understatement. It is also surprising to read his determined statement, citing another author, that 'universities were not established to train lawyers' (219-20). It is true that they adopted a canon of broader studies derived from the Roman Seven Liberal Arts, but that canon of 'inferior' studies was preparation for professional or 'superior' studies. The issue was settled more than a century ago when Hastings Rashdall uncovered the roots of the medieval university in the professional needs of court and city.

Western nations may embrace some version of market economics, albeit intermixed with distributionist policies—social democracy is not exactly dead as Neary believes. Governments are often short-sighted in their higher education policies and burdened with bureaucratic structures, but modern liberal societies are also pluralistic, multi-ethnic, reasonably tolerant while riven with disagreements, open to public and voter pressure, and far more partial to individual experiments than one would gather from reading theorists of the class determinants of social space.

No one denies that the public financing of higher education in an era of competing social demands is a problem, although it is not the same problem nor the same degree of a problem in all advanced societies. We suffer from an overload of social problems, all of which demand a slice of the public purse and the consent of taxpayers. Every year brings another expensive problem: water shortages in California, prison overcrowding, gun violence (an American disease), aging, the decline in the population of frogs, the spread of mutated viruses, drug abuse, unemployment, poverty, corrupt politicians, an unsafe and dangerous world requiring military expenditures. The list is unending. However much we hope that the citizens of free societies make the funding of higher education into the highest of priorities, disagreements over how to distribute resources is a never-ending dispute. It is difficult to imagine a political or economic system that makes decision-making simpler. History does not justify much hope. However, it is not difficult to imagine that no problem can be addressed by societies failing to generate sufficient wealth, however much we might hope that income disparities be less acute.

Market discipline has demerits, transforming culture into getting and spending as Matthew Arnold phrased it 150 years ago. The appeal to consumers varies from utter trivia and vulgarity to smooth advertising layouts. Read correctly, markets also provide needed information. What we term open markets in education are hardly new, extending back in America to virtually the founding of the Republic. They were certainly a feature of the important increase in student access in the Victorian period. Furthermore, we have to remember that the word 'market' also includes the education purchased by states. Market economies are hardly without merits. Market differentiation now includes every conceivable kind of institution at every conceivable cost. Ted Tapper and David Palfreyman remind us that 'higher' really means 'tertiary' education.[11] No advanced democracy has yet to demonstrate that a mass educational system can be funded at elite levels.

The role of the state in Britain has changed, Tapper and Palfreyman explain in a comprehensive and empirical analysis. Government interacts with markets in complex and diverse ways to the point where 'regulated markets' and central 'steering' have been reshaping tertiary education in the United Kingdom.[12] More bureaucratic 'meddling' is one outcome; but complaints notwithstanding, the directions of this outcome are seldom uniform. The late Burton R. Clark closely investigated new, market-oriented universities in various countries and demonstrated that active campus leadership, when combined with energetic professorial co-operation, outreach, and imaginative programming, can breathe new vitality into the world of post-secondary education.[13]

Generations of writers, professors, intellectuals, advocates of every stripe have raised our expectations of the importance of education to the point where hardly anyone appears satisfied with the systems of tertiary education that have emerged. But insofar as modern society rests upon the advanced knowledge coming out of universities, so much of it exhilarating and promising with respect to how lives may be led, it is irritating to encounter glib conclusions like Neary's that higher education is in 'crisis'. What we have are a staggering number of disagreements over the meaning and purpose of higher education. This cannot be surprising if we but state the obvious. Our advanced societies are composed of competing interests and demands, from government agencies, educational specialists, research organizations, religious groups, lobbyists, identity groups, affinity groups, special interests to other forms of public pressure. Universities and colleges struggle to accommodate these interests. Contributors to the volume do

---

[11] David Palfreyman & Ted Tapper, *Reshaping the University, the Rise of the Regulated Market in Higher Education* (Oxford, 2014), pp. v-vi, 5, 21.

[12] And elsewhere. See Guy Neave, *Prometheus Bound: the Changing Relationship between Government and Higher Education in Western Europe* (Oxford/New York, 1991); Neave, *The Evaluative State, Institutional Autonomy and Re-engineering in Higher Education in Western Europe: the Prince and His Pleasure* (London, 2012).

[13] Burton R. Clark, *Creating Entrepreneurial Universities: Organizational Pathways of Transformation* (Oxford/New York, 1998).

recognize this difficult context, although they may state the issues differently or more passionately and arrive at different remedies.

If we turn from what planners and architects hope to achieve to how students actually inhabit spaces, the contribution on China deserves special attention. Zhongyuan Zhang opens his chapter with a tribute to Lefebvre for inspiring his analysis. That is entirely possible. Yet his account of how students carve out special enclaves, or translate existing university norms into features more congenial to them, could arguably be written without the spatial theories framework of the French thinker.

We would expect a communist and authoritarian government that is the principal founder and funder of universities to pay particular regard to political and ideological dimension. It does; but the story has fascinating byways. As the author explains in a fine chapter on the creation of a new (deliberately unnamed) university in China, campus planning also incorporates features associated with China's rapid concern for modernization. It is reflected in white and gray modern buildings, the architectural grouping of disciplines connected by roads and pathways to support interdisciplinarity but also for the convenience of managers and bureaucrats. A sameness of design and endless corridors are bewildering to students. Cyclists and pedestrians once had their run of the campus, but the explosion of automobiles in a China of growing wealth, and expensive cars into the bargain, has produced a contest for parking space to the detriment of those unable to pay parking charges.

The monolithic character of the campus is softened by attention to landscaping and by the provision of a large lake. Other features are those typically found in American universities: residence halls, sports grounds, and restaurants, the latter almost unimaginably huge. Numbers matter.

The story that is being told is not just about a gigantic version of a new campus, or an expanding older one that may be found in other parts of the world. As the author well understands, it is the charivari element that is so arresting. Chinese students are no more comfortable with vast scale and homogeneity than students elsewhere. They continually undermine, reject, or mock the spatial assumptions regarding scale, authority, and management embedded in their given learning environment. Much as an American student will remake campus landscapes by cutting across lawns instead of staying to paths or soften the bland aspect of a dormitory room by hanging pictures and posters, spreading assorted objects around, and positioning family photos as reminders of home, so do Chinese students personalize their new university.

The examples are delightful. First, students choose sites in which to gather that lie outside the stifling spaces created for them, or rather for the benefit of a government programme of modernization. The sites contain cheap food stalls, some of them illegal (cheap and not so cheap food trucks now line the streets outside major campuses in the United States, providing exotic alternatives to cafeteria food). Second, they carve out private space around the campus or create lovers' lanes in the area of the lake. Third, they rename spaces or mock them, as well as tampering with the statues of heroes of the communist realm. (I have seen this done with respect to the statue of a prominent philosopher of Lund University, who occasionally sports a clown's red nose.) Fourth, they establish individual space within libraries or other structures, piling up personal possessions and scaring off possible student invaders, or leave their mark on benches and tables with inscriptions and graffiti. Fifth is the use of social media for derisive and satiric remarks about campus authorities. A reverse politicization appears to be occurring says the author. The conclusion appears rather elevated given the long history of student pranks. Could it be just a mild and passing challenge to ideological egalitarianism, or what is so often the case, a need to annoy adults in students coming of age?

But if these daily efforts to countermand the intentions of a locality created by officials have a lasting benefit, this might be in the form of memories of a period of life in which individuality and personality gave special purpose to campus life. And perhaps those memories were more important as an expression of self-identity than any knowledge gained from books. Might we say that in the day of the huge, bureaucratic and managed university, students are finding the means to create their own versions of a rounded education?[14]

The study of the campus as a built artifact, as a space made into place, and its intersection with other constructed spaces such as cities, has a fairly long history. As stated in the introduction to the book, hundreds of novels about universities—the genre goes back to at least John Henry Newman's *Loss and Gain* about Oxford—convey a sense of the university as a place with its own character. But it is true, judging from the chapters in this volume, and from the references and citations to so many writings, that far more attention is being paid to the many ways in which walls, paths, rooms, and landscapes are arranged, can be arranged, or should be arranged depending upon use and purpose. Since all of human activity, actual and imaginary, is locational, the campus, the city, the corporate headquarters, the military post, the shopping mall, the transportation hub

---

[14] My own version of how student sub-cultures eventually alter the received university culture appears in Rothblatt, *The Revolution of the Dons: Cambridge and Society in Victorian England* (Cambridge, 1981).

are fair game. Scholars have risen to the challenges, works in these areas now being abundant.

Paul Temple, in his introductory remarks, identifies some of the salient problems that arise as investigators attempt to make sense of a built environment. One, as noted elsewhere in this review, is that 'texts' (buildings, grounds, sculpture, frescoes) are read differently across the generations and across cultures. Whatever the architect or designer intended, and it is fascinating to read about those intentions, no universal reading is guaranteed. Furthermore, mistakes are made, as on the Chinese campus where automobiles have pushed walkers and bikers aside. The original conception is then defeated by unanticipated changes. This is virtually an historical law.

A bigger issue is always one of trying to evaluate whether anyone notices or cares whether this bush is chosen in preference to another or whether, at the end of a walk, a statue awaits, or whether a particular roof line echoes one across the campus, or whether an older building paraphrases a newer one. Contributors disagree on the appeal of glossy brochures and virtual or actual tours as recruitment devices, but university public relations officers will continue to use any means to attract notice to the campus. After all, haven't the authors represented in this volume repeatedly told us that we inhabit an overwhelmingly market culture? And is it not the case that our campuses have large supporting staffs that are not directly engaged in the work of education but rely upon outreach efforts for their careers?

But as advertising goes on, we are still left with the question of how much of the elaborate investment into place-making has yielded results. How much does the busy city-dweller notice as he or she rushes about? Does it make a difference? Is the quality of life itself improved, or the opposite, the anxiety of coping with the madding crowd? The lavish attention paid by an architect to the design of a building's upper storey is missed when, head-down, a pedestrian dashes into an underground passage. The undergraduate, in my experience, also head-down, rushes across campus to lecture, library, and examination hall, seemingly unaware of the care taken in creating arresting surroundings. If the campus is designed to be educational, perhaps students need to be systematically instructed in its virtues, a good subject for orientation week.

Yet for a moment, let us set aside some of the more sophisticated reasoning about the 'contours of space and place' and pursue the view-point that time, effort, and money spent on the campus as a place for learning has positive results. Perhaps the results cannot be precisely tabulated in learning outcomes, as 'outputs' and 'outcomes' as Temple puts it. But as education ideally should reach beyond itself, the results may be rewarding in other ways. If, as Aristotle says, we achieve our fullest humanity within the *polis,* then perhaps our higher educational selves are realized within the campus setting. What follows is an American example, where the whole business of campus place-making first commenced.

A half-year or more before graduating high schools, thousands of pupils visit campuses around the nation in the hope of finding a suitable fit before submitting multiple applications for admission. These brief sojourns, usually accompanied by parents and sometimes involving scheduled meetings with admission officers, professors, or undergraduates already in residence, are scraps and clues as to the kind of educational experience awaiting prospective candidates. The smallest bits are recorded, assessed, weighed, and pondered. Were the meetings hospitable? Were the institutional representatives welcoming? What questions did the seekers forget to ask? Comparisons are made, a list of priorities and hopes compiled, and then follows the long waiting period in which the mysteries and rituals of selection are undertaken.

Objectively, we might think that little can be gained from such campus visits beyond impressions, with some prior hearsay tossed into the backpacks, or perhaps reports from friends or relatives who have attended prospective colleges and universities. After all, classrooms appear the same throughout the world. Instructors drone on in much the same way. As a collection of structures, plantings, lakes, and art scattered about the grounds has by now fairly common sources, colleges and universities resemble one another. Despite the hype and claims, few colleges and universities among the thousands are genuinely unique, especially since the academic profession consists of interchangeable parts. And no simple formula exists to predict the jumble of courses, examinations, essays, friends, instructors likely to be encountered. The undergraduate experience occurs during late adolescence and the transition to young adulthood. It is intermixed with the personal problems of detaching from home and adjusting to far-away circumstances, never uniform across a student population and varying with the historical ages. Consequently the contemplation of any academic future is initially fraught with insecurities.

But let us not underestimate the visual wonders of artfully constructed environments. Busy urban-dwellers do notice and love spaces designed for their benefit. *Pace* Lefebvre: the High Line in Manhattan, a pedestrian walk recovered from an unused elevated railway and lined with plantings, seating, food vendors, and offering wonderful vistas, is crowded with people in the act of gaining pleasure from the city. If this is 'unproductive space' or 'controlled consumption', so be it.

I should not reduce the campus to a simple formulaic level. Nor collectively do the contributors make this mistake. The American campus, and now its many spin-offs and copies around the globe, has been carefully nurtured, spatially developed, and filled with artifacts, symbols, follies, visual attractions, landscaping, and structures precisely to beckon to students, persuade parents to support them, and appeal to the alumni who will remember Alma Mater with affection and largess. The Victorian poet Matthew Arnold noted that Oxford whispered its enchantments (the last enchantments of the middle ages). The American campus may not always whisper so much as bludgeon, but the effect is meant to be similar. Even if the appeal of the campus to potential students falls short of the expectations of administrators and trustees, no institution can ultimately attempt to do without beckoning spaces.

These observations nevertheless require a caveat. Those contributors to the volume who view the campus as a collection of privileged and expensive spaces, or territory manipulated by a managerial and profit-hungry elite with 'disenfranchised' others will welcome it. The thousands of young Americans seeking matriculation through the mechanism of campus visits are still but a small portion of those transitioning from secondary to tertiary education. The majority enter public institutions nearer to home, sometimes private colleges and universities in accessible urban settings. Cost is the dominant factor, since residence is too expensive for most. The campus seekers, if they are not being recruited from lower-income families, are relatively affluent, sometimes very comfortable, who, along with their supporting parents, are searching for the right place that will provide both a special learning experience and a leg-up in career chances.

The real challenge is therefore finding ways in which any educational experience that provides learners with a sense of pride and self-confidence, of being humanly important, can be offered to those whose academic careers will not take place on the campus *qua* campus. We have to follow in the lead of those who believe that people are most at home when they know that they matter. Whatever doubts we may entertain about the measurable contributions of space dedicated to academic achievement, what is certain is that no-one derives any educational benefit from working in an environment that is dangerous and degrading.

We still have to believe that education at its best is a liberalizing and a civilizing experience—the almost hidden theme that Ossa-Richardson finds winding its way through all kinds of new construction. The purpose of the campus goes beyond what is directly gained in the classroom. Any spatial setting that is beautiful, that encourages the making of friends, that provides places for individual reflection, that strengthens a freedom of mind and whispers the enchantments of the middle ages or any other age is beneficial to all. We need to believe that because in the finest sense it is true.

Besides, the opposite is unthinkable.

Department of History
University of California, Berkeley

In Mary Lyon's Footsteps:
The Historiography of Mount
Holyoke College

Joel T. Rosenthal

This is not a history of Mount Holyoke College.[1] Rather, it is a survey of the imposing body of historical writing that has focused on and told the story of Mount Holyoke, the oldest women's college in the United States. Mount Holyoke was founded in 1837 as Mount Holyoke Female Seminary, in 1888 becoming Mount Holyoke Seminary and College, and finally, in 1893 becoming Mount Holyoke College, as it has been ever since. Its founding and guiding genius was Mary Lyon (1797–1849).[2] The seminary came into existence as a result of her crusade for women's education, now (that is, in 1837) taking shape with a dedicated building and with sufficient funding to stand on its own—a mecca for the education and training of young women who would go out to become teachers and/or missionaries and/or missionaries' wives. Lyon's vision of the education of women, her labours to establish her institution, and her success in setting it on its feet constitute an important and, indeed, an awe-inspiring chapter in the Horatio Alger tales of nineteenth-century America.[3]

---

[1] My thanks to Leslie Fields and Deborah Richards of the Mount Holyoke archives and special collections, to Amber Douglas of the Mount Holyoke Department of Psychology, and to Judith Bennett, alumna and distinguished medieval historian. The open resources of the New York Public Library and the Library of Congress have been invaluable. Errors of fact rest at my door and the opinions expressed are solely those of the author.

[2] Standing first among the 'seven sisters', their subsequent dates of foundation being: 1861 for Vassar, Matthew Vassar founder; 1871 for Smith, Sophia Smith founder; 1885 for Bryn Mawr, founded by the will of Joseph W. Taylor; 1870 for Radcliffe, Elizabeth C. Agassiz, founder; 1870 for Wellesley, Henry and Pauline Durant, founders; 1889 for Barnard, Annie Nathan Meyer principal founder.

[3] For basic information, the Mount Holyoke College web site; Kathryn Kish Sklar, 'The Founding of Mount Holyoke College', in Carol Ruth Berkin & Mary Beth Norton (eds), *Women of America: A History* (Boston, 1979), 177–201. On women's higher education in

A survey of the vast body of literature about Mount Holyoke—historical, biographical, administrative, official, literary, personal, distant, devoted, fictionalized, nostalgic, romanticized, or defying easy categorization— gives us a rich and complex case study in the larger tale of the emergence of women's higher education in the nineteenth century. A look at this whole body of literature places this particular story very much in the centre of the mega-narrative of women's history, of the social history of the Republic, and of that of higher education. The sheer volume of writing generated by and contributing to the many-handed and many-tiered enterprise of historicizing the seminary-college in South Hadley, Massachusetts, is most impressive. As an experiment that worked—a bold and novel venture that took root from the very start—Mount Holyoke has been chronicled and lauded by a long queue of admirers and friends, alumni, faculty, staff, academic historians, 'amateur' historians, and others who put pen to paper. Beyond this, Mary Lyon herself has been the subject (and heroine) of a virtual cottage industry of biography, figuring in work focused on her life and accomplishments and being drafted as a regular member of those diverse teams of men and women assembled in volumes of collective biography designed to offer role models, tales of adversity overcome, and 'real life' snapshots giving moral encouragement to readers young and old, male and female. And while these Mount Holyoke authorial-historiographic ranks are comprised mostly of women who turned to this task, a fair number of men have also contributed to the enterprise, one that has now run for almost two centuries. Even in a world where innumerable colleges and universities have had their history enshrined in a pious volume or two, Mount Holyoke still stands out for the attention it has received. As a ground-breaking experiment Mount Holyoke moved, from quite early in its history, to see that its tale was told and to support (and often to publish) an ever-growing body of material in the direction of what we can think of as an enterprise in 'self-historicization'.

To deal with this vast amount of material and to impose some order upon its diversity we will divide our material into several categories. For a college's history the traditional and customary way is to begin with a

the U.S.: Helen Lefkowitz Horowitz, *Alma Mater: Design and Experience in the Women's Colleges from their Nineteenth Century Beginnings to the 1930s* (New York, 1984): Mabel Newcomer, *A Century of Higher Education for American Women* (New York, 1959), written for the Vassar centenary: Thomas Woody, *A History of Women's Education in the United States* (1929; rprn New York/Lancaster, PA. 1970): Barbara Solomon, *In the Company of Educated Women: A History of Women and Higher Education in America* (New Haven, 1985): Margaret Nash, *Women's Education in the United States, 1780–1840* (New York, 2005). On the 'seven sisters', Elaine Kendall, *'Peculiar Institutions:' An Informal History of the Seven Sisters Colleges* (New York, 1975): Joan Marie Johnson, *Southern Women at the Seven Sisters Colleges: Feminist Values and Social Activism, 1875–1915* (Athens, GA, 2008).

narrative, that familiar (and largely chronological) saga that usually runs from the school's genesis (or even a bit before) to some point near the date of publication. Histories of this sort are a distinct and fair-sized genre of historical writing; hundreds of American institutions of higher learning have had their story set forth in this fashion.[4] After offering a survey of the various narrative histories of Mount Holyoke—some long, some short, some official publications, some individual or personal efforts—we can turn to biography. And though this obviously steers us to Mary Lyon—she being treated in and by an amazing number of books and book chapters—there also is a reasonable body of work on the very distinguished Mary E. Woolley (president, 1900–37), along with some studies of and memorials to other stalwarts of the Mount Holyoke family. But biography is mostly Mary Lyon, still more than holding her own in the annals of higher education, and comparing well in this regard even when set against or alongside her famous male counterparts from the nineteenth century.

However, neither narrative histories nor biographical studies, whether full-length or as chapters in volumes of collected essays, exhaust the full spread of historiographic material. There are various other types of publications (plus some valuable material still in manuscript form in the Mount Holyoke archives) that, if not always produced explicitly or deliberately to be a historical source or synthesis, nevertheless lend themselves to such an analysis, an example being the many biographical and alumni directories produced over the years. Then, beyond such material there are some sub-genres or side fields we can turn to such materials as works from the pens of Mount Holyoke's presidents, at some of the many student and alumnae efforts, at various creative writing and media presentations that merit a quick glance, at biographies of several early friends of the fledgling seminary, and at such miscellaneous items as the histories of 'daughter' colleges that were direct historical and ideological offspring of Mount Holyoke. For an institution that was never large and never impressively rich Mount Holyoke worked from the start to impose and export its mission, its sense of its history, and its keys to success. Furthermore, it did so in a rather outspoken fashion. It was never shy about proclaiming its path-breaking role.

A healthy view of self-worth emerged early in Mount Holyoke's history. Though no narrative history was to come for several decades, the 25th birthday in 1862 was, quite properly, considered as sufficient occasion for some looking back-looking forward. On what we are told was fairly short notice, there was both a birthday party and, of value to us, a volume that

---

[4] Joel T. Rosenthal, 'All Hail the Alma Mater: Writing College Histories in the U.S.', *History of Universities*, 27 (2013), 190–222.

chronicled the events for all to read. The commemorative volume was dedicated to 'the scattered daughters' of the Seminary and one does wonder if there is a touch of irony in the lament that—because of the short notice—*only* 800 guests came to the reunion. As would be the case with some subsequent volumes designed to record birthday festivities, that of 1862 covered events in numbing detail, telling us that some 600 people attended the official church service to hear Reverend Dr Kirk, President of the Trustees, deliver a very long address as a tribute to (the late) Mary Lyon. Other high spots were an original hymn (by Mrs L.H. Sigourney), the reading of letters of regret from alumni unable to attend, a sad greeting from a fading Zilpah Grant Banister (Mary Lyon's closest associate from early days), and still another sermon, this one by Rev. Mr Laurie of West Roxbury, who had been at Lyon's deathbed. In 1862 even 25 years for a women's institution was creditable and the numbers in each class (as well as those actually on hand) argued for success of the seminary, the classes growing larger almost every year. But while the 1862 volume is heavy on data and texts, it is light on analysis or any sort of synthetic narrative, virtually to the point of total absence. Perhaps in 1862 the founding years were still so fresh in memory that there was little need for an official wordsmith, though the ceremonies did catch enough of the public eye to get extensive coverage in the local papers, as fame grew and success seemed assured. A note of some interest: as far as the published proceedings are a guide, there was no mention of the Civil War.

Narrative history of Mount Holyoke properly began in 1876, the nation's centennial year, and it came in the form of a booklet of 21 pages, *Historical Sketch of Mount Holyoke Seminary, Founded at South Hadley, Mass., in 1837* (Washington DC). This brief history had been written in 'compliance with an invitation from the commissioner of education representing the Department of the Interior in matters relating to the National Centennial of 1876'. This little booklet seems to have touched all the bases: a campus now of 15 acres, buildings, early history, the course of study, expenses and fees, the lack of an endowment, the role of religion in the curriculum and in college life, etc. It was written by Mary Nutting (old girl, class of 1852; now the seminary's librarian) and published by the Government Printing Office, it being Mount Holyoke's response to a nation-wide call for college histories.[5] Though short, it was a very legitimate predecessor of more elaborate volumes that would follow:

---

[5] Much of the national impetus behind the move to write college histories came from Herbert Baxter Adams of Johns Hopkins: John Higham, 'Herbert Baxter Adams and the Study of Local History', *American Historical Review*, 89 (1984), 1225–39.

statistics, tabular presentations of classes and numbers, and a balanced discussion of the role of fervent but non-denominational Protestantism.

Full-fledged narrative history was introduced with the 50th birthday celebrations in 1887. Sarah D. Locke Stow, class of 1859, not only wrote a full-volume history (372 pages; much of it data, lists, etc., rather than narrative) but also edited a second volume designed to cover and report on the birthday festivities.[6] The Seminary—just about to become a college— had now come of age, forever to be first among the increasing number of women's colleges in the land and with a past worth trumpeting. Stow's narrative picked up with women's education from the seventeenth century onwards and then moved to and then beyond Mary Lyon: the years of Miss Chapin (1850–67), Miss French (1867–72), Miss Ward (1872–83), and now the reigning head, Miss Blanchard. We have what had quickly become the basic statistical presentations: numbers of students, their states of origin, class size, plus testimonials from alumni. There is a full chapter (chapter 21) on the institutions—still mostly seminaries in the 1880s— that had sprung from or had been modelled on Mount Holyoke (more on this, below). Stow's edited volume—chronicling the celebrations of June, 1887—was much in the footsteps of the comparable volume of 1862. Every faculty member from the beginning onwards got her own paragraph and her moment for reminiscences of the old days, in addition to reports from far-flung alumni groups, discussions of the medical and missionary work of alumnae, a talk on role of science in the curriculum, and those interminable sermons that audiences seemingly sat through (and then went home and read?).

Except for two small pamphlets this body of commemorative and historical material sufficed to bridge the years between 1887 and 1937. In 1893 Sara G. Snell, class of 1866, published, in 25 pages, *A Sketch of Mount Holyoke College, South Hadley, Massachusetts* (Florence, MA) in which she gave a brief but adequate account of the founding and subsequent success. In 1897 Henrietta E. Hooker's 21 page guidebook, first published in the *New England Magazine* and then printed on its own, served as both a brief history and a visitors' guidebook.[7] The celebrations of birthday 75, in October of 1912, were marked by the usual

[6] Sarah D. Locke Stow, *History of Mount Holyoke Seminary, South Hadley, Massachusetts, during Its First Half Century, 1837–1887* (Springfield, MA, 1887), and *Semi-Centennial Celebration of Mount Holyoke Seminary, South Hadley, Massachusetts, 1837–1887* (Springfield, MA, 1988: published by the Seminary).

[7] Henrietta E. Hooker, 'At Mount Holyoke', *Century Magazine* 49/3 (January 1895), 431–2; 'Mount Holyoke College', *New England Magazine* 15 (1897), 545–63.

commemorative volume but not by any burst of historical narrative. There was a considerable effort to use the 1912 birthday and reunion as a focused occasion for some serious fund raising; Mount Holyoke's role as the 'mother' of numerous 'daughter' schools and the launching pad for missionary activity—in the United States and abroad—and for women's higher education received considerable attention (and space in the volume). Probably for the last time, a significant number of class representatives from the mid-nineteenth century were there to be honoured; still one living member of the class of 1843, five from 1845, and a few others from the early decades. As a serious tribute to the College's historic role, the presidents of Bryn Mawr, Smith, Wellesley, and Vassar—sister schools and rivals—each had a turn at the podium, while the president of Lake Erie College, a daughter institution, received an honorary degree, as did the emeritus principal of the Huguenot College, Wellington, Cape Colony (a missionary daughter institution). The greeting from President Taft was particularly appropriate; his mother, Louisa Torrey, was an early alumna of the seminary.

There was little for our basket between the 75th birthday in 1912 and the great centennial celebrations of 1937. One piece of creative writing does stand out, a slight filler for that gap that covered both World War I and the worst days of the great depression. While hardly history, a play written in 1924 by Alzada P. Comstock, 'Mount Holyoke Milestones', contributed—in so far as it was produced, seen, or read—to the idea of how events, lives, and memories of the past just seemed to glide into those of the present, with the present an ever-moving point along the time line. Comstock's young heroine enters the seminary in 1872, her daughter enters what is now a college in 1896—very much a decade of change for the college—and finally her granddaughter comes along as a new student in 1923, the latter now having a boyfriend who, having seen the glories of a woman's college, comes out in favour of women's suffrage. The climactic line of the drama is 'this place is just the same and yet so different', a line that probably sums up the views of virtually every 'old girl' who ever came to a reunion.

Publications of the centennial year of 1937 are the high water mark of Mount Holyoke historiography; nothing that had gone before could measure up against the works produced in and in honour of that year. The many items published in that year give us a sort of international date line, everything else falling on one side or another—before and after the 100th birthday—and the flood of material centring around 1937 gives an idea of the strength of tradition that had built up by then and of the varieties of commemorative publication devised for the occasion. When Mount Holyoke celebrated a full century of existence it had no rivals for longevity among the women's college of the land.[8] Accordingly, as the college approached its famous birthday it had been decided to commission a comprehensive narrative history of the traditional sort: '100 years of Mount Holyoke and still counting' sort of volume. This would be a capstone to whatever else was planned by way of ceremonies and commemorations (and self-congratulation). Toward this end Arthur C. Cole, a respected American historian and professor at Western Reserve University, was chosen for the assignment.[9] Though various problems held up publication until 1940, Cole produced a fairly standard and a fully satisfactory narrative history.[10] The in-house committee that planned the centennial indicated, in the preface to Cole's history, that they wanted a history that would offer 'authoritative information' about Mount Holyoke while also covering the changing role of women in higher education since 1837. Though Cole followed the usual top-down style of most college histories he picked up the Mary Lyon tale well before 1837 and then he went on to offer a full and generally complimentary appraisal of the women who presided over the seminary (and then the college) after Lyon's death in 1849. Nor did his *A Hundred Years of Mount Holyoke College: The Evolution of an Educational Ideal* (New Haven, 1940) neglect student life, athletics, student publications, or other side-issues that gave some balance to the narrative, and he included tributes to Mary Woolley, now moving toward retirement after 37 years as president. As a special touch, Cole published some Emily Dickinson letters from her student days at the seminary. Like the majority of early women, the famous poet had left before completing the full course of study.

It seems a bit strange for a famous women's college with distinguished historians on its faculty to turn to an outsider, and to a man, for its centennial history, though there are other instances of choosing an outsider (and of successful college histories that resulted from it).[11] Since Mary Woolley was to be succeeded by the College's first male president—the transition taking place in the centennial year—one wonders if the

[8] Wheaton Women's Seminary, in Wheaton, Massachusetts, can trace itself back to 1834. However, it does not emerge as a full-fledged college until later in the nineteenth century and it never challenged Mount Holyoke's claim to seniority.

[9] Arthur C. Cole, a social historian, authored volume 7 of the 'History of American Life Series' and served as managing editor of the *Mississippi Valley Historical Review*, the leading scholarly journal devoted to American history (later to become the *Journal of American History*).

[10] It ran to 426 pages and was published by the Yale University Press for the College.

[11] Indiana University turned to Thomas D. Clark of the University of Kentucky for its four-volume history: *Indiana University: Western Pioneer* (Bloomington, 1970–7), and the University of Pittsburgh asked a non-academic writer to tell its tale: Robert Alberts, *The Story of the University of Pittsburgh 1787–1987* (Pittsburgh, 1986).

trustees, overwhelmingly male, had already deemed it time to alter heavy female and feminist face to the College and its image, the choice of Cole being a signal of this.[12] But against such speculation we should note that the preface, written by the centennial committee, does says that he was a strong choice, whatever the reality of the politics behind the decision. Nor, needless to say, is there any reference to outgoing President Woolley's campaign against the choice of her successor, Roswell G. Ham, coming from the Yale English Department and of no great distinction.[13] Though nothing in the record indicates that such distinguished in-house historians as Nellie Nielson or Bertha Putnam or Viola Barnes had sought this prestigious assignment, 1937 was a year of great transition—not all of it smooth—as well as of celebration. But regardless of the turmoil Cole's history does seem to have satisfied those who had commissioned him; no one has sought to replace his soup-to-nuts volume and it still stands, many years on, as the basic tale of Mount Holyoke's first century.[14]

While Arthur Cole's book is the noteworthy and very standard historical narrative written to mark the centennial year, it is only one of a large number of publications of 1937—some explicitly meant to be part of the official celebration, others perhaps independent efforts but no doubt timed for that great and famous year. Here we ignore our own boundary lines regarding the various categories of writings, focusing rather on 1937 as a collecting point for so much material. In addition to Cole's official history there was a detailed account of the birthday party as such; *The Centenary of Mount Holyoke, Friday and Saturday May Seven & Eight, Nineteen Thirty-Seven* (South Hadley, 1937), published by the College itself (whereas Yale University Press had published Cole's history). This volume, dedicated to the 17,472 daughters of the first century, covers the birthday party, sermons, speeches, and letters of congratulation from the U.S. and abroad, among its many riches. Speakers of all sorts, topped by old girl Frances Perkins, now Secretary of Labor in FDR's cabinet, addressed the role of women and higher education. Distinguished alumni awards were distributed

[12] In 1852 the principal's position—they were not 'presidents' until Elizabeth Mead in 1890—was offered to Albert Hopkins of Williams College, brother of Mark Hopkins, an offer that seems to have raised no gender-based objections, though Hopkins declined and Mary Chapin, acting principal after Lyon's sudden death, was now formally appointed.

[13] Woolley's opposition to Ham's appointment and her unsuccessful efforts to mobilize support for her position figure largely in her biographies: for the story in detail, see Ann Karus Meeropol, *Male President for Mount Holyoke College: The Failed Fight to Maintain Female Leadership, 1934–1937* (Jefferson, NC, 2014). Woolley had hoped to be succeeded by Mary Ashby Cheek, class of 1913, and the choice of Roscoe Ham, coming from the English Department at Yale, was a considerable shock to many.

[14] Cole's history has extensive notes but no bibliography. An appendix treats the portraits of Mary Lyon.

to fourteen recipients, alongside honorary degrees to Malvina Hoffman, the sculptor, and Eileen Power, the English medieval historian, among others. If those who attended the great occasion chose to take a break from the talks, there was an exhibition of alumni and faculty art as well as displays mounted by various academic departments. A representative from each year's class, going as far back as 1861, was also singled out for applause amidst the air of festivity and self-congratulation.[15]

This, we might say, is the official material produced by the college to note its 100th birthday. However, we are far from the sum total of publications spurred by and coinciding with the centennial. Louis Porter Thomas's *Seminary Militant: An Account of the Missionary Movement at Mount Holyoke Seminary and College* (South Hadley, 1937)—published by the English Department and running to 117 pages—explored one of the prime purposes behind the creation of the school. The background of the New England missionary movement, Mary Lyon's personal devotion to the cause, and then the fortunes of many of her students are all set forth. Young women came out of Mount Holyoke fired with evangelical zeal, though many went into the world as wives rather than on their own to teach, to convert, and to heal. It was a tale bespeaking great devotion: 'if counted worthy I should be willing to go', as Fidelia Fiske said on her way to Persia, presumably speaking for at least many of the 175 women who had been to 40 countries by 1887. Frances Lester Warner's *On a New England Campus* (Boston, 1937: published by Houghton-Mifflin) combined autobiography, a rather meandering biography of Mary E. Woolley (who did not want a formal biography), and anecdotes and reminiscences about the campus and campus life, looking at such incidents as when dinosaur bones had been uncovered on the grounds. Warner offered a survey of academic departments and college traditions, thereby adding a touch of gravitas to her breezy prose. The obligatory obeisance to Mary Lyon included some unflattering comments about the great lady's penmanship, though such frivolous touches were more than offset by quotations from students who had personal memories of Lyon. So while Cole's volume stands as the official history of the College, others also explored aspects of the story and some did so in a more reader-friendly style.

Moreover, if these books are college histories in the accepted sense, there are still other volumes in the honor roll of 1937. One item of note is the *One Hundred Year Biographical Directory of Mount Holyoke College,*

---

[15] In addition to Perkins's talk there were speeches from Mary Beard, on women's education, from Francis Sayer, undersecretary of state, on women and peace, and from Helen Monchow on a century of Mount Holyoke scholarship. Monchow was the daughter of Mary Chapin, Lyon's successor as principal.

1837–1937. This was produced by the Alumni Association, edited by Mary C.J. Higley, secretary of the association. It was not an official publication of the college but rather a complementary or co-sponsored volume, listing virtually *everyone* from the entire century: faculty, trustees, recipients of honorary degrees, each year's class (naming both graduates and non-graduates). For each alumna we get an address, birth dates along with those of children (plus their names and sex), the husband, a death date when relevant, and careers or professions. Though this wealth of detail comes with almost no historical narrative or analysis it is a goldmine of data, another of those labours of love that testify to the college's hold upon its family, and a tribute to the network of women who collected and arranged the data (often through widely scattered alumnae chapters, and long before the computer). The college's tradition of publishing student verse was still alive and well and in 1937 Ada L.F. Snell, chair of the English Department, edited *Mount Holyoke College Verse*, giving permanent form to a body of work that the undergraduates clearly were encouraged to produce.[16] Snell's *History of English Studies in Mount Holyoke Seminary and College, 1837–1937* (South Hadley, 1942) must also have been part of the centenary retrospective, though it was not published until 1942. And while it will be mentioned below when we turn to biography, Marion Lansing's *Mary Lyon through Her Letters* also appeared in 1937, the only item of that memorable year primarily focused on the founder. Finally, to bring home the significance of the 100-year span of the school in parallel with the nation's history, there was an exhibition of 100 volumes, each one marking, in its date of publication, one year of Mount Holyoke's existence. Nor was all the centennial attention devoted to written work. The 'Cavalcade of America', a popular middlebrow network radio programme, turned to the Mount Holyoke story for its October 6, 1937 broadcast. Lastly, hard on the heels of the centennial and seeking to capitalize on the nostalgia and publicity it had generated, in 1938 the College published a booklet, *Mount Holyoke College: Manual of Money Raising*, explaining that now to launch the second century, 'the outstanding need [is for] endowment'. The booklet contained form letters designed to simplify the paperwork for would-be donors, plus a chart pegging a good bequest against the age of a prospective donor.

After 1937 there may well have been a sense of anti-climax; short of the far-distant bicentennial of 2037 little was likely to match this great burst of publication, retrospection, transition, and publicity? There seems to have

---

[16] The 1937 volume, an official part of the centennial publications, was actually published by the Oxford University Press as the second volume of a collection: Ada L.F. Snell (ed.), *Mount Holyoke College Verse* (2 vols, Oxford, 1928–37).

been little by way of festivities in 1962 to mark 125 years. In 1973 the Alumni Association celebrated its own centennial year; Mary Higley Mills, class of 1921 and long-time secretary of the association, edited *The First Hundred Years of the Alumni Association of Mount Holyoke College,* giving another valuable reference book or directory with what was by now the standard categories of material: trustees, recipients of honorary degrees, class members and numbers, and more of such biographical and historical data.[17] But by 1987, when the school was coming up to an impressive and unrivalled 150th birthday, the world of higher education was changing. Narrative history was not in vogue among academic historians, some of the Seven Sisters were undergoing major changes (Radcliffe being subsumed into Harvard, Vassar going co-ed, others including Holyoke wrestling with this issue), and the future of private liberal arts colleges was uncertain, with both finances and enrolments as worrisome factors. So, for a combination of reasons, Mount Holyoke decided as early as 1983 against celebrating and then chronicling another birthday party, as least as far as a written record would stand: instead it was arranged to bring a series of high-level speakers to campus, and their talks were published by W. W. Norton, a commercial house, as John Mack Faragher & Florence Howe (eds), *Women and Higher Education in American History: Essays from the Mount Holyoke College Sesquicentennial Symposia* (New York, 1988). There was nothing here explicitly devoted to Mary Lyon, as presumably her stature was a given and hardly in need of more polishing. Rather, talks turned to such leaders in the field of women's education as Alice Mary Baldwin and Lucy Sprague Mitchell, alongside talks (and then papers) on the education of black women, the history of co-education, careers (past and future), and the links between women's liberation and the professions. The speakers were all women, all with impressive credentials. In addition to these essays the College produced a guide for visitors and returning alumnae in the form of a historical map of the campus, prepared by Cynthia Krusell: a 20" x 24" affair, 'An Historical Map of Mount Holyoke College, 1837–1987, Prepared for the Sesquicentennial'. This gave a brief, mostly one-line, historical and geographical introductions to the buildings, a key to which buildings had been built in each presidential reign, and a guide to territory from the 1852 pump house (the oldest still-standing building) to the new equestrian centre. The map may have drawn more admirers than any of the serious volumes listed above.[18]

---

[17] The Alumnae Association has continued to publish registers; that of 2008 approaching phone-book proportions in size.

[18] The notes on the map call attention to Skinner Hall, built with money pledged and then given by the Skinner brothers at the 1912 birthday; we are also directed to notice

This is almost the tale of Mount Holyoke historiography—but not quite. A pamphlet of by Mary Chandler Lowell told *The Story of the Big Fire: Mount Holyoke College, September 27, 1896* in 18 pages (Dover Foxcroft, ME, 1946). Other relevant materials have never seen the bright light of publication but rest in the college archives and special collections. Bertha E. Blakely, who worked her way up from assistant librarian in 1895 to librarian (1901–36), published two articles in the *Mount Holyoke Alumnae Quarterly:* in 1928 on 'The Library' and in 1935 on 'The Library Building', and she then followed this up, in her capacity as librarian emeritus, with a 350 page typescript (preserved in the college archives), 'The Library of Mount Holyoke College, Its Character and Development through Three Periods'.[19] There are other items of historical focus and analysis, dissertations that attest to the College's role in the history of higher education. A 1954 Columbia dissertation by Hilda Stahl Wagner, 'A History of the Forms of Dramatic Expression in Mount Holyoke College, 1837–1950', surveys the many kinds and levels of dramatic work presented over the years, looking at how such activities were seen as an appropriate part of the seminary's training. As befits a dissertation, we have a mountain of detail; the study covers every play and every dramatic presentation that left any record as well as in-house writings and student productions of work by the masters, ancient and modern.

Charlotte King Shea, class of 1960, wrote a Cornell dissertation, 'Mount Holyoke College, 1875–1910: The Passing of the Old Order' (1983). This covers the great transition from seminary to college: 'the integration of nineteenth century evangelical tradition . . . with the culture of professionalism'. Shea explores how, with strong alumnae support, President Mead was able to push the conservative trustees into the new century. A PhD thesis for the University of Massachusetts by Tiziana Roth, 'Between "True Women" and "New Women": Mount Holyoke Students, 1837 to 1908', was an analysis of a student body that in effect through the course of the nineteenth century went from enrolling farmers' daughters to recruiting daughters of white collar families. Persis Harlow McCurdy (class of 1895) published 'The History of Physical Training at Mount Holyoke College', *American Physical Education Review* 14 (1909), 138-50, covering an early focus of the seminary and giving still one more

---

Mead Hall, named for Elizabeth Mead (1890–1900), the president who led the transition from seminary to liberal arts college. In 1989 the College produced an aerial view map, keeping up with the new technology.

[19] The periodization is from 1837–70, 1870–1901, and then 1901–37, presumably delineating stages in the library's growth.

insight into how 'well rounded' the curriculum and student life had been from the start.

Novels and even dramas about college life are not uncommon, and at least one of each figures in this sweep. Julia Redford Tomkinson's novel, *Doris, A Mount Holyoke Girl* (New York, 1913) picks up Doris at age 15 when she is told of the opportunities offered by the College and is being steered to apply (as she does, and with success). This novel was published by the American Tract Society, publisher of much of the earlier Mount Holyoke material that had such a pronounced evangelical slant, indicating perhaps that that original mission of the school had not completely faded from sight. A more recent dramatic effort is in the line of the famous *The Group* by Mary McCarthy (who was concerned with Vassar 'girls'). Wendy Wasserstein wrote a play about a reunion of college friends— *Uncommon Women and Others*—and the 1978 televised performance (a Phoenix Theater play) lived to become a video recording in 2002.

A final area in which the Mount Holyoke's early lead in women's education has been chronicled (and much admired) is in the role accorded from the start to science, both as component of the basic curriculum for the students and as an area of serious faculty research. Here, once again, the seminary—even before it became a college—took a bold position among institutions for women. Bonnie S. Handler and Carole B. Shmurak offered 'Mary Lyon and the Tradition of Chemistry Teaching at Mount Holyoke Seminary, 1837–1887', *Vitae Scholastica* 9/1–2 (1990), 53–73. This paid tribute to one of Lyon's pet interests; she herself had studied chemistry with Edward Hitchcock, perhaps at Amherst College (and she also studied art from Mrs Hitchcock), and she then taught both chemistry and botany when her seminary opened. But the major tribute to and analysis of how the school yoked science with religion—and this began 22 years before Darwin's *Evolution of Species*—is the 2005 study by Miriam R. Levin, *Defining Women's Scientific Enterprise; Mount Holyoke Faculty and the Rise of American Science.*[20] In this scholarly treatment the early influence of Edward Hitchcock (an important geologist), Lyon's concern to bridge what might have been seen as competing world-views, and the endurance of this tough-minded aspect of her legacy, are extensively covered. As with so many of Lyon's innovations, what she began was maintained and even enhanced by her successors. Important figures in the history of nineteenth-century science like Lydia Shattuck and Cornelia

---

[20] Published by the University Press of New England (2005), and favourably reviewed by Auden D. Thomas, *History of Education Quarterly*, 43/3 (2006), 459–62. On women in science, the basic study remains that of Margaret W. Rossiter, *Women Scientists in America: Struggles and Strategies to 1940* (Baltimore, 1982).

Clapp (in zoology) were long-time faculty members, and widely shared and accepted views about the equality of women's minds meant a curriculum that included lab work, field trips, a natural history collection, and an observatory. Science had been incorporated into the course of study from the beginning. This emphasized that women could master such fields of enquiry just as well as could their brothers. It also reinforced, as a complement to the idea of intellectual equality between the sexes, the message that Mount Holyoke was *not* to be (just another) finishing school with a training for domesticity as the goal. This precocious and aggressive inclusion of 'hard subjects', should temper any inclination to focus too heavily on the religious and missionary priorities of the 1830s.

After History comes Biography, which pretty much means Mary Lyon et alia, though the ranks of the et alia category are also quite respectable. Since there is far too much material on Mary Lyon to deal with on a piece-by-piece basis, especially as much of it is repetitive and rests heavily on a few basic studies and/or on works that tell her story by way of her own letters, some categorization again seems advisable. We will look first at various individualized and exclusive treatments of Mary Lyon; some are book-length, some just of pamphlet or booklet style and scope. Then we have the many volumes of collective biography wherein she figures for a chapter among each book's particular aggregation of worthies. Lastly, there are miscellaneous bits and pieces, 'Mary Lyon periphery' or even, with all due respect, 'Mary Lyon trivia', with the number of items in this category perhaps being more impressive than some of the items themselves. And taken all in all, the record of interest in Mary Lyon, beginning in the mid-nineteenth century and running well through the twentieth, seems truly amazing.

After Lyon's death in 1849 a major tribute seemed called for. Appropriately, by 1851 a large volume—*The Power of Christian Benevolence Illustrated in the Life and Labor of Mary Lyon*—appeared in its first edition (Northampton, MA). This was edited and written in part by her friend and mentor, Edward Hitchcock, then president of Amherst College, the memorial biography being something he undertook at the request of the Mount Holyoke trustees, or so he assures us. His original idea was that he would simply be the 'arranger of material prepared by others', though, as we are not surprised to learn, he eventually wrote or co-authored the account of the Mount Holyoke years of Lyon's life. Her earlier years had been well covered by her friends and associates, Zilpah Grant Banister, Hannah White, and Eunice Caldwell Cowles.[21] The biography rested

---

[21] Cowles also wrote a 'Notice of Mary Lyon', for the *Massachusetts Teacher,* 2 (1849), 113–28.

heavily on Lyon's letters—her main form of literary endeavour—and it set the stage, with its wealth of personal information, for much of what was to follow. Its popularity can be gauged by the fact that the American Tract Society, the publisher, brought out twelve editions of *The Power* by the early 1860s, and that by the eighth edition (of 1858) it had dropped the names of those who had put it together, its anonymous preface now stating that 'the work is intended as a monument, not to its author, nor to Miss Lyon, but to His most holy praise'. Not surprisingly, later biographers said that Hitchcock and fellow authors may have placed undue emphasis on Lyon's piety at the cost of a more rounded presentation. Moreover, the team committed a major historiographical sin: they actually destroyed some of her letters after incorporating them into the narrative or publishing them in an edited version. But the book stands as a powerful tribute, coming a mere two years after Lyon's death and with so much information from close associates who had played a significant role in the creation and success of *her* seminary. Despite its scholarly shortcomings and its particular perspective, the 1851 volume was a worthy starting point for what was to become a long string of successors.

After the 1851 life, biographies of Mary Lyon came in a steady stream. Some were scholarly efforts, building upon Hitchcock, offering better versions of primary materials, mining the last personal recollections, and setting Lyon into a broader context that would move her to some extent away from that early emphasis on evangelical Protestantism. Nevertheless, the *Recollections of Mary Lyon* that Fidelia Fisk brought out in 1866 was very much a volume with Lyon's mission-orientation in the fore, Fisk having been a prize pupil and having written her own tribute after returning from a stint as a missionary in Persia.[22] In 1910 Beth Bradford Gilchrist, having been asked by President Woolley to undertake the project, published a life for which 'all known manuscripts bearing intimately or remotely on Miss Lyon's life have been read'. Gilchrist's 462 pages certainly cover the ground, including a critical survey of her historiographic predecessors—some being praised, some taken to task. Gilchrist's observation that Lyon was 'not a profound thinker; she added nothing to the sum of the world's speculation', is more than balanced by her assertion that 'Mount Holyoke was all in Mary Lyon's head'.[23] In the centennial year of 1937 Marion Lansing published *Mary Lyon Through her Letters* (Boston,), using material covered by Hitchcock along with letters that he

---

[22] *Recollections of Mary Lyon, with selections from her instructions to the pupils in Mt. Holyoke female seminary* (Boston, 1866); reprinted (Olive Press Publications, Los Olivos, CA, 1995), with no editorial comments or introduction to explain the reprinting.
[23] *The Life of Mary Lyon* (Boston, 1910).

and his co-authors had not used (and, therefore, had not destroyed). Lansing's style or method was to incorporate Lyon's words into the running narrative (rather than publishing the letters separately) and there is more personal flavour here than in previous biographies. This work had presumably been timed so it could be part of the centennial year's offerings.

Sydney R. McLean of Mount Holyoke had been at work on a Lyon biography when she had to abandon the project, it then being picked up and completed by Elizabeth Alden Green in 1979: *Mary Lyon and Mount Holyoke: Opening the Gates* (published by the University Press of New England: Hanover, NH). Much of this major study covers Lyon's early years; her close relationship with Zilpah Grant and Joseph Emerson, her split with Catherine Beecher, and her search for supporters and financial backing.[24] And to remind us that Lyon is still a figure to conjure with, in 1997 Amanda Porterfield returned to the evangelical theme with her *Mary Lyon and the Mount Holyoke Missionaries,* published by Oxford University Press in a 'Religion in America' series, and not so much focused on Lyon's life as on her seminary as a hotbed of missionary enthusiasm and training. Porterfield looks at how Mount Holyoke women fared when they heard the call that led them to many parts of the globe, going almost everywhere, mostly it would seem with limited awareness of either local cultures or of their own elitism.

Though this list would appear to cover what we can read as serious (and scholarly) biography it comes nowhere near exhausting the long roster of material on Mary Lyon—educator, devout Christian, crusader for women, role model for so many good causes. Popularized versions of Lyon's life appeared, early and late. In 1859—a decade after Lyon's death—William Makepeace Thayer used all of 353 pages for his version of the tale: *The Poor Girl and True Woman, or Elements of Women's Success drawn from the Life of Mary Lyon and Others.* This appeared in an 'Aimwell series', meant for girls of 10–18, a companion to such as *The Poor Boy and Merchant Prince,* no doubt aimed at their brothers. And Lyon, for young readers, has had a long life, the most recent retelling of her life being that of Dorothy Rosen, a Mount Holyoke alumna, a children's librarian, and the author of mystery stories for young readers. Her *Fire in Her Bones: the Story of Mary Lyon* (Minneapolis, 1995), part of a 'Trailblazer Biographies' series, has, among its newly commissioned drawings and old pictures, a photograph of Lyon herself from 1845, 'taken on a day when 48 year old

---

[24] On Lyon's split with Catherine Beecher, Andrea L. Turpin, 'The Ideological Origins of the Women's College: Religion, Class, and Curriculum in the Educational Visons of Catherine Beecher and Mary Lyon', *History of Education Quarterly,* 50/2 (2010), 133–57.

Mary was not at her best' but rather showing signs of wear and tear.[25]
Between Thayer in 1859 and Rosen in 1995, and apart from the 'serious'
biographies covered above, there were numerous lesser or popularized
lives, some long, some short. From the late nineteenth century we have
*Life and Its Purposes Illustrated in the Life of Mary Lyon and Others: A Book
for Young Ladies* coming out of London and Edinburgh in 1880, with
some insightful generalizations and comparisons in its 192 pages. This was
followed, in 1886, by Walter Scott's *Mary Lyon, The Christian Teacher*
(New York) in a 'church and home series of biographies' in which Lyon
stood alongside such worthies as Peter Cooper of Cooper Union, and Sir
Titus Salt, 'captain of industry'. Scott, in his twelve-page booklet, said of
Lyon that 'among the great and good women of history no small place
belongs to this daughter of New England'.

Nor did this crowded shelf deter Elizabeth Bronson Hatch Douglas from
still another biography, *The Life Story of Mary Lyon: founder of Mount
Holyoke College* (Minneapolis, 1897; 106 pages). She rested heavily on
Hitchcock's life but said that 'the object of this sketch is to give in the
fewest words the essence of a noble life'. Oxley Stengel's *The Story of Mary
Lyon* was, in 1922, in a 'famous Americans for young readers' series,
alongside volumes on Washington, Jefferson, Lincoln, Franklin, Harriet
Beecher Stowe, *et. al.,* his 181 pages covered familiar ground but offered
many details as well as the usual pieties. Still a few more efforts: Isabel Hart's
sixteen-page *Sketch of Mary Lyon*, written for the Women's Foreign Missionary Society of the Episcopal Church and offered at 3 cents per booklet;
Martha H. MacLeish, 'Mary Lyon: Pioneer in Women's Education, Mount
Holyoke's Founder and her Dream', published in the *Journal of the Ameri-
can Association of University Women*, 30–1 (1937), 152-6; Mildred Fenner
& Eleanor C. Fishburn's 'Mary Lyon, and Mount Holyoke', Personal
Growth Leaflet (no. 82) of the National Education Association.

After all this we can turn to the Mary Lyon chapters in those many
volumes of collective biography. Those who wrote or edited books in this
popular format of instructive reading would create an all-star team of one
sort or another, exemplifying some virtue or mark of success, now to be
emulated and admired, usually by young readers. Volumes in which Mary
Lyon figured first appeared in 1883 and 1886, and as recently as 1975
they were still making their mark. For Mary Lyon, it is a fairly standardized abridgement of a tale of early dedication and ultimate success. Amidst
the uplifting tales Lyon's story is often teamed up with such all-stars as

---

[25] As Elizabeth Green did with her 1979 *Mary Lyon and Mount Holyoke: Opening the
Gates,* Rosen dedicated her book to Sydney McLean, clearly a much revered faculty
member.

Harriet Beecher Stowe, Clara Barton, Florence Nightingale, Elizabeth Barrett Browning, Julia Ward Howe, Louisa May Alcott, and the like. In the more recent volumes figures like Jane Addams, Maria Mitchell, Alice Freeman Palmer, Eleanor Roosevelt, and even Lady Astor might be brought in for inspiration and diversity of focus.

Of the many volumes of this sort only a few give serious attention to Lyon's actual efforts as an educational innovator and those that do set her alongside some towering figures. In 1928 Mark De Wolfe Howe, in his *Classic Shades: Five Leaders of Learning and their Colleges* (Boston), bracketed Lyon with Timothy Dwight of Yale, Mark Hopkins of Williams, James McCosh of Princeton, and Charles William Eliot of Harvard. Heady company indeed. In 1931 (and reprinted, 1970), Willystine Goodsell edited *Pioneers of Women's Education in the United States* (New York), and she concentrated on three foundational figures: Emma Willard, Catherine Beecher, and Lyon. In 1975 Mary W. Burgess's *Education: Contributions of Women* (Minneapolis) put Lyon alongside Patty Smith Hill, an innovator of the kindergarten, Florence Sabin for medical science and education, and Mary McLeod Bethune for black women's education.

While all the other volumes in the list of collective biographies deal with Lyon with great admiration, she does tend to get swamped—as does everyone else who is covered—by each volume's unbroken string of success stories. In 1883 it was in Joseph Johnson, *Noble Women of Our Time*, in 1886 the collective volume was Bolton's *Lives of Girls Who Became Famous*. Then came a veritable flood of such volumes in the new century: nine by 1920 and a few more in succeeding decades. Mostly they were organized along the lines of 'great women' or 'brave women who have made good' or 'religious life of famous Americans' or 'heroines of modern service', or with some comparable principle to give a semblance of unity and coherence. Though Lyon usually kept company with women, including Queen Victoria, Jenny Lind, and Clara Schumann, she was sometimes teamed up with men: Lincoln, Horace Greeley, Cyrus Hall McCormick (of the mechanical reaper), Cornelius Vanderbilt, and Franklin, among others (including Robert Raites, 'father of Sunday schools'). As a heroine of service she ran with Madame Curie, while as a prominent American woman she might line up with Emily Dickinson and Louisa May Alcott. The most idiosyncratic of all these volumes is that of Grace Humphrey, *The Story of the Marys* (1923), where Mary Lyon is paired (for readers of 10–14) with Mary Queen of Scots, Mary Ann Evans (George Eliot), Marie Antoinette, Mary Lamb, and the Virgin Mary, among others.[26]

---

[26] This impressive list is probably not a complete one. The volumes with a chapter devoted to Mary Lyon, are, in chronological order: Joseph Johnson, *Noble Women of Our*

A final aspect of the Mary Lyon cottage industry is what I offer as the Mary Lyon periphery. Reference must be made to a few of what must have been a flood of sermons, some immediately after her death, some at later anniversaries (as 1897, her centenary year), and all deemed worthy of publication and preservation. There is not much historical material in these though they shed light on the power of the Lyon cult or myth. Hitchcock included the funeral sermon of Reverend Humphreys in *The Power of Christian Benevolence* (357–9: 'The Shining Path'), and we can follow this sermon-printing trail with Philip Moxom on *Mary Lyon Centennial and the Higher Education of Women* (Springfield, MA, 1897), delivered in the South Congregational Meeting House in Springfield in 1897, perhaps in competition with Reverend G.H. Bailey's sermon of February 28, 1897; and the one he delivered at Ashfield and Buckland on Lyon's 100th birthday—'An Address on the Hundredth Anniversary of Mary Lyon's Birth' and including, in its 38 printed pages what we are told was her favorite hymn. Or we go back a few years for Reverend W. A. Nichols, preaching in 1887 at the unveiling of a plaque in Lyon's honour at Buckland: *Mary Lyon in her Birth and Life. Distinctive Plan of God for the Development of Womanhood, Especially in the Middle Classes* (Boston, 1890), which, even in nineteen pages, sounds like heavy going. The Founder's Day sermon of 1902, Henry Hopkins's *The Power of Personality as Illustrated in Mary Lyon* (South Hadley) seems to have been a hit, given how frequently is it referred to. Or we can leave the sermon trail to track the *Mary Lyon Year Book* (1895), a day-by-day calendar of biblical quotes and of poetry, presumably presenting some of

---

Time (London, 1883); Sarah K. Bolton, *Lives of Girls Who Became Famous* (New York, 1886); Louis Albert Banks, D.D., *Religious Life of Famous Americans* (New York, 1904); Sherman Williams, *Some Successful Americans* (Boston, 1904); Elmer C. Adams, *Heroines of Modern Progress* (New York, 1913); Edith Horton, *A Group of Famous Women: Stories of Their Lives* (Boston/New York, 1914), advocating 'biography as a means of education'; Lilian Whiting, *Women Who Have Ennobled Life* (Philadelphia, 1915); Cecil Ker, *Women Who Have Made Good* (New York, 1916), in a series, 'Inspiration Books'; Mary R. Parkman, *Heroines of Service* (1916; rprn Freeport, NY, 1969): Gamaliel Bradford, *Portraits of American Women* (1919; rprn Freeport, NY, 1969); Mabel Ansley Murphy, *Greathearted Women: Biographies of Sixteen Women Leaders* (Philadelphia, 1920); Grace Humphrey, *The Story of the Marys* (Philadelphia, 1923): Jane Y. McCallum, *Women Pioneers* (Richmond, NY, 1929); Elsie E. Egermeier, *Girls' Stories of Great Women* (Anderson, IN, 1930), assuring readers that 'you will discover...that in your girlhood [you] are sharing some of their experiences'; Mildred S. Fenner & Eleanor C. Fishburn, *Pioneer American Educators* (Port Washington, NY 1944; reissued 1960): Sonia M. Daugherty, *Ten Brave Women* (Philadelphia/New York, 1953); Marguerite Vance, *The Lamp Lighters: Women in the Hall of Fame* (New York, 1961); Mary W. Burgess, *Education: Contributions of Women* (Minneapolis, 1975). Burgess, like Howe and Goodsell, deals with Lyon in the context of comparable leaders in education.

Lyon's favorite passages (though this is inferred, not explained) and published by the Congregational Sunday School Publishing Society.[27]

There are still other variations on this theme: 'The Reminiscences of Mary Lyon', were collected between 1905 and 1908 and preserved in the College archives to enshrine the distant memories of some who could still recall personal contacts with the founder.[28] In 1916 the National League of Women Workers had Jessie V. Budlong write a three-page pamphlet on Mary Lyon, 'A Woman Who Cared'. Fannie Shaw Kendrick, *The History of Buckland, 1779–1935* (Buckland, MA, 1937), gives much attention to the town's most famous citizen (and the book was published in the College's centennial year).[29] In 1933 *The Ladies' Home Journal* and *The Christian Science Monitor,* to coincide with the Century of Progress World's Fair in Chicago, ran a campaign to choose 'America's Twelve Great Women Leaders during the Past Hundred Years' (128, 882 ballots cast). Lyon received over 40,000 votes and made the elite dozen, though the accolade that 'the quality that brings Mary Lyon now to this company . . . is durability. She wore well', could also be applied to a good pair of shoes.[30]

Even this long and disparate list does not end the various manifestations of the cult-cum-memory of Mary Lyon. A pleasant novel—a fictionalized biography—from 1965, Evelyn I. Banning's *Mary Lyon of Putnam's Hill. A Biography* (New York) is frank and insightful about her split with the Beechers and her differences with Zilpah Grant, although a bit sentimental about would-be romances in Lyon's younger days. There were probably but few productions of *Mary Lyon—Pioneer in Higher Education for Women,* a narrative dramatization by Barbara J. Rugg (class of 1950), written around 1962 for the Franklin County Mount Holyoke Club (and Kate Carney's 2001 monologue, 'Mary Lyon of Mount Holyoke' probably had a similar fate). A short pamphlet (twelve pages) was written for the Girard Trust Company of Philadelphia to salute Mary Lyon as *The First Woman in the American Hall of Fame* (Philadelphia, 1933). One suspects that Lyon would have been flattered by her 2005 induction into

---

[27] This volume of devotional and uplifting passages puts Mary Lyon into the company of such 'devout thinkers' as Martin Luther and Madame Guyon.

[28] The Alumnae Association of the Midwest also collected reminiscences of Mary Lyon, assembled in 1879 for the sixth reunion of the Association in Chicago. The volume of loose sheets in the Mount Holyoke archives preserved 41 written reminiscences plus 21 that were dictated and then transcribed: 'from the pen' or 'from the lips', as it says on the cover sheet.

[29] A tablet honouring Lyon was unveiled in Buckland in 1887. In 1924 the town established a scholarship to send a local girl (or girls) to Mount Holyoke.

[30] Mary Woolley, the college's president in 1933, also made the elite dozen with some 37,000 votes. Mary Baker Eddy led the tally with 103,000 votes, hardly surprising as the Christian Science Church was one of the poll's organizers and sponsors.

the Western Massachusetts Entrepreneurship Hall of Fame, now being established by Springfield Technical Community College. A 1987 documentary film and video, coinciding with the College's 150th birthday, had Julie Harris (working from a script by Jean M. Mudge) tell the tale of 'Mary Lyon: Precious Time'. It ran for 30 minutes and could be rented for $45 (or bought for $525). In 1997, for Lyon's 200th birthday, the U.S. postal service issued a 2 cent stamp in her honor. And to conclude—and to step on my own toes—in 1975 Nancy Perrin Jandl (class of 1964) prepared a 35-page bibliography on Mary Lyon, another in-house effort now resting quietly in the college archives. Though becoming dated, it is a useful survey of works by, about, and even casually referring to the great lady.

In terms of Mount Holyoke biography there is some life after Mary Lyon, though obviously nothing to match what we have just surveyed. Of the many imposing figures to be found in the long history of the college it is Mary E. Woolley, president from 1900 until 1937, who stands in an honourable second place. She was a very prominent public figure and her life (and letters) have come in for considerable attention. Her eminence and public image ran far beyond the bounds of academia: nominated by President Hoover to international commissions on disarmament, she was an outspoken figure on on behalf of the League of Nations and on numerous progressive issues (including protesting against the execution of Sacco and Vanzetti). Her long-time friend and companion Jeannette Marks published *Life and Letters of Mary Emma Woolley* (Washington, DC, 1955), giving an informal and personal biography, much of it by way of Woolley's own writings and conversation. Though Woolley's years of success and prominence as a long-serving college president take centre stage in the biography, her bitterness over the way she was followed by a man from Yale at her retirement in the centennial year receives much sympathetic attention. Marks details Woolley's unsuccessful campaign to rally faculty and alumnae in a protest against the choice of Ham and then tells how Woolley departed, in anger and bitterness, never to return to the campus before her death in 1945. Woolley's personal life, a topic of prurient interest that ordinarily would be out of place, does figure here because of Anna Mary Wells's *Miss Marks and Miss Woolley* (Boston, 1975: Houghton Mifflin), a biography of Woolley with a heavily Freudian approach which leaves little doubt about the two women as lovers. We have a tale of sublimation, lesbianism, a father who wanted a boy instead of a girl, emotional dependence, and perhaps even some platonic relations—all treated and speculated on at length. Francis Lester Warner's *On A New England Campus* (Boston: another product of 1937, that *annus mirabilis* for the college) was written with Woolley's life and career as its central focus but, in keeping with Woolley's wishes, it was a weaving of her life into a history of the college rather than a biography as such. And like Lyon, Woolley was included in one of those all-star collections; Philip B. Lotz (ed.), *Creative Personalities*, ii: *Women Leaders* (New York, 1940) where she shared billing with Jane Addams, Edith Cavell, Amelia Earhart, and Harriet Beecher Stowe, among others, her chapter being written by Grace Sloan Overton.

Lesser Mount Holyoke figures were not totally ignored in the ranks of college biography, though their accounts came mostly in the form of an in-house tribute, usually a eulogy. Fidelia Fiske, one of Lyon's prize pupils, who wrote about her mentor, merited her own chapter, along with Mary Lyon, in Johnson's *Noble Women of Our Time,* pages 71–102 highlighting 'Fidelia Fiske and her Persian Girls'. Sarah D. (Locke) Stow, author of those two volumes in 1887, presided over a 23-page sketch of the life of Lydia W. Shattuck who had worked with Agassiz of Harvard. The memorial booklet offered the funeral sermon and various tributes to a major college figure and scientist: *Memorials of Mary W. (Chapin) Pease and Lydia W. Shattuck* (Boston, 1890). Shattuck, who died in 1897, had been a member of the American Association for the Advancement of Science, an honour rarely bestowed on nineteenth-century women. The memorial tributes published alongside Shattuck's, to Mary W. Chapin (Pease), class of 1843, president from 1852-67 (and acting president, 1850-1), also tell, in the words of Helen Norton, of another long Mount Holyoke career, though Chapin had resigned as 'principal' in 1865 and went off to marry Claudius Pease.

Stow, the *de facto* if not the *de jure* historian of the College, also presided over the memorial booklet for Elisabeth M. Bardwell, another of the science faculty—a mathematician and astronomer in this case. Bardwell, class of 1866, taught at her alma mater for 33 years and the booklet carries excerpts from some of Bardwell's own talks to the alumnae: *Memorial of Elisabeth M. Bardwell: of Mount Holyoke College, South Hadley, Mass.* (South Hadley, 1899). But there was a long interval before the next full-length Mount Holyoke biography, which came in the form of a full-length study of the life and career of one of the history faculty: John G. Reid's *Viola Florence Barnes, 1885–1979: A Historian's Biography* (Toronto, 2005). Though Barnes was not the most distinguished of the history faculty, her long career, from her arrival in 1919, had caught the author's attention; historians often like to write about other historians.[31]

---

[31] Barnes had a burst of publication in the 1920s: *Dominion of New England: A Study in British Colonial Policy* (New Haven, 1923: reprinted, 1960), and *Richard Wharton: A Seventeenth Century New England Colonial* (Boston, 1926). There are no references to

Most of the material that is, explicitly or incidentally, focused on the history of Mount Holyoke has been covered. However, there is a still a considerable amount of related or semi-related work that would be of value were one to re-tell the narrative that Cole offered in 1937 or if one were to turn a hand to a historical-statistical analysis of the college. One source of information, though presented with little by way of analysis, is to be found in that long (and large) series of biographical directories issued by the college and by the alumnae association; we have referred to them above. These give comprehensive lists of students and thumbnail information about the subsequent life of so many women: marriage, children, careers, residence, death dates, etc. While Mount Holyoke's student numbers were always small, as befits a liberal arts college, the biographical directories are an impressive presentation of *how many* and *from where* and *going on to what*. They are reference books that testify to alumnae loyalty and to a life-long desire to 'keep in touch' that began in South Hadley. In the 1895 directory the College could talk of 2355 graduates since the first class had left the campus, along with another 5073 women who did not go all the way to a degree (or whatever had been the terminal award of the early days). The *One Hundred Year Biographical Directory* was part of the 1937 publications, much like earlier volumes and helping set the mould for its many successors.

There is a lot of other material, mostly historically peripheral but worth a quick mention. Unfortunately, none of the writings of Mount Holyoke's presidents has dealt in any explicit fashion with the history of Mount Holyoke or, even more broadly, with the school's trailblazing role in the tale of women and higher education. In the 1830s Mary Lyon wrote a number of descriptive pamphlets—virtually sales promotions with an eye on fund-raising, recruiting, and explaining purpose and curriculum—but her only 'real' book was her 1843 *Missionary Offerings, or Christian Sympathy. Personal Responsibility, and the Present Crisis in Foreign Missions,* a short book (103 pages) concerned with missions and missionary activity, not with *her* seminary as such. Much in keeping with the culture of genteel

---

the history of Mount Holyoke in a volume honouring a retired economist: Lucile Tomlinson Wessmann (ed.), *'Those Having Torches . . .': Economic Essays in Honor of Alzada Comstock, Presented by her Former Students* (South Hadley, 1954). All contributors had been Mount Holyoke undergraduates and some also earned masters' degrees there. For two of the college's distinguished historians, Margaret Hastings & Elisabeth G. Kimball, 'Two Distinguished Medievalists—Nellie Neilson and Bertha Putnam', *Journal of British Studies,* 18 (Spring 1979), 142–59. Mount Holyoke had a number of important medievalists, all covered in Jane Chance (ed.), *Women Medievalists and the Academy* (Madison, WI, 2005), incorporating David Day on Bertha Putnam (157–66), Anne R. DeWindt on Nellie Neilson (167–81), Carolyn P. Collette on Charlotte D'Evelyn (295–309), and Kevin J. Harty on Ruth Dean (565–74).

ladies of her day, Lyon was a prodigious letter writer, giving us the material on which the biographies would be based, and the letters have been collected, edited, and well mined. But, as Lyon died rather suddenly, there never was any move on her part to organize the letters or the ephemeral material; no volume of collected writings, no retrospective thoughts about her great crusade.[32] However, as an indication that the cult of Mary Lyon still lives there is a 2008 reprinting of her collected works, mostly her letters: James E. Hartley (ed.), *Mary Lyon: Documents and Writings*.[33]

Mary Woolley did publish a fair amount of material, though almost exclusively focused on her role on various peace commissions and League of Nations, activities in which she was a prominent player—as shown in such as her *Internationalism and Disarmament* (New York, 1935: 30pp.). She aired her liberal views on the emerging role of women as early as 1906, when she spoke at the National Suffrage Convention: the talk being published as *Miss Woolley on Woman's Ballot* (Warren, OH). Much of her material, like the pieces cited here, appeared in pamphlet or article form, and none of these, even when talking of the value of a college education, deal in any direct way with Mount Holyoke, even if they were inspired and informed by her 37 years as president. Her introduction to a 1932 booklet, *Study Course on the League of Nations,* as well as her *The College Women and The New Epoch,* testify to her active public role but, as we noted, they take us far from South Hadley.[34] Some of her talks were also incorporated into miscellaneous pieces: for example her *Life of Shaw King: An Appreciation by Mary E. Woolley, President of Mount Holyoke*

---

[32] Lyon as an author, beyond her letters, has a thin record. Her *Missionary Offerings* (Boston, 1843) is 'a plea for financial support and (for) the widespread missionary movement', and that, plus seven versions of circulars promoting Mount Holyoke that 'present her educational philosophy in crisp form', are all we have: Linda Eisenmann, 'Mary Lyon' in John A. Garraty & Mark C. Carnes, (eds), *American National Biography* (24 vols, Oxford, 1999), xiv. s.n.

[33] Clearly a labour of love and published by the Doorlight Publication of South Hadley. The reprinted documents begin with a letter of July 21, 1821, Mary to her mother, and the volume reprints much of the Lyon-Zilpah Grant correspondence. Many letters stem from Lyon's campaigns to raise money and to find supporters in the years just before the seminary opened.

[34] The booklet (68 pages) on the League of Nations was published by the League's Education Committee, the talk on women and college was given at Randolph Macon Women's College and published in the *Bulletin of the College,* April-June, 3 (1916). There is a paper from Woolley's graduate student days: 'Early History of the Colonial Post Office', *Rhode Island Historical Society: Studies in Colonial History* New Series 1 (1894), 270–91. Ironically, Woolley's companion, Jeannette Marks, wrote a book that comes closer to reflecting on the college experience with a kind of 'how to do it' approach: *A Girl's Student Days and After* (New York, 1911), with an introduction by Woolley.

College, privately printed in 650 copies in 1923, or her talk on 'Mrs. Howe's Work for the Advancement of Women', printed as part of the *Memorial exercises in honor of Julia Ward Howe, held in Symphony hall, Boston, on Sunday evening, January 8, 1911, at 8 o'clock* (Boston, 1911), under the auspices of the Mayor and City Council. The closest Woolley may have come to writing about *her* school was an article on Mary Lyon, for a student publication, 'Mary Lyon', *The Mount Holyoke* 14 (1904-5), only running to eleven pages.

This presidential pattern of *not* publishing material on Mount Holyoke, let alone on its history, covers everyone from Mary Lyon, at the start, to Lynn Pasquerella, the philosopher who currently presides over the college. Though many of the presidents of the twentieth century published scholarly material appropriate to their discipline, none ever went the way of such figures as Clark Kerr, talking about the University of California, or Robert Hutchins, about his college at Chicago, let alone Joseph Quincy, writing a history of Harvard in the mid-nineteenth century while presiding over it. Woolley did contribute a chapter to a rather peculiar collection of essays, *What I Owe to My Father*, in which she offers a happier picture of her early family life than what we find in Marks, let alone in Wells's study.[35] After President Woolley—and whether he was a good choice or not—came Roswell G. Ham (1937–57), author of *Otway and Lee: Biography from the Baroque Era,* a 1931 study of two very minor seventeenth-century dramatists. Elizabeth Kennan, (1978–95, and a strong opponent of co-education) co-edited and translated some of the voluminous twelfth-century works of Bernard of Clairvaux. Joanne V. Creighton (1996–2010 and then leaving to preside over Haverford), wrote numerous books on recent authors like William Faulkner and Margaret Drabble. David Truman (1969–78) was a prominent political scientist with numerous works on American government. Meribeth Cameron (acting president, 1968-9) published widely on modern China and the Pacific. But none of these leaders, whether prolific authors or not, ever gave any extensive or book-length attention to the college, either while in the chair or afterwards.

Most of the student publications—and there have been many—cover current events and bring literary efforts (mostly of students, sometimes by alumni) to the light of day. We have those volumes of Mount Holyoke verse, 1928 and 1937. One student publication, the *Llamarada* began life as the junior class's yearbook and soon proved to be such a good chronicle

---

[35] Edited by Sydney Strong (New York 1931; rprn 1992). This work contained essays by Jane Addams and by the sons of such celebrities as Theodore Roosevelt and the poet Vachel Lindsay. Woolley's essay is at 167–79.

of events that in his 1937 history of the College Arthur Cole praises it as a reliable source of material, so thorough was its coverage. But this is unusual and, in fairness, student publications are usually meant to record the ephemeral, leaving long-term reflections to others with other interests. In the long history of Mount Holyoke numerous student publications, mainly focused on creative writing, have appeared; *Pangynaskean* (which became the *Pan*), *Pegasus, Tempo,* and the *Mount Holyoke,* among others. From the perspective of social history there is actually much to be gleaned from the advertisements in these publications. They offer a running commentary on the fashions and tastes of young women of the day (whatever day that was), as they speak to the variety of and competition between local stores and merchants, to the pricing of by-gone times, and to the possibility that Mount Holyoke women could afford autos, jewellery, silk underwear, and trips to Springfield and Boston.

Several other categories of material shed light on the proud history of the College; some of this explicitly focuses on the legacy, while in other cases it can be read in reflected light. In addition to the biographical material on Mount Holyoke's own there are biographies of two important figures from Mary Lyon's early days. One is Zilpah Banister, née Grant, her closest friend and long-time associate; her life is fully and piously chronicled in L.T. Guilford (ed.), *The Use of a Life: Memorials of Mrs Zilpah A. Grant Banister,* published some years after her death in 1885, and, like other early works relating to Mount Holyoke, by the American Tract Society of New York (1885). Much of the information for this life came from Mrs E.C. Cowles, one of that team from the 1851 biography of Mary Lyon, and the volume on Grant is tilted toward her years of friendship and co-operation with Lyon. And though Lyon and Grant went separate ways in the 1830s, they always kept in touch. The other figure whose biography informs the story of Mary Lyon, though he died before the seminary was on its feet, is Joseph Emerson. The 1834 life was written by his second cousin, Ralph Waldo Emerson: *Life of Rev. Joseph Emerson* (Boston). The lesser known Emerson was perhaps the strongest influence of all on Mary Lyon—as her teacher and then, as her wings began to spread—as one of her most devoted supporters. She clearly benefited immensely from being exposed to Emerson's egalitarian views about women and men, girls and boys. 'He seemed to regard neither male nor female, but all as one in Jesus Christ' (420), and though Emerson died too early, from a Mount Holyoke perspective, Zilpah Grant-Banister lived long enough to be able to send apologies for not attending, due to failing health, the 1862 birthday commemoration.

As a pioneering institution Mount Holyoke soon became a mother school from which many daughters (and step-daughters) would spring: seminaries, women's colleges, two-year institutions, and (eventually) full-fledged colleges. Some of these schools *also* have had their histories written, and their strong and direct debt to Mary Lyon and Mount Holyoke and to those who left South Hadley to serve as pioneers in an educational wilderness is a strong theme in these histories. Mount Holyoke women went out to teach, to help create, and to administer, to maintain links between the home base and the colony; missionary work did not have to be in the far corners of the earth. The genealogy of Mount Holyoke's daughters was a source of pride at both the old and the new institution. The link placed each new enterprise along a great chain of being, so to speak, and Mount Holyoke's influence, its towering status as a role model, and its generosity in sending out faculty and alumnae for this form of outreach were noteworthy from the beginning.

As the written histories of the daughter schools take us away from the main theme of Mount Holyoke historiography it does not seem necessary to go through these volumes, one by one or school by school, in order to offer still more evidence of the influence and the prestige of Mount Holyoke. One way to assess the reach of this legacy is by naming the various daughters that sent a representative to South Hadley to be on the spot for the 75th birthday party in 1912. This is an impressive list, both in numbers and in geographical spread, and it reminds us that in the decades after 1837 much of the mid-west and the rural south were still pioneer country (as we recall from tales of Lincoln's boyhood). In 1912 there were representatives of Lake Erie College in Painsville, Ohio, of Mills College in California (founded by an old girl and her husband), of the Western Women's Seminary in Ohio (merged into Miami University, Miami, OH, in the 1970s), of seminary-colleges in Rockford Illinois, Kalamazoo, Michigan, and Albert Lea, Minnesota. From abroad, greetings and congratulations from Mount Holyoke's daughter school in Barcelona (whence it had migrated from Santander and Madrid), from one in Wellington in Cape Province of South Africa, and from schools in Bitlis and in Marsovan, both in Turkey. This does not include Fidelia Fiske's school at Oroomiah in Persia, nor either of the two Cherokee Nation schools that Mount Holyoke had staffed and helped shape in the second half of the nineteenth century. One of the Cherokee schools was in the deep south, the other in the Oklahoma territory. Nor does this impressive list include Wheaton Seminary-College, and it does not try to count the number of Mount Holyoke faculty and alumnae who occupied critical positions in the early days of the other seven sisters' colleges in the latter decades of the nineteenth century.[36]

---

[36] For Lake Erie College, Margaret Geissman Gross, *Dancing on the Table: A History of Lake Erie College* (Burnsville, N.C., 1993): Elias O. James, *The Story of Cyrus and Susan Mills* (Stanford, 1953); Narka Nelson, *The Western College for Women, 1853–1953*

In toto, this body of material is a tribute to the widespread interest in the success and influence of Mount Holyoke, to the loyalty it has inspired, and to a recognition of the vision of its founder. In a sense no conclusion is needed; the volume of material, its span from the mid-nineteenth century into very recent years, and the variations in theme and approach in the appreciation of Mount Holyoke all point in the same direction. Mount Holyoke did not quite create the 'game' of women's higher education (as a single-sex institution) and Mary Lyon was not the only brave figure whose thoughts and efforts ran in this direction. But her force of personality, her ability to enlist friends and colleagues, and her ability to combine the visionary with the practical, somehow worked. A combination of ideology and early success helped assure that those early efforts would be enduring ones, affecting others both near and far. In 1837 one might have had some doubts about the new seminary's future. Mary Lyon, on the other hand, would have taken strong issue with the doubters. 'History' has proved that she was right.[37]

Stony Brook University

(Oxford, OH, 1954); Rev. Samuel Haskell, *Historical Sketch of Kalamazoo College* (Ann Arbor, 1864): 12 pages; Althea Bass, *A Cherokee Daughter of Mount Holyoke* (Muscatine, IA, 1937); Devon A. Mihesuah, *Cultivating the Rosebuds: The Education of Women at the Cherokee Female Seminary, 1851–1909* (Urbana, IL, 1995). For Wheaton College, with a slightly different pedigree but much in the mould of Mount Holyoke, Paul C. Helmreich, *Wheaton College, 1834–1912: The Seminary Years* (Norton, MA, 1985) and Lucy Larcom, *Wheaton Seminary: A Semi-Centennial Sketch* (Cambridge, MA, 1895).

[37] A full narrative history, were one to be written today to bring Cole's 1937 volume into the new century, would be expected to explore the debates over whether to become co-educational or to remain a women's college. It would also look at the issues surrounding sexual activity and identity. The College now has a website for lesbian and trans-gender issues and these topics, and the questions and problems they pose, are very much part of today's agenda (as is sexual abuse). I thank Judith Bennett for directing me to the relevant web sites.

Reviews

Jacopo Zabarella, *On Methods*, i: *Books I–II*; ii: *Books III–IV, On Regressus*, ed. and trans. John P. McCaskey (Cambridge, MA/ London: Harvard University Press, 2013), 352pp; 480 pp. ISBN: 9780674724792; 9780674724808

Per Landgren

Of all European universities during the sixteenth century, Padua had probably the strongest attraction for medical students. An impressive amount of the foremost Renaissance physicians had studied there.[1] Students of medicine, however, had to spend at least two years in philosophical studies before they could turn their attention to medicine. During those years they concentrated on Aristotelian logic and natural philosophy.[2] After the middle of the century, the dominant teacher in these subjects was Jacopo Zabarella (1533–89).

Zabarella was descended from old Paduan nobility. He devoted his whole life to academic work, finishing his doctorate in 1553 and becoming professor of logic in 1564 and professor of natural philosophy five years later. His lectures were comprehensive, his writings prolific, and his arguments often provocative but convincing. His authority as an original and critical advocate of Aristotle and the Aristotelian commentary

---

[1] Paul F. Grendler, *The Universities of the Italian Renaissance* (Baltimore/London, 2001). 37

[2] Heikki Mikkeli, *An Aristotelian Response to Renaissance Humanism: Jacopo Zabarella on the Nature of Arts and Sciences* (Helsinki, 1992), 133. Charles B. Schmitt 'Aristotle among the physicians', in A. Wear, R.K. French & I.M. Lonie (eds), *The Medical Renaissance of the Sixteenth Century* (Cambridge, 1985), 1ff.

tradition was widely recognized by academics of Roman Catholic and Protestant persuasion alike. His published works in Italy were soon republished by transalpine publishers and covetously read by Protestant scholars, who were in need of powerful logical tools in their theological debates with scholars of rival and opposing confessions. Professors in logic at various northern European universities displayed their modernity by lecturing on the works of Zabarella and letting their students defend *pro exercitio* and *pro gradu* various statements plucked like flowers directly from his *Opera logica.*

Modern scholars seem to be in complete agreement that the influence of Zabarellian Aristotelianism was widespread and pervasive.[3] Heikki Mikkeli contends without hesitation that Zabarella 'is considered the prime representative of Renaissance Italian Aristotelianism'.[4] In his seminal work *Die Logik der Neuzeit,* Wilhelm Risse called Zabarella 'einer der scharfsinnigsten und klarsten Logiker aller Zeiten'.[5] William F. Edwards in his important but still unpublished doctoral dissertation 'The Logic of Iacopo Zabarella' finds that Zabarella 'was praised by all of his biographers (even Antonio Possevino, who for the rest found much to criticize in him) for the marvellous clarity he was able to bring into even the most difficult and obscure passages in Aristotle, a judgement the modern reader can scarcely help but concur in'.[6] Finally, Dr John McCaskey, the editor and translator of the present works, describes Zabarella as 'the leading logician at Europe's leading centre of secular Aristotelian scholarship'.[7] For several decades either side of 1600, Zabarellian Aristotelianism dominated the teaching in logic at the transalpine academies.[8]

---

[3] See e.g. Wilhelm Schmidt-Biggemann, *Topica Universalis: Eine Modellgeschichte Humanistischer Und Barocker Wissenschaft* (Hamburg, 1983), 89ff. and Howard Hotson, *Johann Heinrich Alsted, 1588–1638: Between Renaissance, Reformation and Universal Reform* (Oxford, 2000), 29 See also e.g. Ian Maclean, 'Mediations of Zabarella in Northern Germany, 1586–1623', in Gregorio Piaia (ed.), *La presenza dell'aristotelismo padovano nella filosofia della prima modernità* (Padua, 2002), 173–98, and, in the same volume, Sachiko Kusukawa, 'Mediations of Zabarella in Northern Europe: the Preface of Johann Ludwig Hawenreuter' (199–213), and Heikki Mikkeli, 'Zabarella and Piccolomini in Scandinavian Countries in the Seventeenth Century' (257–72).

[4] Heikki Mikkeli, 'Giacomo Zabarella' in Edward N. Zalta (ed.), *The Stanford Encyclopedia of Philosophy* (Winter 2012 Edition): http://plato.stanford.edu/archives/win2012/entries/zabarella/.

[5] Wilhelm Risse, *Die Logik Der Neuzeit,* i: *1500–1640* (Stuttgart, 1964), 278.

[6] William F. Edwards, 'The Logic of Iacopo Zabarella (1533–1589)' (Diss New York, 1961), 11.

[7] Introduction, p. ix.

[8] Concerning Cambridge and Oxford see Jonathan Woolfson, *Padua and the Tudors: English Students in Italy, 1485–1603* (Cambridge, 1998); and Marco Sgarbi, *The Aristotelian Tradition and the Rise of British Empiricism: Logic and Epistemology in the British Isles (1570–1689)* (Dordrecht/London, 2013).

It has taken considerable time for some of Zabarella's most influential logical works to appear in English-language translations and editions with commentary.[9] The well justified choice of texts by the translator fell upon the four books of *De methodis* (*On Methods*), and the much debated and smaller piece of work *De regressu* (*On Regressus*). Both are now published in the Harvard series *The I Tatti Renaissance Library*, in two handsome volumes. The first volume, of about 360 pages contains the first two books of *On Methods* and an introduction by the translator to Zabarella and to modern research on the Paduan philosopher. The second volume of about 470 pages contains books three and four of *On Methods* and *On Regressus*. Both volumes are equipped with general notes on the text, translation, and references as well as specific notes on the texts and translations in the different volumes. Indexes are to be found in each volume, that in the second volume being cumulative.[10]

The edition is based on four printed texts. Two were published in Venice during the lifetime of the author, in 1578 and 1586, and two were published posthumously in Cologne and Frankfurt. My only critical comment to this new Latin edition is that it should have been punctuated more strictly according to modern standards and harmonized with the punctuation of the English text (e.g. note 18). This would have increased its readability. The Renaissance practice of punctuation is confusing to modern readers. Apart from this, the Latin text runs smoothly and accords with the overall practice of the series in having parallel translation. There are some textual errors, but these are rare.[11]

In his introduction, McCaskey presents a possible context to the works by describing the debate between Ramists and Aristotelians in Cambridge. The same controversy 'in Padua' is then said to have 'engaged innovators and conservatives in natural philosophy and in medicine'. By way of introduction, one ought also to add that the four books *On Methods* offer a highly critical assessment of the methodology of the contemporary *medici*, the Galenists, who had taken command of the methodological discussion. An empirical and experiential surge among academic physicians together with crucial discoveries, culminating with Vesalius' *De*

---

[9] Other modern translations that I am acquainted with are *Über die Methoden, De methodis, Über den Rückgang, De regressu*, trans. Rudolf Schicker (Munich, 1995) and *La nature de la logique*, trans Dominique Bouillon (Paris, 2009).

[10] I will refer to these volumes in the following way: e.g. I.ii.3. which means volume one, chapter two, paragraph three. A page number alone, e.g. '(p. x)' in the text refers to the Introduction page x.

[11] Such as 'libi' for 'libri' in book I, chapter ix and paragraph 8, (i.e. I.ix.8) or 'si omnis essent huiusmodi' for 'si omnes essent huiusmodi' in I.xiv.24,

humani Corporis Fabrica in 1543, shaped a decisive trend in medicine which Zabarella followed with great interest.[12]

In book one of *On Method,* Zabarella defines *methodus* as a *habitus logicus,* which includes *ordo* as the ordering of the material in question and *methodus stricte* or *proprie dicta* as method in a strict or proper sense which leads us from knowledge into new knowledge (I.iii.2). In book two, he describes the three Galenic species of order, the compositive, resolutive, and definitive, but refutes the last one. The proper method is defined in book three. This method has *vis illativa,* or in McCaskey's translation 'inferential power', and it leads from the known to the unknown. According to the translator's introduction, this is the only book that is 'dedicated specifically to method' (p. xv). Zabarella asserts that method is syllogism. Division is rejected, not only as order, but as method as well. The only approved methods are two syllogisms, more specifically *demonstratio compositiva* and *demonstratio resolutiva,* since they have inferential force and lead to new knowledge. In the fourth book, Zabarella argues that the *Posterior Analytics* concerns the strongest type of syllogism, the compositive method or *demonstratio potissima.* McCaskey maintains that *On Methods* 'is not a treatise about scientific discovery'. Rather, in his view, it is Zabarella's proposal for the proper way to convey knowledge between the master and his pupil. Method in its more restricted sense 'is how each step in the presentation leads to the next' (p. ix). I am bound to disagree.

Admittedly, it is not easy to dissect the different layers of content in Zabarella's work. McCaskey often repeats that *On Methods* is about teaching, and, of course, in a sense it is all teaching. However, it is definitely not all about *ordo.* Instruction on how to arrange the material in lectures is to be found in the two first books: that is the part concerning *ordo.* Certainly, *On Methods* is also about the demonstration of new knowledge, about demonstration of effects as well as discovery and demonstration of causes. The goal of *methodus demonstrativa* was to gain distinct knowledge of the effects, and the goal of *methodus resolutiva* was to gain distinct knowledge of causes or principles. It is instruction about syllogisms as instruments for discovering new knowledge, i.e. teaching about scientific discovery, which McCaskey denies.[13] But does McCaskey really equate syllogistic reasoning with 'how each step in the presentation leads to the next'? Perhaps, the translator has interpreted *docens* in the explanation by Zabarella of *methodus* as a *habitus logicus* in too narrow a way, i.e. only as teaching? I.iii.2, But, irrespective of this, in this context 'scientific discovery' reasonably means discovery of *principia,* in the

[12] Edwards, 'Logic of Iacopo Zabarella', 88 ff.
[13] See Introduction, p. ix.

Aristotelian sense, which according to Zabarella was the goal of *methodus resolutiva* (*partium seu principiorum inventio* e.g. III.xvi.7 and III.xviii.3). If successful, it leads to *scientia*, i.e. distinct knowledge of causes (e.g. III. iv.3 and IV.iii.2).

As we have seen, Zabarella has a broad definition of *methodus*, which includes both *ordo*, i.e. order in teaching, and *methodus* properly taken (I. ii, III.i). The first two books are devoted to *ordo* and the last two are devoted to *methodus* in its more strict sense of way of acquiring knowledge, i.e. necessary syllogisms. (III.iii) In book I.ii.3 Zabarella compares *De methodis* with his work *Natura logicae*, in which he declares that logic has a double structure just like method. Logic can be separated from the *res* and reality (*logica docens*) or put in use (*logica utens* or *logica applicata*).[14] In the first case, logic is taught and in the second it is applied in a way so that logic even becomes the science it is applied to. When logic is applied to physics it becomes physics. Now, Zabarella writes that method works in the same way. When method is taught it is not yet applied, and when it is applied it becomes that very discipline it is applied to. Zabarella wrote primarily about logic and physics, and physics is one of the three *scientiae* in theoretical philosophy. So, of course, *De methodis* concerns teaching, but it is teaching about both *ordo* and *methodus stricte*, and this strict method even becomes the science to which it is applied. Therefore, Zabarella's *De methodis* is about the scientific discovery in e.g. physics that formed the foundation for medicine. But obviously, *De methodis* is not a work on natural philosophy. In McCaskey's understanding, *ordo* seems to prevail over *methodus stricte dicta* and deprive it of its specific signification.

McCaskey's translation is helpful on many difficult occasions and in several ways. It is clear and faithful to the text of Zabarella. According to the translator's own admission the translation is 'rather literal, even wooden' (i. 285). Perhaps the main reason for this judgement is that the

---

[14] I.ii.3.: 'Quoniam autem Methodus est habitus logicus, non est ignorandum, duplicem esse Methodum, quemadmodum et duplicem esse logicam alias declaravimus in eo libro, quem de natura logicae scripsimus, ex quo multa sumi possunt ad praesentem tractationem conferentia. Ibi quidem logicam duplicem esse diximus, unam rebus applicatam et iam in usu positam, alteram a rebus seiunctam. Hanc scientiam non esse, sed scientiarum instrumentum seu instrumentalem disciplinam demonstravimus; illam vero non amplius instrumentum, sed scientiam, fit enim scientia illa, cui dicitur applicata. Eadem ratione methodum appellare possumus tum ipsum instrumentalem habitum nulli adhuc rei seu disciplinae applicatum; tum etiam disciplinam ipsam, cui est applicatus. Propterea Aristoteles multis in locis scientias ipsas ac disciplinas methodos appellare solitus est, nam methodo utuntur omnes, methodoque consistunt; siquidem nihil aliud sunt, quam logicae methodi in usu positae'. Cf. Iacobus Zabarella, *Opera Logica* (Hildesheim, 1966), Cap. V. cols. 10–11.

translator has chosen to reproduce many Latin words in the translation with the exact counterpart among the Latin loan words in early modern English. Even though there seem to be good reasons for this strategy, exploiting terminology that, according to McCaskey, 'would not be far from what Zabarella's contemporary English readers and discussants used in their own writings on the same subjects' (i. 285), there are also substantial arguments against it. The most important one concerns readability. The English text is now much less accessible, since crucial Latin words are too often just anglicized into the translation. Some Latin words have, of course, kept their meaning in the English language. When that is the case, it is reasonable enough to use them. But some have not. Some notes are absolutely essential to the reader who is not familiar with the technical terms of Renaissance Aristotelianism. An illuminative example is the Latin word *affectio*. Zabarella and other contemporary writers used it for *accidens*, which means 'a contingent characteristic'. In Aristotelian ontology, substance and accidents are concepts fundamental to the understanding of all things, but in McCaskey's translation this useful ontological couplet becomes 'substance' and 'affections'. The reader finds the explanatory note about this on page 294 in the first volume and on page 426 in the second volume, but is it not far too optimistic to believe that readers will turn there before they start to read the text?

Another problem I should like to draw attention to in more detail concerns the concept of *cognitio confusa*. Here there is a fully understandable temptation, reasonably triggered by the strategy McCaskey generally adopts, to translate the obscure word *confusa* or the similarly obscure concept *cognitio confusa* as the equally obscure English word 'confused' or concept 'confused knowledge', as he does in I.viii.5, I.ix.3, I.ix.13, I.ix.14, II.viii.4 etc. But this concept is of no trivial significance for Zabarella. The word *confusa* occurs e.g. in the the Latin translation of the first book of Aristotle's Physics, 184a, which Zabarella used for his commentary. He even claims, in commenting on the passage, that the full understanding of this rough sentence hinges on grasping the precise meaning of the word *confusa*: 'if it is understood the whole text will be manifest'.[15] Now, McCaskey writes in his introduction that the distinction between imperfect and perfect knowledge is 'central to Zabarella's theory' (p. x). However, he does not penetrate any deeper so as to reveal to

---

[15] Iacobus Zabarella, '*Commentarii in Magni Aristotelis Libros physicorum* (Francofurti, MDCII), 50: 'Haec est sententia rudis huius contextus, cuius plena intelligentia consistit in declaratione eius vocis (confusa). Haec enim intellecta, totus textus est manifestus. I have used the facsimile of this edition, *Jacobi Zabarellae, Opera Physica*, edited by Marco Scarbi, (Verona, 2009).

the reader that 'imperfect knowledge' actually is 'confused knowledge'. As a result, unfortunately, these two concepts of imperfect and perfect knowledge and the distinction between them are not really explained at all. All that remains is for the reader to meet the challenge of understanding the concepts from the contexts in which they occur, not from the introduction, nor from the translation.

Why is the concept of *cognitio confusa* so important? Zabarella explains this himself. The concept *cognitio confusa* occurs some seven times in book one of *De methodis*, five times in book two, five times in book three, and twice in book four. It also occurs eighteen times in the much smaller *De regressu*. This is not even taking into account all derivatives such as *confuse* (e.g. *confuse cognita*) or *notitia confusa* etc. To begin with, irrespective of *ordo* and *methodus*, Zabarella maintains in *De methodis* as well as in his other logical writings that we have knowledge of two kinds which are basic to Aristotle's positition: perfect and imperfect knowledge, *cognitio perfecta* (also called *cognitio distincta*) on the one hand, and *cognitio imperfecta (also called cognitio confusa)* on the other hand. (I.viii.3) We need to know two things in everything: a thing's essence or nature, and its accidents. (I.xiv.4) Accidents are contingent and sensible (I.xiv.7). Essences are necessary and insensible. Order uses disposition to make learning easier and method in the strict sense is the way to know things which were unknown before (I.iii). In teaching, the normal route goes from knowledge of substances and universals to knowledge of particulars, but in using method *proprie dicta* the route goes from knowledge of known things to knowledge of unknown things. Accidents or effects are near and more easily known to us. Substances and, normally, causes, are known according to nature: that is to say, they are 'known by their own light' (III.xix.6). This means that we can know accidents and effects through our senses, but not substances and, normally, not causes. Now, to know a thing in a perfect way, one has to have knowledge of both accidents and substance, or effects and cause. When this condition is fulfilled, our knowledge is perfect, in the sense of being complete. As Zabarella explains in his commentary to *Physics*—and I leave the word *confusus* untranslated—'*confusum* seems to signify something whole, which consists of many parts, all of which, when they at the same time are composite and *confusae*, is, as that whole, called *confusum*'.[16] In his *De naturalis scientiae constitutione* Zabarella writes along the same lines that to get to know something *confuse* is to get to know something without knowledge of its parts, and to get to know something *distincte* is

---

[16] Ibid. 50: 'Confusum hic videtur significare totum aliquid, quod ex multis partibus constet, quae cum simul iunctae et confusae sint, totum illud vocatur confusum'.

to get to know something through knowledge of its parts.[17] And as we have noticed, our senses experience the whole, and the goal of *methodus resolutiva* is to discover the parts (principles or causes) of that whole. To know accidents without knowing their causes is to have confused knowledge about the accidents. Knowledge in this sense is incomplete. One can also have *cognitio confusa* of causes, since such knowledge only becomes distinct through *methodus resolutiva*. But *cognitio confusa* refers to *cognitio sensilis*, and that is experiential or empirical knowledge. Knowledge of causes and substances is, of course, rational knowledge. Aristotle and Zabarella nourished both kinds, but all knowledge originated from the senses.[18] Therefore, to translate *cognitio confusa* with 'confused knowledge' is in itself confusing and even misleading to a remarkable degree for the reader. In other words, *cognitio confusa* is a very important concept for our understanding of Zabarella as well as of Aristotle and various forms of Renaissance Aristotelianism. Behind it lies an enormous treasure of empirical knowledge that had to be formed into generalized statements through induction. This treasure of empirical material was the source for premises which were needed for the work of the natural philosopher and for the implementation of Zabarella's two approved methods. That crucial emphasis on ratiocination in his logical works crowns the mountain of empirical facts in *historia naturalis*, but the empirical background to the work of the natural philosopher tends to be disregarded. Therefore, bearing a mass of *cognitio confusa* in the mind was, I believe, a most important stage for scientific research according to Zabarella. He was highly effective in delineating this process in the *Regressus,* with its three stages: *demonstratio quod,* that something is the case, *consideratio mentalis,* which was supposed to lead to a distinct knowledge of the cause, and, finally, *demonstratio potissima,* the most potent demonstration, from the cause to a distinct knowledge of the effect. The latter was to become an important and crucial tool, not least for the next transalpine generation of scholars. The acute problem, though, which was realized only gradually,

---

[17] Iacobus Zabarella, *Liber de naturalis scientiae constitutione,* (Venetiis, MDLXXXVI), 39: '... cuius rationem declaro hoc exemplo, si sit cognoscendum animal genus cognitione, quantum fieri possit distincta, necesse est ut, quum sit totum quoddam confusum, cognoscatur per cognitionem partium. (Hoc enim est distincte cognoscere. Confuse autem cognoscere est confusum cognoscere ut confusum. Hoc est sine cognitione partium)'.

[18] Book III.xix.8: 'Omnis enim nostra cognitio a sensu originem ducit, nec potest aliquid a nobis mente cognosci, quin prius sensu cognitum fuerit, proinde inductione omnia eiusmodi principia nobis innotescunt, nec propterea demonstrari seu probari dicuntur, ea namque proprie dicuntur probari, quae demonstrantur per aliud. Inductio autem non probat rem per aliam rem, sed modo quodam eam per se ipsam declarat, universale enim a singulari reipsa non distinguitur, sed ratione solum'.

was that the treasure of empirical facts was largely unreliable. The Baconian answer to that was the urge for experimentation. But that is another story and not within the province of this review.

In conclusion, McCaskey has done an enormous service to the scholarly community with his work. Although the introduction to the texts contains some notable gaps, his translation is a big step forward for the accessibility of a difficult and extremely significant text by one of the most influential Aristotelians of all time.

Wolfson College
University of Oxford

Sari Kivistö, *The Vices of Learning: Morality and Knowledge at Early Modern Universities* (Leiden/Boston: Brill, 2014), viii+304 pp. ISBN: 9789004264120

Arnoud Visser

As a general rule, vice tends to be a much more interesting subject matter than virtue. In this lucid and stimulating book, Sari Kivistö proves that scholarly literature forms no exception. Based on the study of an impressive number of academic treatises and dissertations, Kivistö charts the moral discourse about scholarly vices in late Baroque and early Enlightenment Europe. As Kivistö points out, several hundreds of treatises about scholarly sins were published in this period, mostly in Latin. Apart from the voluminous source base, the discourse itself also proves remarkably rich and detailed, ranging from analyses of ambition and vainglory to taxonomies of arrogance and pedantry, from critiques of abuses within the intellectual community, such as plagiarism and quarrelling, to treatises about the anti-social nature of academic life, as exemplified in slovenliness (*misocosmia*) and lack of hygiene.

Kivistö concentrates largely on dissertations written by German intellectuals between approximately 1670 and 1730, building on previous investigations of literary *Gelehrtenkritik* by scholars such as Gunter Grimm, Martin Gierl, and Alexander Košenica, as well as on social historical studies of German universities in this period by historians such as William Clark and Marian Füssel. In this period academic self-criticism became a flourishing genre of publication. The gradual rise of a more empirical and experimental scientific culture generated new tensions between traditional academic values and reformist ideals of critical independence and scientific usefulness. Kivistö's main purpose is to investigate how scholarly vices were conceptualized in this period of change, exploring in particular the connections between knowledge and morality. Her exploration is divided into five thematic chapters that explore the vices of self-love (ch. 2), the desire for fame (ch. 3), quarrelling (ch. 4), curiosity (ch. 5) and bad manners (ch. 6). Although these vices regularly prove to overlap, Kivistö explains the division by stating that these sins are the most prominently discussed in the primary sources. A key overarching argument in her account is that traditional religious norms remained at the heart of the discourse about scholarly ethics (or at least, as presented in these treatises and dissertations).

A good example of how this process worked can be seen in Kivistö's chapter about pride and self-love. Patristic authorities such as Augustine had portrayed pride as not just a capital sin, but in fact the source of all other vices. Pride created a dangerously unchristian attitude in humans, which made them forget their dependence on divine grace. Echoing such early Christian views, scholarly critics such as the Augsburg Lutheran minister Gottlieb Spitzel pointed at the dangers of pride for intellectuals, suggesting it made them pursue knowledge for selfish reasons rather than out of concern for the truth. Spitzel provided many examples to illustrate his point, ranging from the ancient scholar Palaemon who claimed to have invented literature and the alphabet (suggesting that learning would die out again after his death), to the scholastic philosopher Simon of Tournay, who was said to have claimed he could refute all Jesus' teachings. The Leipzig philosopher and legal scholar Jacob Thomasius similarly cautioned against self-love as something that obstructed a man's intellectual development. Although Thomasius acknowledged that recognition was a universal human need, he knew that proper, legitimate self-love easily degenerated into a misguided desire for pleasure, causing scholarly quarrels and opportunism. According to Kivistö the traditional vocabulary to describe Christian vices was exploited by both traditionalist and reformist intellectuals. As a consequence, 'the sins remained the same', she writes, 'even if they had different manifestations on different sides of the conflict' (74).

In contrast to the versatility of pride, other sins prove to be more exclusive in their application to scholarly culture. In the context of the desire for fame Kivistö discusses several types of scholarly abuse that were applied to humanist culture in particular. Bibliomania or obsessive book collecting, for instance, was an old-style scholarly disease, according to the moralists, that could take various perverse forms. Kivistö discusses treatises by Petrus Ekerman, Daniel Friedrich Jani, and Michael Lilienthal that criticized collectors who assembled a great number of books without really paying attention to their contents. Such frantic collecting indicated ostentation and vainglory.

More pernicious, however, especially in the context of Enlightenment ideals of scholarly sociability, was the practice of bibliotaphy, which denoted the 'burying' of books by collectors who kept their treasures to themselves and withheld from others the knowledge that they had assembled. With this type of behaviour these scholars erred in two ways, as Kivistö points out. Besides displaying a form of intellectual avarice, they also overestimated the value of bookish knowledge at the cost of wisdom. And yet, it also becomes clear that the moralists were hard to satisfy. The same critic who warned against ostentatious collecting also vilified the austere opposite, the reluctance or downright refusal to possess books. Apart from a few laudable examples of *abibloi*, such as Philipp Melanchthon who was said only to have owned the Bible, Aristotle, Pliny, Plutarch, and Ptolemy, this attitude could easily reflect contempt for the knowledge of other people.

In this competitive social context the longing for personal recognition was increasingly expressed, as Kivistö notes, through the use of titles. This trend originated in the political arena and subsequently spilled over in the Republic of Letters, where it provoked a series of critical pamphlets about *titulomania*. Such visible signs of professional status were clearly a highly sensitive issue in a community that had long prided itself as an environment where social distinctions were subordinate to intellectual values. In his Leipzig dissertation (1723), Karl Heinrich Heege ridiculed the elaborate titles that some scholars had fabricated for themselves (giving examples such as 'librarian of the most elegant literature and admirable from top to bottom'), as well as the use of misleading abbreviations, such as the person who wrote S.Th.D. after his name, which suggested he was a doctor of theology, whereas in fact it meant he was deacon from Salfeld in Thüringen. These and many other cases formed a reservoir of stock examples that served to clarify scholarly decorum. As such, the treatises about title-mania do not just reflect a moral discourse that is rooted in Christian criticism of secular fame, but also reflect a social world in which these titles were increasingly prominent (for good reason the archivist Eckart Henning recently suggested that *Titulaturenkunde* would make a promising ancillary discipline).

In her general conclusion, Kivistö underlines the central idea that the acquisition of knowledge was not a morally neutral activity. The ethical perspective of the Protestant critics that dominated the treatises on scholarly vices was predicated on the idea that only a righteous scholar, who possessed the Christian virtues of humility and modesty, could attain true knowledge. Yet apart from this general conclusion, Kivistö's study also shows in rich detail how together these treatises on scholarly vices formed a literary tradition in their own right. With their wealth of topics and examples these texts shaped discussions on scholarly culture for decades, not just in German contexts, but also in Sweden and Finland. According to Kivistö the impact of this tradition was to some extent to instil ethical pessimism in the reader. With their learned references and lengthy citations the treatises became detached from their immediate social context, giving the arguments an air of universal validity. And still, Kivistö argues, all this strenuous critical reflection did not necessarily imply a complete lack of trust in scholarly morals. Instead, it should be regarded as an exercise in scholarly ethics in itself. The authors themselves certainly seem to have regarded it as a useful activity. Indeed, as the Erfurt archivist Johann Gottfried Büchner claimed, the treatises on scholarly vices could evoke 'fear or outright terror' in their readers and thus help them avoid the most serious errors (263).

Department of Languages, Literature and Communication
Utrecht University

Maximilian Schuh, *Aneignungen des Humanismus. Institutionelle und individuelle Praktiken an der Universität Ingolstadt im 15. Jahrhundert* (Education and Society in the Middle Ages and Renaissance, Vol. 47), (Leiden/Boston: Brill, 2013), xiii+286 pp. ISBN: 9789004230958

Richard Kirwan

Maximilian Schuh's *Aneignungen des Humanismus* is an informative and valuable study of the manner in which humanist learning took hold at the University of Ingolstadt in the late fifteenth century. The monograph is the outcome of a PhD dissertation examined at the University of Münster in 2011. Its findings are established through sensitive investigation of the manifestations of humanism in a variety of forms and contexts at Ingolstadt. What emerges is a story of the gradual and piecemeal assimilitation of humanist tendencies which were advanced not alone by an intellectual elite, for example in shape of Konrad Celtis, but also, in a more fundamental yet subtle way, and indeed from the university's inception, as a result of the interests and activities of less studied masters and students. Schuh's 'ground-up' approach allows him to meet the stated aims of the work: to understand the social, economic, and institutional factors which facilitated the embedding of new intellectual norms and habits.

The author's sense that manifestations of humanism at the grass roots could be subtle and halting leads him to adopt two methodological positions. In the first instance, he intentionally eschews any sustained focus on the figure of Celtis. The tendency heretofore to focus on the renowned humanist within the scholarship, the author suggests, has led to an inattention to the existence of humanism at Ingolstadt prior to Celtis' intervention in 1492. This traditional approach has also been at odds with the extent to which Celtis is reflected in the archival materials of the institution. The second position adopted by Schuh is to follow the relatively inclusive methodology of Paul Oskar Kristeller in the latter's observation of the gradual infilitration of humanism. Thus Schuh endeavours to avoid a doctrinaire approach in his attempts to detect the first stirrings of humanism among Ingolstadt's students and masters.

The book is arranged in three main chapters (aside from the introduction and conclusion). These focus on the contexts in which humanism emerged at the university. This leads primarily to the scrutiny of developments within the faculty of Arts and the Poetics *Lektur*. The first of the main chapters examines the intellectual dispositions and activities of the masters of the Arts faculty and the incumbents of the Poetics *Lektur*. The second chapter explores the infilitration of humanistic elements into the curriculum of the faculty of Arts with particular reference to grammar and rhetoric and the revision of the faculty's statutes. It also examines the stocks of the faculty library with a view to unearthing the shift towards humanistic studies. The third main chapter again examines pedagogical developments but on this occasion with a focus on the reception of humanism at the level of the individual rather than institution. Here Schuh unearths evidence of the assimilation of humanist concerns in text-books, student lecture notes and glosses, books possessed by individuals, and individual writing and linguistic styles.

A range of interesting observations follow from Schuh's exploration of the early manifestations of humanism in Ingolstadt. One such observation is that the Poetics *Lektur*, established in 1477, was not the prime mover in terms of the introduction of humanism since its status within the university and the curriculum remained rather uncertain and ambigious until the sixteenth century. Rather, the primary setting within which humanism emerged was the faculty of Arts. Another important finding of Schuh's work relates to the importance of non-elite actors in the assimilation of humanism. The process it appears was facilitated in first instance by masters of varied status as well as by their students. Ingolstadt, as the author demonstrates, was subject to broader trends and fashions in the academic circles of the Empire. Masters and students were exposed to humanistic ideas during their studies and careers in the Empire's other universities and also in Paris. Following their 'academic socialization' such scholars became the carriers of humanistic interests. This 'academic socialization' continued at Ingolstadt, thus strengthening the foundations of humanism in the institution. This mobility it seems rarely extended below the Alps. Schuh suggests that such limited contact with Italian humanism allowed a certain flexibility in the integration of humanism into the curriculum in Ingolstadt facilitating a gradual and relatively easy transition from the scholastic method in the study of the Arts. Another significant observation relates to the relative importance of students as drivers of curricular change. In this respect the author emphasizes the power of student demand, especially when it came to tuition on the margins of the curriculum. Dependent as they were on the income that accrued from such tuition, masters were inclined to respond to and attempt to stimulate student demand. This encouraged a certain of level of innovation in the effort to court student interest.

This book offers a carefully researched, stimulating, and insightful exploration of the advancement of humanism at the University of Ingolstadt in the late fifteenth century. Schuh interrogates a relatively wide range of source material in this study and a variety of institutional settings in order to detect the gradual assimilation of humanism at the university. His methodological approach is one which allows a great sensitivity to change in this regard. The resulting findings are both stimulating and convincing. Certain questions and issues might have been probed a little deeper. For example, the author might have elaborated further on how exactly 'academic socialization' operated in daily practice. Or indeed, the author might have offered a greater depth of information in relation to the corresponding developments at other universities in the Empire. In conclusion, Schuh offers a richly observed and insightful study of the emergence of humanism at the Ingolstadt in the years following its foundation.

Department of History
University of Limerick

Elizabeth Harding, *Der Gelehrte im Haus: Ehe, Familie und Haushalt in der Standeskultur der frühneuzeitlichen Universität Helmstedt* (Wiesbaden: Harrassowitz, 2014), 388 pp. ISBN: 9783447102865

Asaph Ben-Tov

The University of Helmstedt was founded by Duke Julius of Brunswick-Wolfenbüttel in 1576 and closed by Jérôme Bonaparte in 1810. Its foundation, flourishing, and decline are closely linked to the academic history of the post-Reformation Holy Roman Empire—it closed four years after the Empire itself had ceased to exist. Its inauguration was part of a wave of later sixteenth- and early seventeenth-century university foundations in the Empire,[1] and its end under Bonaparte was part of the wave of university closures of those tumultuous years.[2] Unlike the University of Erfurt (closed in 1806) the University of Helmstedt has no medieval history and unlike its neighbour and successful rival in Göttingen, or Wilhelm von Humboldt's university in Berlin (which opened the very same year Helmstedt expired) it has no modern history. From foundation to liquidation it was an early modern phenomenon. Though it was long gone by the time late nineteenth- and twentieth-century scholars were composing voluminous histories of universities, and there

---

[1] E.g., Jena (1558), Altdorf (founded as an academy in 1575 and elevated to university status in 1622), and Giessen (1607); and Rinteln (1620) and Dillingen (founded as a Latin school in 1549 turning into a Jesuit university 1553) to name two Catholic examples.

[2] E.g. Erfurt (1804), Altdorf and Rinteln (1809), or Frankfurt an der Oder and Wittenberg which were effectively closed and later incorporated into other universities (1811 and 1817 respectively).

is, as yet, no comprehensive history of the university,[3] it has by no means been overlooked by scholars. Shortly after it was closed the orientalist and former Helmstedt professor Paul Jakob Bruns published his *Verdienste der Professoren zu Helmstädt um die Gelehrsamkeit* (The scholarly accomplishments of the professors of Helmstedt), to which one can add Friedrich Koldewey's 1895 account of classical scholarship at this university.[4] Apart from these and other earlier studies, the university has been at the focus of more recent scholarship.[5] To these can also be added studies devoted to prominent scholars, mostly of the seventeenth century, who taught at this university, such as Johann Caselius (1533–1613), the theologian Georg Calixt (1586–1656) or the polymath Hermann Conring (1606–81). The history of the *Academia Julia*, thus named after its founder, is also the subject of an ongoing research project at the Herzog August Library in Wolfenbüttel, which houses much of the university's paper remains.[6] It is in the context of this project that Elizabeth Harding's study has emerged.

Rendered into English the book's title reads: *The scholar at home: marriage, family, and household within the class-culture* (Standeskultur) *of the early modern University of Helmstedt*. In other words, this study is dedicated to a scrutiny of professorial families and households in Helmstedt as part of the culture of a self-fashioning class (or rather estate— *Stand*) in early modern society.

The work opens with a detailed introduction, where, apart from surveying the existing relevant scholarship the author considers some of the basic terms underlying this study—e.g. family and the evolving scholarship on early modern families in Europe. Surprisingly it is the pivotal category of *Standeskultur* (class/estate-culture), which is taken as

[3] Comparable e.g. to Walter Friedensburg's *Geschichte der Universität Wittenberg* (Halle, 1917) or to collaborative ventures like Wilhelm Doerr & Gisbert zu Putlitz (eds), *Semper apertus: 600 Jahre Ruprecht-Karls-Universität Heidelberg 1386–1986* (6 vols, Berlin, 1985) or more recently *Geschichte der Universität Leipzig 1409–2009* (5 vols, Leipzig, 2009–10).
[4] Friedrich Koldewey, *Geschichte der klassischen Philologie auf der Universität Helmstedt* (Brunswick, 1895).
[5] To name but a few: Sabine Ahrens, *Die Lehrkräfte der Universität Helmstedt (1576–1810)* (Helmstedt, 2004), several studies by Peter Baumgart collected in his *Universitäten im konfessionellen Zeitalter: gesammelte Beiträge* (Münster, 2006), Richard Kirwan, *Empowerment and Representation at the University in Early Modern Germany: Helmstedt and Würzburg, 1576–1634* (Wiesbaden, 2009).
[6] This project has produced a volume of collected articles on the university, accompanying an exhibition at the library in 2010: Ulrike Gleixner & Jens Bruning (eds), *Das Athen der Welfen. Die Reformuniversität Helmstedt 1576–1810* (Wiesbaden, 2010), as well as Jens Bruning's study *Innovation in Forschung und Lehre: Die philosophische Fakultät der Universität Helmstedt in der Frühaufklärung 1680–1740* (Wiesbaden, 2012). In addition, much, including scans of historical sources on Helmstedt, has been posted online by the Wolfenbüttel Helmstedt project. The links can be found under: http://www.hab.de/de/home/wissenschaft/forschungsprofil-und-projekte/laufende-projekte. (last visited 2.6.2015).

a given. Much of what Erich Trunz (1931) and later scholars have identified as the cultural and social characteristics of the *Standeskultur* of late-humanists around 1600 is relevant to the social and cultural self-fashioning Harding traces in discussing Helmstedt professors.[7] It would be instructive to further consider which of these aspects of professorial social habits were typical of a broader landscape of Ancien Régime scholars (e.g. learned clergymen, Latin School teachers or scholars active at the Empire's many aristocratic courts) and which were more distinctly academic. While early modern professors clearly saw themselves as belonging to a well-defined corporate body with the social status and legal privileges this entailed—Harding's discussion of the legal privileges of Helmstedt professors is one of the book's strengths—at the same time they saw themselves as belonging to a more amorphous, yet no less real, Republic of Letters as well as to a social estate within their own society, not strictly defined by academic corporate privileges.

Harding formulates the book's thesis at the outset: the so-called private spheres of marriage, family, and household were fundamental for constituting the estate/class of university professors (12). While doubtless true, I am unconvinced that this very general argument is the best vantage point from which to consider the rich array of sources from Helmstedt.

The introduction is followed by four sections:

1) Framework conditions: the economic position of scholars in practice and discourse.

2) Production and consumption: domestic regimes.

3) The marital ideal and the joys of singledom: matrimonial regimes.

4) Representation and celebration: settings of order.

The more general institutional context set by Harding for Helmstedt is an incremental regularization of early modern universities in the process of which they gradually lost their earlier autonomy to become part of the growing state apparatus (36). After dwelling on the precarious mess of early modern university funding—here as elsewhere in the study, Helmstedt is convincingly taken by the author as a representative example of broader trends among Protestant universities of the Holy Roman Empire, rather than as an exception—Harding stresses the competitive, supply and demand oriented nature of professorial additional income (i.e. private instruction) embedded in the pre-modern porous distinction between

---

[7] Erich Trunz, 'Der deutsche Späthumanismus um 1600 als Standeskultur', in *Zeitschrift für Geschichte der Erziehung und des Unterrichts* 21 (1931), 17–53. Needless to say, much work has been done since Trunz's famous essay.

gift and exchange. The eighteenth century witnessed a gradual monetarization (and thus depersonalization) of these services. A case in point is the varying fees charged in Helmstedt (as elsewhere) for the *privata*. Here too the author identifies a growing regulation and standardization in the course of the eighteenth century. Such attempts at regulation, welcomed by the territorial rulers, were often resisted both by students and professors. Harding quotes an instructive case from 1729 where mitigating fee exceptions were suggested for both poor and particularly diligent students; neither side was eager to jettison the personal nature of these arrangements for an impersonal and well-ordered regulation (58-9), though, as the author points out, gradual regulation and monetarization also brought greater stability for the professors themselves (64).

In this, as well as in the following section on domestic consumption and production, Harding offers an overview of trends of monetarization and sharpening social distinctions and their spatial expression within the professorial household. Much of this is instructive but I find the author's choice of focus regrettable. The need to contextualize the findings from Helmstedt within a broader framework is clear and yet Harding's decision, especially in the first section of the book, to offer a very broad narrative and use Helmstedt material as illustrations thereof rather than engage in a closer study of the localized social history of Helmstedt professors and then see if and to what extent this conforms to, nuances, or indeed undermines grand narratives is, to my mind, regrettable. The wealth of material in the opening sections notwithstanding, embedding information from Helmstedt as illustrations of very broad arguments about early modern universities and private life misses the opportunity offered by such focused case studies. Thus this detailed study in learned habits and professorial households in Helmstedt tells us less than the present reviewer would like to learn about local contexts—first and foremost about the concrete urban setting of Helmstedt. This is all the more regrettable since what the author does reveal about the local context in the first part of her book is of considerable interest—thus Harding offers an interesting (but tantalizingly brief) discussion of the evolving architecture of professorial households in Helmstedt, brewing as a source of income and its gradual fall from favour, professors' deteriorating relationships with Helmstedt artisans as neighbours, and the intriguing case of Helmstedt's Wednesday Club (*Mittwochklub*) opened in 1784. Such localized cases do more than 'add colour' to a traditional social history with its predilection for impersonal longue durée trends. They bring case studies into a more nuanced and instructive dialogue with grand narratives. Long-term developments could here have been complemented by a closer scrutiny of individual professors making economic, social, and cultural choices—these are not absent from the book, but I believe they have been underprivileged. Furthermore, a closer consideration of the way professorial households dealt with *events* would have potentially been an instructive complement to tracing long term trends—e.g. attempts to cope with the ravages of the Thirty Years War or bubonic outbreaks which challenged academic life (and academics' lives).

The section on 'the ideal of marriage and the joys singledom' is in many ways the core of this study and is by far the best part of the book—in great part due to the careful study of trends and exemplary cases taken from Helmstedt. Of particular interest is Harding's discussion of the legal autonomy of Helmstedt professors and their standing in questions of family morals and recruitment of new teachers. The author finds among Helmstedt professors evidence for a broader trend among late-seventeenth- and eighteenth-century scholars. In Protestant territories marriage and the family household had been established as the scholar's ideal setting, but there arose in the later seventeenth century a new scholarly ideal, the learned bachelor, not replacing the former but offering a valid alternative. Harding offers some interesting case studies on this point. Among them is the case of the professor of oriental languages and idiosyncratic biblical scholar Hermann von der Hardt, his last-minute renouncement of his betrothal (1711) and the ensuing legal feud with his young fiancée and her family. Of equal interest is the author's careful consideration of the Helmstedt jurisprudent Karl Friedrich Paelicke (1736–1780). Paelicke married his pregnant housemaid, an act which almost terminated his academic career. Revealingly it was not so much the sexual relationship outside wedlock which the privy councillor and several of Paelicke's colleagues in 1766 found so offensive; it was rather for his marriage to someone below his estate that they wished to thwart his appointment to a chair in the law faculty. Interesting too is the fact that Paelicke was eventually appointed to the post in 1768 following his students' petition (222–3). In these and other such cases of marital norms and their violation among Helmstedt academics, Harding identifies a shift in post Reformation era attitudes to marriage. It was no longer necessarily seen as a moral safeguard or as an ideal. From the professors' point of view, this allowed a certain freedom in the eighteenth century to abstain from marriage—as singledom was itself becoming a distinguishing mark for many scholars. The book concludes with a final section 'Representing and celebrating' of which the opening chapter, 'Family as a political argument', traces the gradual separation of family and office with further chapters considering the academic festive and commemorative culture

In the concluding remarks Harding reiterates the claim made in the introduction, that her study of professorial habitus in Helmstedt is intended as a contribution to the study of the early modern communicative significance of seemingly private affairs. From the standpoint of a reader interested in the history of universities and in the University of Helmstedt in particular, this is not an ideal vantagepoint—with the fine exception of the substantial section on marriage and single scholars. And while, from this point of view, readers may regret Harding's decision to arrange her study according to such a broad interpretive blueprint rather than a more localized scrutiny of the case at hand, it offers much that is of interest to students of early modern academic life.

Forschungszentrum Gotha der Universität Erfurt

Roger L. Geiger, *The History of American Higher Education: Learning and Culture from the Founding to World War II* (Princeton: Princeton University Press, 2015), 551 pp. ISBN: 9780691149394

W. Bruce Leslie

The History of American Higher Education implies that the titled volume is definitive. In this case, the work justifies the implicit boast, at least to 1940, the delimiting chronology of the sub-title.[1] This is the new gold standard, a volume which every specialist in our field must read. In this volume Roger Geiger confirms his place as the pre-eminent historian of American higher education. Unfortunately this daunting volume will not reach many beyond the readers of this journal—more on that later.

But first, let's travel through the four centuries from the Massachusetts Bay's audacious transplantation of the Oxbridge model in the virgin New England soil to an America about to assume world supremacy in the nuclear age. Or, in Geiger's words, analyse how colleges in 'an isolated, provincial colonial society evolved into a system that served an incipient economic powerhouse by 1940'. (p. ix)

He anchors his account of the first century in two premises. First, that the founders carried with them the academic traditions of arguably the most literate society in the world, an England in which higher education

---

[1] This review has benefited considerably from the insights offered in a panel discussion on this book at the 2014 Annual Meeting of the History of Education Society (US). I am indebted to my fellow participants: David Hoeveler (University of Wisconsin at Milwaukee); Jim Turner (University of Notre Dame); Lester Goodchild (University of Massachusetts at Boston); and Roger Geiger, (Penn State University). I have also benefitted from the insights of James Axtell (College of William and Mary).

included 2.5% of seventeen-year-old males. Early seventeenth-century Oxford and Cambridge had benefited from a broadening social base, particularly among the gentry, and from a fiery intellectual life stoked by scientific breakthroughs and religious fervour. Second, that the English heritage contained the dynamic interaction of three goals: culture, careers, and knowledge. Geiger maintains that despite being tethered by the European traditions of close oversight by the state, Harvard, William and Mary, and Yale showed surprising intellectual diversity in the century after Harvard's founding.

Geiger's account of the half century from George Whitefield firing up the Great Awakening through the early years of independence expertly places colleges at the centre of the intellectual ferment of the rapidly maturing and eventually rebellious society. Each college is described within its particular context as competing religious forces, especially Calvinist and Anglican, sought to retain or challenge orthodoxy and the Enlightenment increasingly challenged sectarian-based founding identities. The result was dynamic institutional developments as the colleges proved surprisingly open to new ideas, especially as Enlightenment writings became familiar on the western side of the Atlantic. Geiger masterfully connects intellectual history and early institutional development to create an exciting account of the foundation of a truly 'American' higher education.

Geiger casts the post-independence decades in less glowing light. Innovative attempts to create 'Republican universities' largely failed. Colleges lacked the intellectual and financial resources to exert much influence and early state governments either showed little interest in funding the experiments or even became overtly hostile to them as hotbeds of Enlightenment thought.

Then Geiger makes a second major contribution, rescuing the antebellum years from a reputation for intellectual and institutional stagnation characterized by Richard Hofstadter's phrase, the 'Great Retrogression'. Instead, Geiger convincingly demonstrates that the 1820s and 1830s were 'the takeoff years for the American college' (213). He further describes surprising growth and innovation in the last two antebellum decades. Geiger places the antebellum colleges into a broader historical context, framed particularly by his clear grasp of technological and economic change. No reader of this book will think of higher education in the Early Republic in the same way again.

His depiction of the years straddling the Civil War is similarly innovative. Attempts to deal with this period have often missed its intellectual fervour due to focusing only on colleges and imposing a modern definition of 'higher education'. Geiger does a superb job of detailing the multifarious attempts to deal with a rapidly changing world, though one without a clear role for traditional colleges. He tackles the dilemma of explaining institutions before our modern categories existed by expanding the terminology to 'higher learning'. Thus academies, Normal Schools, Female Institutes and Seminaries, and schools of science are added to the mix. Our modern distinction between secondary and higher education has no place for institutions that straddled that line and were losers in post-1890s systemization. He also shows that even the term 'college' misleads us as most were multi-purpose institutions in which college students were a minority. Free-standing colleges were rare.

Geiger finishes revising our understanding of mid-nineteenth-century higher education with a rich depiction of the land-grant movement. That umbrella term covered deep curricular divisions among land-grant colleges with differing balances of vocational, applied, and liberal arts courses. The land-grant colleges also differed by region and according to whether they were added to existing institutions or created new. Most strikingly, he points out that surprising proportion of early philanthropy to colleges was directed toward giving 'mechanics' (i.e. engineering) a more theoretical base through attachment to formal institutions of higher education.

As the narrative approaches the twentieth century, Geiger adroitly intertwines the seemingly contradictory rise of the research university and the collegiate revolution. 'As long as higher education was defined by the collegiate course, the university ideal was indeed remote. Conversely, any approach that ignored the undergraduate college was doomed to failure' (316). Most of the strands are familiar, but two aspects may surprise readers. First, Geiger gives much less importance to German and English influences than most scholars. Second, he demonstrates that professional schools played a much bigger role and posed a much greater challenge to colleges than usually perceived. With forty per cent of students, few of whom had college degrees, enrolled in medical, law, and theology schools in the 1890s, professional schools were an alternative to college rather than a logical next step. This highlights the significance of subsequently assimilating professional schools into universities and making them a sequential post-baccalaureate step—a practice that still distinguishes American from European practice.

Having focused on elite institutions in his explanation of the emergence of the university and the collegiate revolution, Geiger moves to normal schools, junior colleges, urban colleges, and historically Black colleges and universities into the post-WWI chapter. This creates some chronological confusion but weaves often-overlooked institutions into the saga of the creation of the world's first mass higher education. One striking omission is Catholic colleges and universities, which are barely mentioned despite having been the major alternative to the historically Protestant institutions.

Geiger concludes his four-century narrative with the triumph of what he calls 'The Standard American University'. Using his knowledge as the leading historian of research universities, Geiger makes a convincing case that the 1920s and 1930s saw more fundamental change than normally assumed, underwritten by unprecedented philanthropic support for a coterie of elite institutions. The resulting standardization created a true system for the first time and one poised to take advantage of the opportunities WWII and the post-war world offered. If others find Geiger's case as persuasive as I do, his unlikely ending date of 1940 will change our conventional periodization.

This comprehensive and massive work will become the leading single-volume study on the subject for specialists; a second volume on WWII to the present is promised. No other work provides so much detailed information and insightful analysis with such sure-footed historical sense based on up-to-date scholarship.

The History of American Higher Education serves up an impressively complex and hard-driving interpretation that should become the touchstone for readers of *History of Universities.* It is a daunting tome that I read with delight, but is unlikely to draw many others. Its heft and style will limit its influence to a small band of specialists. In addition to its length (551 pages), long paragraphs, lengthy chapters (averaging over 45 pages), lack of photos and inclusion of only one table will narrow its readership. The lack of a bibliography is regrettable, though the plentiful and informative footnotes partially compensate.

The decision to divide the history into two volumes will further limit its influence, especially as a textbook. Thus, instructors seeking a text accessible to students will probably continue to rely on Rudolph's increasingly dated work or Thelin's delightfully anecdotal but less ambitious synthesis.[2]

General readers seeking a comprehensive history may still turn to Brubacher & Rudy's venerable but dated *Higher Education in Transition.* Cohen's *The Shaping of American Higher Education* continues to be useful on post-WWII developments but is less sophisticated historically. Lucas's *American Higher Education* sweeps across the ages from classical Greece but lacks Geiger's historical grasp of American developments.[3] Thus, when

---

[2] Frederick Rudolph, *The American College and University: A History* (New York 1962; 2nd ed. Athens GA 1990 with an essay and updated bibliography by John Thelin); John Thelin, *A History of American Higher Education* (Baltimore, 2004).

[3] John Brubacher & Willis Rudy, *Higher Education in Transition: A History of American Colleges and Universities* (New York 1958; 4th ed. New Brunswick 1997). Arthur Cohen, *The Shaping of American Higher Education* (San Francisco 1998; 2nd ed. 2010). Paul Lucas, *American Higher Education: A History* (New York 1994; 2nd ed. 2006).

Geiger's second volume is published we will have a new definitive work, but will lack a one-volume work that condenses his impressive synthesis into more accessible form.

By moving our understanding to a new level, Geiger's work offers a platform from which to look in other directions that synthetic works could incorporate. Most fundamentally, *The History of American Higher Education* is an avowedly institutional history that focuses on 'colleges and universities legally empowered to award the degrees that certify advanced education' (539). Future syntheses could give more attention to the social and intellectual context, particularly on student life and the educational process. The architectural and physical dimension, especially at a time when the future of 'brick and mortar' campuses is being debated, could be usefully discussed. The unique social space occupied by higher education in American culture is an important aspect worthy of a place. Finally, future scholars could try to answer the question of what impact higher education has had on society and ask whether a more European style academic world would have made America a different place?

But to suggest adding further dimensions to a saga Geiger only partially told in over 500 pages raises questions about the role and utility of writing a national synthesis, particularly one encapsulating a large country with such a de-centralized (non-?) system. Is it possible to tell a coherent 'American' story? How useful is the nation-state as an organizing concept? Are the histories of demographic groups, regions, types of institutions, genders, more important than the ties that bind 'The Standard American University'? How can a synthesis reflect the diverse institutions and experiences without Balkanizing the field? Can we depict central tendencies without cutting off the outer standard deviations?

Given those complications, is it possible to write such a national synthesis in a readable and reasonable length? How much complexity must be sacrificed to write an accessible account for students, policy-makers, and general readers? Whatever the challenges, at a time of fierce international competition measured by league tables that shape and even warp educational policies, national studies will have current importance as well as historical interest. And given the dominance of American research universities and the profound misunderstandings of the unique American system, they are vitally important. How do we tell the American story to other cultures and, in turn, what are the barriers to learning more from other nation-states' experiences?

Princeton University Press has made a fundamental contribution to the history of higher education by commissioning Geiger's two volumes as well as a history of the university from Paris to the present by

James Axtell.[4] These synthesize a generation of scholarship and should be the new bedrock on which works our future scholarship stands.

Department of History
The College at Brockport
State University of New York

---

[4] James Axtell, *The University: from Medieval Origins to Global Ascendance* (Princeton University Press, forthcoming 2016).

Noël Golvers, *Libraries of Western Learning for China. Circulation of Western Books between Europe and China in the Jesuit Mission (ca.1650–1750)*, ii: *Formation of Jesuit Libraries*. (Louvain: Ferdinand Verbiest Institute K.U. Leuven, 2013), 559 pp. ISBN: 9789082090901

Alexander Statman

Formation of Jesuit Libraries is the second volume in Noël Golvers's *Libraries of Western Learning for China*, a comprehensive account of Western book collecting in China during the seventeenth and eighteenth century Jesuit mission. The first volume, *Logistics of Book Acquisition and Circulation*, dealt with how the Jesuits selected and acquired Western books in Europe, and the third volume will address their presentation of Western books to Chinese audiences. This volume, *Formation of Jesuit Libraries*, focuses on the crossroads between the two, the libraries of the individual missions established all over China, describing in detail how they were built, maintained, and finally dismantled.

The Society of Jesus was the most important conduit for literary exchange between China and the West during this period, and its libraries were the main sites of contact. As a source book and a starting point for research, *Formation of Jesuit libraries* will find an audience. It is also a display of extraordinary erudition. Golvers relies almost entirely on archival documents, with lengthy quotations throughout the text in at least six European languages and many supplemental graphs, tables, and lists. The empirical contribution is tremendous. It also makes it hard to generalize about the material, though Golvers does not seem overly determined to try. The main argument is that in the early seventeenth century, the missionaries Nicolas Trigault and Niccolò Longobardo formulated a centralized program for procuring European books and organizing them in China, but this comes off largely as an afterthought. What this volume actually shows is just how diverse the Jesuit libraries in China really were.

Formation of Jesuit Libraries is primarily concerned with the individual libraries and their particular histories. Golvers begins with a discussion of his missionary sources and prosopographical methods, while also introducing the Jesuit library master plan. The core of the book uses archival documents to tell the stories of nearly every known Western library in China, including those of the first mission at Macau, the four churches in Beijing, and some smaller outposts in the provinces. The short conclusion offers some general remarks on Jesuit book collecting, addressing themes such as the division between communal and private libraries, the circulation of books, and the continuity of collections. At the back are numerous appendices describing the contents of the Jesuit libraries as well as an extensive bibliography, together comprising about half the book's length and no small part of its value.

Golvers argues that almost from the beginning of the China mission, the Jesuits had a 'library policy' or 'master plan' to coordinate book collecting around a 'central library' in Beijing. Trigault and Longobardo implemented a systematic program for organizing book collections and catalogues, based on theoretical instructions such as Claude Clément's *Musei sive Bibliothecae* and realized prototypes such as the *Collegio Romano*. The conceptual blueprints for the formation of Jesuit libraries were therefore exclusively European: Jesuit libraries were supposed to be more or less the same, no matter where they were located. In this account, the Chinese context closes off more possibilities than it opens up, entering mostly in the form of floods, fires, and the occasional invasion. One would like to know more about what made Jesuit libraries in China different from those in Europe; unfortunately, sources are scarce. No early modern Jesuit archives survive in China, and important collections of rare Western books are, for the moment anyway, inaccessible. The Chinese contexts of Western collections will be the subject of the next volume of *Libraries of Western Learning for China*. But it seems as if the Chinese setting might have figured more prominently here, too, since that is just what makes the formation of Jesuit collections of Western books in China special.

Formation of Jesuit Libraries is nevertheless a useful resource for scholars of the Jesuit China missions, who will not mind that it sometimes sacrifices elegance for content. This is certainly the most significant work on the topic since Hubert Verhaeren's catalogue of the European books in the collection of the North Church in Beijing was published in

1949, just before research in China became more difficult. Golvers expands on Verhaeren's work by exploiting the extraordinary wealth of Jesuit archives all over Europe. He seems to have read every last letter and found all the references to books and libraries, reflecting many years of careful and diligent research. This could have potentially allowed for more sustained prosopographical analysis of the mission as a whole, but Golvers leaves that opportunity for others to pursue.

The focus is instead on the history of the individual Jesuit libraries throughout China, which is the best part of the book. For each collection, Golvers shows how it changed over time and what books it included, where they came from, where they were stored, and how they were used. *Formation of Jesuit Libraries* clarifies some issues that can be confusing even to specialists, for example, the changing names and locations of the four main churches in Beijing. Sections on provincial collections in places such as Jiangsu and Hubei and on the separate libraries of the *Propaganda Fide* and the *Missions Étrangères de Paris* may be the only recent studies of these topics available and should suggest many new avenues of investigation.

The inevitable barrier to entry for such an erudite tome could have been lowered a little by better editing. The style is scholarly to the point of dense. Footnotes are numbered over the whole book rather than by chapter, so that by the end they run into the 1000s. Long and frequent quotations in Latin are usually translated into English, though even longer and more frequent quotations in modern languages are not. In the style of a textbook, sections are numbered (for example, '4.3.3.3.2. The French Residence') and key words are often in italics or boldface or, sometimes, both. Perhaps some of these editorial decisions simply suggest that the book is designed to be used rather than to be read.

In sum, *Formation of Jesuit Libraries* focuses on questions of 'how' rather than 'why', reveling in the diversity of the evidence without trying to impose a single narrative upon it. Golvers is satisfied just to reconstruct the formation of Jesuit libraries in meticulous detail. So much so that if the Jesuits in China had indeed written a general 'library policy', one imagines that it might have looked something like this book. *Formation of Jesuit Libraries*, along with its companion volumes in *Libraries of Western Learning for China*, will undoubtedly become the standard reference on the topic and will likely remain so for a long time.

Department of History, Stanford University
Lane History Corner
450 Serra Mall
Stanford, CA 94305

Tamson Pietsch, *Empire of Scholars: Universities, Networks and the British Academic World 1850–1939* (Manchester/ New York: Manchester University Press, 2013). ISBN: 9780719085024

'Networking' is a common idea today, given particular currency by tele-communications and internet developments in the creation and strengthening of longitudinal associations. The word or concept has its theorists, sociologists, and historians, such as Manuel Castells (*The Rise of the Network Society*, 1996). It has been amply employed by the late city planner, Sir Peter Hall, in his monumental work on the history of cities,[1] especially with regard to the integrating and geographical features of early industrialization in the English Midlands and North, the coming together of labour supplies, capital, transportation, technical innovation, market discipline, and entrepreneurial skills. Other authors have joined in (e.g., Francis C. Moon, *Social Networks in the History of Innovation and Invention*, 2014), the result being a complex picture of the multiple interconnections established and required by societies undergoing major transformations, often enough under the heading of 'modernization', although that idea tends to limit the chronological possibilities of networking.

Broadly, 'networking' diminishes the role of individual genius in the creation of new structures, systems, and discoveries and concentrates attention on the congress of cooperating actors involved in the social and technical revolutions now daily expected. Far be it to conclude that exceptional individuals do not exist—*pace* Tolstoy and Marxist thinkers—,

---

[1] Peter Hall, *Cities in Civilization* (New York, 1998).

but even the Noble Prizes in science or medicine are now usually shared amongst researchers who sometimes work together. Nevertheless, even if discoveries are made independently and simultaneously, a larger environment of influences is always present. The Nobel Prize Museum in Stockholm has a display that indicates the loci where discoveries are made, usually indicating a bunching of talent, the striking interactions of which are beautifully illustrated in Michael Frayn's drama about the Copenhagen School of physics in the 1920s, *Copenhagen* (1998).

Tamson Pietsch's very readable account of the networking phenomenon with respect to higher education within the British Empire in its heyday does not weigh the reader down with a networking lexicon. Although her discussion is based on a very impressive acquaintance with scattered archival sources and wide reading, her analysis is lean and disciplined. Digressions are few, if any, the main points always uppermost.

Pietsch concentrates on the circulation of academic elites within established and newly created universities or research stations during the period of the growth of 'informal empire'. The net effect of such movement was twofold. British cultural values and systems were spread to what used to be called the 'white Dominions' and Asian and African regions. Simultaneously, scientists and scholars from overseas had an impact on research activity within the United Kingdom, especially and particularly because of the two world wars of the twentieth century. In sum, the networks constructed from about 1850 to 1939–45 were more than a result of a dominant homeland influence. They were in and of themselves instrumental in creating a shared sense of empire, adding to its pre-existing base of intellectual and cultural content and substantially contributing to a worldwide, self-conscious, and identifiable community of highly educated scholars, scientists, and intellectuals. Unlike the United States, which broke its ties to Majestic Empire through defiance and war and subsequently recreated its system of schools, colleges, and universities to correspond to new sets of national understanding, the academics who criss-crossed the Atlantic and the Pacific retained a sense of their British identity for the better part of a century. This would inevitably change under new global circumstances following the defeat of Japan and Germany.

As a prologue to Pietch's discussion, a reviewer might desire to refer back to the inherently expansive nature of university activity itself. As knowledge-based institutions, universities continually reach beyond their borders in search of new constituencies and opportunities. They add to the existing corpus of ideas, disseminating them to adjacent and distant regions. Today's talk of 'globalization', a staple of public policy discussions and endless publications, rooted in present-minded concerns about financing and branding, hugely underplays the fact (or gives a contrary impression) that from their origins universities were spreading both ideas and educated talent around Europe, and afterwards to colonial possessions wherever they were to be found. This occurred far more slowly than today since travel was arduous and communication tortoise-paced, but occur it did.

Universities became aspects of state-building strategies (their independence and freedom of thought often compromised in the alliance). They were as much a part of the dissemination of values as the trading networks so critical to human progress since the beginning of time. The story of academic networking within imperial Britain is therefore another if later example of a phenomenon instantly noticed from the twelfth century onwards. If we take account of newer speculation about the history of schools and academies in the Middle and Far East, the imperialism of knowledge generation and the institutions in which it was incorporated are even far older. (A subject currently being jointly explored by Roy Lowe in the U.K, and Yoshi Yasuhara in Japan).

The interesting question that arises is the extent to which the export of knowledge, its carriers and its structures created or contributed to specific regional or community identities. Insofar as the universities of the Middle Ages rested their knowledge base on a scholastic curriculum derived and adapted from Aristotle and his Jewish and Arabic commentators, conducted their affairs in Latin and recognized scholars of one institution as entitled to teach in another, historians can speak of a common university culture and values. Yet significant variations existed, differences in scholastic emphases, in a focus on particular disciplines or fields of inquiry, in financial support, in the types of students attracted and in the relationships between universities and royal and papal states or municipalities. Clearly there were pulls in a variety of directions, multiple and competing loyalties and identities within and between academic communities, rivalries for honours and recognition, and a late-developing ethic of the critical interrogation of sources.

Such a broader picture is one provided by this book. As the Second British Empire spread, one of its principal exports, besides the English language, as important as Latin in the creation of common cultures, was the university or the university college, many of which in their earliest years were no more than secondary schools. This pattern of institutional founding was as much domestic as global, for in the same period as the establishment of educational institutions overseas, university colleges were created at home outside Oxford and Cambridge, the educational nurseries of England's governing and ecclesiastical elite. For a long while the new civic universities and university colleges of the kingdom were regarded, and regarded themselves, as inferior to the established universities. In this respect, the newly created overseas institutions were similar. London, founded first as a university college in the 1820s, eventually morphed into an imperial examining university, awarding degrees to colleges abroad. The London model of a university that examined and awarded degrees to students in colleges worked in Toronto, according to Pietsch, and in South Africa and New Zealand, but not in Sydney.

While a plenitude of institution-building at home challenged the monopoly conventionally enjoyed by Oxbridge, and to a much lesser extent by the Protestant Trinity College Dublin, the spread of higher education opportunities actually enhanced the celebrity status and rank of the two senior universities of England. Liberated from basic kinds of teaching that could be undertaken elsewhere, their educational standards rose, and their ability to attract talented students increased. Under competitive market conditions, institutional differentiation occurs corresponding to different levels of demand. Rarely under such conditions do established universities lose their prestige, since they enjoy well-entrenched alumni support and a proud architectural fabric. Their graduates enjoy what sociologists call 'sponsored mobility' or a 'charter' of approval useful in entering labour markets.

The domestic and overseas expansion of higher education therefore strengthened the leading positions held by the senior universities, and it was primarily to these, or, decades later, to London University's collection of specialized schools, hospitals, and university colleges that ambitious academics from what Pietsch calls 'settler universities' resorted. Her story, as she says, concentrates on the elite universities of Britain, not only English but Scottish as well. In fact, the Scottish universities, which reformed themselves (or were reformed) before Oxford and Cambridge underwent major transformations, were well positioned to add to imperial influence, especially because of the importance they accorded to professional studies such as medicine and because the professorial model of instruction was less expensive than the Oxbridge tutorial system. Although understandably the story of Scottish influence outside Britain is not a major part of the history that Pietsch relates, it is useful to recall that Scottish and Scots-Irish educators were critical to the development of higher education in colonial America and that they created what is today a quasi-independent and important research university in Sweden (Chalmers). Within the Empire, Pietsch notes that Capetown academics in South Africa had strong connections with Scotland, and the Scottish model of non-sectarian admissions and education and scientific instruction proved to be critical to colonial settlements that contained the representatives of many faith communities. In this respect, the nonconformist college model that had developed in Britain in the eighteenth century should have been influential, but these institutions lacked funding (and it might be added, never really upgraded from secondary school status).

The revolutions in transportation and communication based on steam and the telegraph (Pietsch also mentions the much later importance of air mail) connected scholarly and educational communities in the imperial domains as never before. As networking analysts rightly contend, the technology of communication is a vital component in the circulation of elites. In the beginning, adopting or attempting one known British educational model or another, the settler universities concentrated on spreading the inherited culture to their young communities, building up feeder schools and inspecting them, and focusing on the customary liberal arts curricula of homeland universities. As in colonial America when the first colleges were founded, character development for local leadership and inculcating broad understandings were the usual educational undertaking. Since books were more accessible than laboratories, text-based studies naturally predominated, and this favoured more or less traditional curricula.

A livelier pursuit of imperial identity occurred in what might be termed a second phase in the story of overseas universities. Networking as a self-conscious activity was established, facilitated by the newer technologies mentioned and by the opening of the Suez Canal linking Britain with India. Now we find the elements of network formation that are being stressed in today's scholarship. First, an innovative environment was emerging, requiring new practical specialties to address economic and technological needs: mining engineering in South Africa and elsewhere; agriculture everywhere and veterinary science; dentistry, architecture. These requirements invited new players who needed access to the forms of knowledge essential for creative undertaking. Second, the cohorts available for entering higher education were increasing as the result of demographic expansion, some of it through immigration and pressure from women, hitherto largely excluded from higher education, and from a loosening of social class boundaries, easier to achieve in some as yet unsettled colonial situations than in the mother country. Third—the priority of push-pull factors is always difficult to identify exactly—state governments after 1880 or 1890 entered more forthrightly into the process of financing education at all levels, stimulating expansion and innovation. And fourth, an ingredient in academic networking that can never be understated, was an awakening ambition, both personal and institutional, allied to a feeling that the settler universities had become provincial, too concentrated on local issues and problems, and needed to gain wider recognition. Since no break with Westminster had taken place, unlike the American situation, the obvious means of advancing self-esteem and enhancing personal opportunities were closer ties to the elite academic communities of Britain.

Pietsch details how networks formed under newer conditions. A rising sensitivity to feelings of academic inferiority led to the adoption of well-known instruments of community building and public relations: learned journals, the establishment of university publishing, the tying of universities to professional societies. Through such mechanisms a strengthened congregation of settler universities secured outlets for a greater role in the imperial community of career-minded scholars and scientists. A larger sense of a community of like-minded individuals now existed within which, as a next step, the most adventurous could move outward and upward. Pietsch specifically and frequently mentions how much of the networking that subsequently developed was of a personal nature, what she terms 'personalized systems of trust'. Individuals secured positions or support for themselves or for their students, sending their leading disciples to the elite British universities, taking leading roles in newly-created associations, advisory bodies, and research programmes, and moving out of their home universities to take positions in Britain, or even in other parts of the imperial domains. Rhodes and Great Exhibition of 1851 scholarships or even earlier schemes of student support were part of the package of connections. At the same time, academics from Britain pursued appointments in the settler universities, or spent part of their careers abroad before returning. In these ways the traffic between the imperial lands and the centre coalesced and solidified.

Recent works on the essential meaning of the British Empire have focused on ambiguities and fuzzy definitions.[2] The search for a 'Britannic Vision', led by historians and politicians, had been around since the later nineteenth century. But one gathers from a reading of Tamson Pietsch that quite possibly it was academic networking that was at the heart of an imperial understanding, the networks providing the common and shared culture that linked the many regions that formally comprised the Empire of Britain. And both ends of the networks contributed. The settler universities introduced sabbaticals and leaves of absence to link centre and periphery before they were common in Britain or, for that matter, in America.

Where the networks proved especially vital was during two world wars. Citing Roy MacLeod and others who have detailed the scientific and technical contributions of overseas academics, Pietsch explains how

---

[2] Aaron L. Friedberg, *The Weary Titan: Britain and the Experience of Relative Decline, 1895–1905.* (Princeton, 2010); W. David McIntyre, *The Britannic Vision: Historians and the Making of the British Commonwealth of Nations, 1907–48* (Basingstoke, 2009).

many critical contributions to the war efforts were made by those who lived or worked abroad. The result of such mutually supporting activity was an even keener sense of a shared transoceanic culture, one understandably enhanced by the knowledge that the very survival of the countries of the empire was at stake.

The decline of imperial dominion, even though a weaker Commonwealth of Nations under a British crown still persists as a fading symbol, adjusted the networking ties. This was as much the coming of age of the imperial regions as the ending of a pervasive conception of empire signalled by Indian independence. The post-1945 emergence of the United States as a world power, its universities assuming a prominent and even dominant position within the international assembly of research institutions, offered alternative models of higher education and new opportunities for networking. Furthermore, American philanthropy abroad, most notably by the Carnegie and Rockefeller foundations, clearly revealed the influence and importance of American wealth and exposed the economic weaknesses of the United Kingdom. Loyalty to the nation eventually replaced ties to the mother country.

Even earlier, Anglophone Canadian universities had been establishing ties south of the Dominion's border, if more hesitant before 1945 from fear of losing a British identity. Many decades earlier, from 1918 in fact, the appeal of America's universities had resulted in a British effort to compete for students and academic talent by introducing the research doctorate. The innovation was also meant to divert overseas students from attending the German universities. Some earlier introductions included greater recognition by Oxford and Cambridge of first degrees taken overseas to counteract a feeling that overseas universities were secondary. Not only was the United States important in the transfer of connecting ties, but the emerging economies and states of Asia and the South Pacific would inevitably attract attention from Australia and New Zealand. Pietsch closes her argument on this development in a passing nod to the more recent phenomenon of 'globalization' driven in part, if not wholly, by government pressures and incentives to develop a variety of educational and research-related markets in the age of cyber-communications.

Networking is a positive phenomenon, or at least it is seen as such today, but the warnings contained in Pietsch's account also indicate another dimension. One might say that two kinds of networks exist, those that are, in an older phrase, 'open to talent' wherever it is to be found (and recognized), and those corresponding more to the 'personalized systems of trust' that joined settler and elite universities within the imperial domains. Academic life has often been described as a collection of status hierarchies within disciplines. Institutional differentiation by mission, funding, public attention, and student quality, while a positive aspect of a democratic opportunity structure, creates or reflects prestige differences. The current practice—or not so current—of ranking teaching and research universities nationally and globally reinforces feelings of superior or lesser standing and, insofar as institutional affiliation is equated with personal academic quality, acceptance into the right network is both a goal and a trial. So from a democratic perspective, the ideal condition of a network is that it be socially inclusive and not exclusive.

While she stresses how essential was networking to the pre-1939 conception of a British Empire, Pietsch is quite clear about its exclusionary drawbacks precisely because the networks were private or informal, nepotistic, a collection of insiders armed with insider knowledge. Racial or ethnic considerations were omnipresent. Academics from the 'white Dominions' were favoured, and those from India or Africa or the Caribbean were marginal. They were not Anglo-Saxons. Nor were the Irish. Furthermore, networks were male: women were by and large left out or for the most part occupied supportive and subordinate roles. J.A. Mangan has written extensively on the importance of competitive games to imperial rule and understanding. The culture was a celebration of masculine virility, and women were not part of a games culture.

Neither the settler universities nor the home universities were warmly disposed to refugee scholars, and elements of anti-Semitism were to be found throughout the Empire in the favoured institutions. The story of the historian Sir Lewis Namier, who came from a Jewish family in Poland, and his rejection by Toronto as well as other slights, is often told. Some accommodations were made for Jewish academics who escaped Nazi murderers, but even when the Carnegie Corporation in New York indicated a willingness to finance 36 fellowships in settler universities for displaced scholars in 1934, some pushback occurred. In short, to use Pietsch's words, the story is one of 'highly uneven landscapes of scholarly access and exchange'. (Anti-Semitism was prevalent in American universities between the wars, and it would be too easy and wrong to attempt to distinguish hiring practices in the United States from those in the British Empire.)

In general, academics tend to flatter themselves as peculiarly enlightened, tolerant, and fair-minded. However, the record does not bear out such a straightforward declaration of self-esteem, neither in the past nor in the present. But since the tale of inclusion and exclusion depends upon the historical formula of time, place, and circumstance, the best way of grasping this fact is the case study, of which this book is a welcome example.

Department of History
University of California, Berkeley

Correction: Dissenting Academies Online: (http://www.english.qmul.ac.uk/ drwilliams/portal.html)

John Spurr

In John Spurr's review of *Dissenting Academies Online*: (http://www.english. qmul.ac.uk/drwilliams/portal.html), *History of Universities* XXVIII/2, Mark Burden is wrongly identified as the editor. We apologise for the error. *Dissenting Academies Online* has been created by a team consisting of Rosemary Dixon, Simon Dixon, Inga Jones, and Kyle Roberts, with the technical assistance of Dmitri Iourinski, and under the direction of Isabel Rivers and David Wykes. Mark Burden is the author of *A Biographical Dictionary of Tutors at the Dissenters' Private Academies, 1660–1729* http:// www.english.qmul.ac.uk/drwilliams/pubs/dictionary.html, which is linked to *Dissenting Academies Online*.